Unraveling the Lie-Knot

Finding Freedom From the Tangles of Discouragement, Deception, and Depression

Sheryl Giesbrecht Turner

Foreword by *Neil T. Anderson*

FREEDOM
IN CHRIST
Transforming Discipleship

Published by Freedom In Christ Ministries International
4 Beacontree Plaza, Gillette Way, Reading RG2 0BS, UK.
www.freedominchrist.org

First edition 2021

A catalogue record for this book is available from the British Library.
ISBN: 978-1-913082-33-8

Cover Design: Amber Weigand-Buckley, #barefacedcreativemedia

Table of Contents

Endorsements

God is FOR YOU! And so is the author, Sheryl Giesbrecht Turner. With clarity, simplicity and biblical wisdom, *Unraveling the Lie-Knot: Finding Freedom From the Tangles of Discouragement, Deception, and Depression* hands you the road map for your path to freedom and victory.

~ Pam and Bill Farrel, authors of 52 books including bestselling *Men Are Like Waffles, Women Are Like Spaghetti,* Co-Directors of Love-Wise

When you start reading *Unraveling the Lie-Knot*, you're going to think Sheryl Giesbrecht Turner has been peeking into your mind and heart. Don't worry, though, her insights apply to everyone. We all, to some degree or another, struggle with believing lies that tie us up in knots and create dysfunctional relationships, missed God-opportunities, and emotional struggles. Turner offers not only hope but practical, biblical truths in a variety of ways that will help to set you free.

~ Kathy Collard Miller, international speaker and author of over 55 books including *God's Intriguing Questions: 60 New Testament Devotions Revealing Jesus's Nature*

If you have ever experienced a traumatic event and processed it incorrectly or not at all, this book will help you to open the wound, understand and accept truth, experience healing, and lead you in the direction of helping others. In *Unraveling the Lie-Knot,* Sheryl Giesbrecht Turner writes with honesty about the personal journey that set her free from discouragement, deception, and depression.

The chapters include biblical applications, discussion questions, an opportunity to journal, and guided prayers. Read this book on your own, or even better, gather a group of friends and go through this important study together. Don't miss it!

~ Carol Kent, international speaker and author of *He Holds My Hand: Experiencing God's Presence and Protection*

Many of us are entertaining the lies of the enemy through negative self-talk, anxiety about the future, and worrying excessively. In *Unraveling the Lie-Knot,* Sheryl Giesbrecht offers biblical truths alongside actionable tools to help lead you out of confusion and discouragement into a new place of freedom in Christ. Sheryl transparently shares her own struggles with these lies and how she was able to break free. She guides you through the text as one who understands strongholds and the process of breaking them down. *Unraveling the Lie-Knot* provides an effective and systematic approach based on the word of God to help you unlearn the lies holding you back.

~ Dr. Saundra Dalton-Smith, physician and author of *Sacred Rest: Recover Your Life, Renew Your Energy, Restore Your Sanity*

Readers can expect transparency, humility, and love from author, Sheryl Giesbrecht Turner, in *Unraveling the Lie-Knot.* They can also anticipate the author's compassion and the power of God's Word to permeate every chapter of the book. With chapter titles that help the readers picture knots — tangled, snarled, or twisted — Giesbrecht Turner guides the audience to see the relationship between those images and their lives. The book provides quotes and anecdotes from a variety of people.

I highly recommend *Unraveling the Lie-Knot*. Be ready to be set free from discouragement, deception, and depression. Buy a dozen copies and give them to your friends, a pastor, chaplain, counselor, or church librarian.

~ Yvonne Ortega, speaker and author of the *Moving from Broken to Beautiful*® Book Series

Most women have experienced feeling less than adequate in their life. The hurtful shots taken by others that penetrate the heart and soul taking on a life of their own actively destroying the person from the inside out. In the book *Unraveling the Lie-Knot: Finding Freedom From the Tangles of Discouragement, Deception, and Depression*, Sheryl Giesbrecht Turner shares ways of healing and escape from the liar and how to become a strong, victorious, and greatly loved daughter of the King.

~ Kathy Bruins, President of Word Weavers, West Michigan and founder of The Well ministries for Christian creatives

Freedom. Healing. Truth. What would these three gifts mean to you in your life right now? Everything? Then you're in for a treat! You'll find these and more in this timely resource by Sheryl Giesbrecht Turner, as she points us, in unique and compelling ways, to the Source of these gifts: God and His Word. Relevant Scriptures, principles, prayers, and study helps come together to equip and encourage us to find freedom from the emotional and spiritual "lie-knots" that have entangled too many of us for too long.

You will love this author's heart, passion, and authenticity. Her friendly tone and masterful writing, along with her refreshing transparency, spiritual insights, and biblical wisdom, make this a valuable resource for us all. She begins with her purpose for writing: "...to help you find a shortcut to freedom.... Daily, I battled anxiety, fear, depression, and despair...unaware of the devil's strategy to distract, deceive, and destroy...to entrap me and hold me hostage...."

In the pages to follow, she shares how she found true freedom, and how you and I can too.

Our stories are all different, but our needs for freedom, healing, and truth are the same. The story of Julia, in Chapter 5, especially resonated with me. After many struggles, Julia found Christ, and made the conscious choice to allow God "to heal the broken and bruised places in her past....She saw herself the way God saw her: dearly loved, secure, and a child of God. She received God's gifts of peace, security, and a new beginning."

The author tells the reader, "I believe you are next. Are you ready?" I was. As I begin now to allow God to unravel the knots and heal my own broken places, I'm finding freedom. I pray you will too.

~ Sandi Banks, speaker, author, and member of Carol Kent's Speak Up Faculty

What a great book! Sheryl's vulnerability, authenticity, and images of personal struggles opens up the reader's heart to fully grasp the insidious power of deception and lies. Her stories ring true because she has lived them. She's not afraid to tackle the tough issues but Sheryl never leaves you in the pit. Lovingly, through other people's testimonies, research and Biblical truths Sheryl sets the reader on a pathway to finding God's truth, wholeness, freedom and ultimately joy. This book is chock full of wisdom and guidance, but most importantly, it upholds the mantle of love. I highly recommend this book for every woman, because each one of us has at one time or another been deceived.

~ Heidi McLaughlin, International speaker and author of *Fresh Joy: Finding Joy in the Midst of Loss, Hardships, and Suffering*

I've spent numerous hours helping my clients move beyond the relational barriers holding them back from experiencing God's best life. Over the years, I've not found anyone who can't relate to being snagged by a lie. Lies from family and friends are often received with blanketed approval because we trust the source. Lies from strangers come disguised as help. Since we are in need, we accept and to our dismay, we experience unwanted pain once again. Yet, it's the lies we tell ourselves that have a deeper and debilitating impact. *Unraveling the Lie-Knot* walks us through multiple lies and offers T.R.U.T.H. to loosen the spiritual tug of war each one has cleverly entangled us in. Sheryl Giesbrecht Turner draws us with real life stories, providing the facts we need to really get that it's possible to untangle our thinking and experience freedom in the plan God has for us.

~ Linda Goldfarb - Board certified Christian life coach, Award-winning author of the *LINKED® Quick Guide to Personalities* series, speaker, and podcaster.

Many of us can admit we've believed our share of lies - lies that curl themselves around our self-confidence and cinch ever tighter whenever we try to move out in faith. Sheryl Giesbrecht Turner masterfully labels them "lie-knots". They keep us mired in mediocrity, incapable of moving forward. In this liberating study, Sheryl uses a powerful acrostic to equip the reader to loosen the *knots* and cut through the lies we have believed about ourselves, our circumstances, and our views of God, bringing glorious truth and freedom.

~ Dawn Scott Damon is a podcaster, speaker, and author of *The Freedom Challenge: 60 Days to Untie the Cords that Bind You*

If you're feeling unable to move forward, tied to your past, or tangled by the troubles of today—prepare to break free! A message of hope and recovery, you'll find freedom while tethered to the transforming truth that you belong to God. Sheryl uses scriptural truths to identify and loosen the lies attached to trauma, addiction, depression, and even negative thinking patterns. Because "We may have some unlearning to do." My friends, I promise that you'll find the best kind of unraveling within the tender pages of this book. You do *knot* want to miss it. Enjoy!

~ Beth Duewel, blogger, speaker, and coauthor with Rhonda Rhea to the *Fix Her Upper* Book Series.

Foreword: Dr. Neil T. Anderson

Stop that! You're making a mess. Can't you do anything right? That was dumb! You should know better than that. Generally speaking, people receive more non-affirming statements than affirmations, and it usually takes several affirmations to negate the effect of one non-affirmation.

If five people say, "Nice job," but one is critical of how well you did; which one will you think about later? We can shrug off negative messages for a while, but eventually they take their toll. Feeling like failures in progress we begin to wonder about ourselves. Maybe there is something wrong with me. I wonder if others struggle with doubts and condemning thoughts like I do.

A person can feel alone in their thoughts and be totally unaware that others are fighting the same mental battles. In one sense it is a good thing that we can't read each other's minds. If there was a way to attach electrodes to our brains so that everything, we thought was flashed on a screen that others could see, would you volunteer? On the other hand, since we can't read each other's minds we are likely to think that we are the only ones who struggle with our thoughts.

I have found that to be especially true about those who are under assault by the evil one. Satan has deceived the whole world and accuses us before God day and night (See Revelations 12:9,10). "The Spirit explicitly says that in later times some will fall away from the faith, paying attention to deceitful spirits and doctrines of demons" (1 Timothy 4:1 NASB). That is presently happening all over the world. Rarely will anyone share with another that they are struggling with blasphemous, tempting, accusing, and condemning thoughts. People are in bondage to those lies and will remain so until they fully repent and believe the gospel.

No natural person inherently feels good about themselves. Don't be fooled by those drawing attention to themselves. They are desperately looking for affirmation as we all are. We are not perfect people. Rebukes and reproofs are a natural part of the maturation process. "All Scripture is inspired by God and profitable for teaching, for reproof, for correction, for training in righteousness; so that the man of God may be adequate, equipped for every good work" (2 Timothy 3:16,17 NASB). We would like to skip the reproof and correction, but it is essential for becoming the people God created us to be.

Seeking affirmation has led many to become people pleasers, which cannot end well. Paul wrote, "If I were trying to please men, I would not be a bond-servant of Christ" (Galatians 1:10 NASB). A bond-servant of Christ is someone who has discovered their own identity and freedom in Christ. They are unconditionally loved and accepted by God. They are new creations in Christ who are affirmed by God. His Holy Spirit bears witness with their spirit that they are children of God. They are used by God to set captives free and heal the wounds of the broken-hearted. Paul shares how we become an instrument in God's hand. "The Lord's servant must not be quarrelsome, but be kind to everyone, able to teach, not resentful. Opponents must be gently instructed, in hope that God will grant them repentance leading them to a knowledge of the truth, and that they will come to their senses and escape from the trap of the devil, who has taken them captive to do his will" (2 Timothy 2:24-26).

Sheryl Giesbrecht Turner is a bond-servant of the Lord. She has a remarkable testimony of overcoming the lies she believed from an abusive childhood that kept her in bondage for years. She has suffered through the death of her first husband, and the spiritual abuse of a Christian leader. She knows how to help you unravel the lies that come from living in a fallen world ruled by the father of lies. This book will help you overcome the world, the flesh, and the devil through genuine repentance and faith in God. Only in Christ are we accepted, secure, significant, and free.

Dr. Neil T. Anderson

Founder and President Emeritus of Freedom in Christ Ministries

Introduction: A note from Sheryl

Therefore, since we are surrounded by such a great cloud of witnesses, let us throw off everything that hinders and the sin that so easily entangles (Hebrews 12:1).

Dear friend,

I wrote this book to help you find a shortcut to freedom. I don't want you to be stuck any longer -- like I was for two decades. And I did not even know I was trapped!

I was a young pastor's wife, expecting my second child, caring for a busy toddler and helping with my husband's vibrant ministry. Daily, I battled anxiety, fear, depression and despair. I expected to live out my happily-ever-after fairy-tale life, but instead, I dreaded facing the challenges of each new day. I was unaware of the devil's strategy to distract, deceive and destroy me. His plan was draw me into temptation by feeling sorry for myself. Once I took the bait, he was able to entrap me, and hold me hostage. I felt powerless as I remained tangled up in the lie that I could never recover from my past mistakes or overcome the traumatic experiences I had faced. Maybe you can relate?

Deception is crucial to Satan's tactics and at an early age, he began planting seeds of discontent, exclusion, hurt and hate in my heart. I did not know what the Bible said about the devil and through my difficulties and trials came to understand what the verse in John's gospel meant. "He (Satan) was a murderer from the beginning, not holding to the truth, for there is no truth in him. When he lies, he speaks his native language, for he is a liar and the father of lies" (John 8:44).

Now, it is clear to me that Satan especially targets women to deceive us. It is his primary mode of operation. He knows we have influential power with men and in our families, and our innocent, yet sometimes sinful choices, can set an example and pattern for others. As a young child, I had no control over the negative comments that were made about my appearance, lack of skills, or personality. As an adolescent, I listened and paid heed to the lie, thinking if I took drugs or drank alcohol I would easily fit in with the cool kids. I numbed my damaged emotions with alcohol and street drugs.

As a teenager, I became dependent on these chemicals, which propelled me into engaging in illegal and immoral means to support my habits. Unknowingly, I had exposed myself to deeper deception, and became helplessly ensnared in the lies of chemical dependence, anger, bitterness, selfishness, and irresponsibility. I share my failures in this book to connect with you. It is my prayer that you may identify with my sense of entanglement, disappointment, and frustration to move through my losses and trials on my own. Your list of what has happened in your past may be different than mine. Or not.

I believe that you did not buy this book or receive it as a gift by accident. I am confident God is working in your life. His desire for you is to better understand the resurrection power of Jesus Christ and He wants you to depend on His grace and not human wisdom. Within these chapters, you will discover the treasure of your position in Christ and how to rely on the authority of the risen Savior. You long to live victoriously through the finished work of the Lord Jesus Christ. Many of your doubts and questions will find resolution, as together, we determine how to move ahead and break free from traps that have ensnared us on our faith journey.

I am excited for you to become more aware of areas you may feel trapped, helpless, or hopeless. I pray, as God reveals Himself through our study of God's Word you will have increased discernment, new resolve, and the ability to overcome. It is gratifying and victorious, to find out how to combat lies, and defeat them. Once we understand how to cut through the lies, we have believed about ourselves, our circumstances, and our views of God we can be triumphant. Implementing our faith, with His help, we can sever ourselves free from anxiety, depression, anger, and bitterness. As we depend on Him and as truth is revealed by His Word, led by the presence of the Holy Spirit, we can learn how to "unravel the lie-knot."

At the end of each chapter you will find a practical workbook section called *Loosening the Lies: Study Questions and Guided Journal Opportunity.* In this segment, there are additional Bible study and group discussion questions, a shepherded journal opportunity and several guided prayers. You can utilize this for your own personal Bible study, in mentoring others, or in a group Bible study setting. This tool will enable you, your mentee, or your Bible study group, with the help of the Holy Spirit, to process how to tell yourselves the truth found in God's Word. In the first part of the Loosening the Lies section, we will use an acrostic to simplify five steps for you to take, highlighting the letters in the word truth. Here is a breakdown of the acrostic:

T - Take time

R – Remember the facts

U – Uncover your fear, unravel the "lie-knot"

T - Tell yourself the truth

H – Help is available by agreeing with God by confession, submission, and declaration of truth.

After the acrostic, you will find study questions to help you engage in the teaching from the chapter. There are how-to techniques and tips that I will teach, describe, and illustrate in detail. You can take these study questions as a unit and move through them all at once, or take one question each day, along with the T.R.U.T.H. acrostic and additional supplemental tools I will explain now.

At the end of each *Loosening the Lies* section, there is a list of suggested scripture references called *Truth Tools,* related to the topics discussed within the chapter. I recommend you use these scripture references as God designed them to be used, as weapons of warfare, essential elements for the process of cutting away the lies, and "unraveling the lie-knot." It's my prayer and hope for you to be equipped and inspired. To assist you in moving ahead, each segment ends with a prayer of adoration and devotion entitled *Freed by Faith.*

I will be sharing my own fears, failures, successes, and joys. I hope you are inspired by my choices to embrace and own God's promises. Although the process may be forthcoming, you are encouraged to keep turning to God's

Word. We are not meant to embark on this healing journey alone, so I urge you to include other trusted believers who are walking the same direction. Additionally, I am excited to share the stories of many others who, with God's help have been victoriously cut free from the bondage of their own "lie-knots."

I may not have met you. I hope to someday. Throughout my twenty-eight years of marriage to a pastor, serving on staff at several churches and non-profit ministries, plus extensive national and international travel, I have heard the cries and prayed with hundreds of women who ask what can I do to break free? Let me assure you freedom is not only obtainable; it is readily available through the finished work of our Lord Jesus Christ.

May I invite you to give yourself permission to find a quiet spot and take a few moments for yourself. Now grab your favorite fun drink, a highlighter, your Bible, and journal, and let's begin as you pray aloud this short prayer. "Lord, speak to me." That, my friend, is a prayer God wants to answer. I am praying you through into victory.

My deep love and constant prayers,

Sheryl

> It is God who enables us, along with you, to stand firm for Christ. He has commissioned us and he has identified us as his own by placing the Holy Spirit in our hearts as the first installment that guarantees everything he has promised us.
>
> (2 Corinthians 1:21, 22 NLT)

The beliefs we hold should hold us up even when life feels like it's falling apart.[1]

Lysa TerKeurst

Chapter 1: Knotted - How Did I Get Here?

Got a minute? I wish we could sit together in my favorite coffee shop with a steaming vanilla latte or Chai tea warming our hands. We connect together as we lean in and share our hearts. Since you've picked up this book, I am picturing you, a woman like me, seeking a deeper walk with God. You are not just any woman; you're one of God's most precious saints. You are His chosen daughter, specially designed to fulfill His purpose and by faith, walk forward in His will.

We want our devotion to God to matter, don't we? We've got a deep desire for our spiritual growth to make an important difference in our journey. We want to influence those around us to be better people because we know the impact this can have on the Body of Christ. We wonder if our direct contributions to our corner of the world and our current culture really do have a lasting impact. When we learn a new truth about God, how to grow closer to Him, or strengthen relationships with our family, we want to share what we learned with anyone who will listen.

Snarled to a Standstill

You're paging through this book, possibly out of curiosity or a desire to find out what to do to get free? The title has intrigued you and you realize you've been tangled up and you want to be liberated, now. You're ready to begin the process. When a necklace or twine becomes tangled, the knot begins with a small kink in the chain or rope, which folds upon itself causing a snag. Often the snag draws in more portions of the chain or rope so the tangle becomes bigger and bigger. The only way to begin to untangle the knot is to find where the kink begins.

Tangles come at the most inconvenient times. Maybe it's happened to you? For weeks, you have looked forward to a much-needed evening on the town—a girls' night out with your best friends or sharing a quiet, romantic dinner with your sweetheart. You're dressed up. The final touch: your favorite necklace. Placing your hands behind your head and elbows to ears, you lock the clasp. Now straightening your little black dress, with your arms to your sides, then your hands on your hips, you glance back to the mirror one last time. Oh, no! The necklace is crooked, and it's hanging off center. Looking closer you see that the dainty gold chain needs to be unkinked. The delicate strands have looped on top of each other and become exasperatingly twisted and ensnared, so the chain will not hang straight.

When the chain is flattened, you can see where the ends are jammed, or which areas are enmeshed. As it is laid out horizontally, we can determine where on the chain the knot begins, we can find the place it's jammed, and we can see the root of the knot. The same principle is true about how we do or do not process negative thoughts about ourselves, people, or circumstances. We wrap them around repeatedly, and so often, we begin to believe them as truth. By weaving together twisted strands of misplaced blame, intertwined with undeserved guilt, further enmeshed with matted half-truths of unworthiness, we craft our own reality. Within the pages of God's Word are answers to help us unscramble every "lie-knot" tangle that ensnares us.

In the same way, emotional knots can hold us back from growing spiritually and emotionally. These knots do not stay the same size. They actually fester, like wounds. If we ignore them, they will be detrimental to our growth as believers in Christ.

A "lie-knot" usually begins with a traumatic event that is processed incorrectly or may not be processed at all. These events may translate into our soul being wounded. These hurts can occur for various reasons.

Sometimes we are injured because of our own bad choices. We can become stuck, trapped, or ensnared and we don't even know it. Other times we are wounded because of things others have done. The snare might not be noticed until it becomes a trap, its cords entangling us, holding us back from maturity. "Lie-knots" may increase in size as we harbor negative thoughts. False and negative self-talk affects how we see ourselves and how we interact with our families, friends, or our husbands. Instead of showing ourselves kindness, we entertain a destructive internal narrative.

In each chapter we will lay out a lie, and then search for the root of the lie. We will share a Bible lesson, and provide a guide to hold you accountable, giving you the tools so you and the Holy Spirit can find the end and begin to "unravel the lie-knot."

Strung Up

I was six years old and some of the girls in my ballet class made comments about my appearance. "You are fat and you look like a sausage in a leotard. Why do you wear your hair that way?" These poison darts affected my self-perception for over two decades. To tame the lies, I was told to use the phrase, "Sticks and stones may break your bones, but words will never harm you." It didn't work. The lies increased in size and were amplified as I entered puberty. Lies never stay the same. Over time they always grow into something bigger and more harmful. That's why we must choose God's truth above what we think and what we have been told about ourselves.

I was an awkward adolescent. I painfully tried to find a place to fit in. After two upsetting family relocations, I urgently desired to get settled in as quickly as possible to our new neighborhood, school, and church. I was a straight-A student, but the results of over-achieving in every class caused the other students in my grade to notice and react with jealousy and competition to my achievements. Besides making fun of my clothes, my nose and my height, they called me "teacher's pet, four-eyes, and brainiac." These names were not meant to compliment but to criticize and lead to my destruction. Trying to cope and compensate, I joined several extra-curricular activities. I thought that these activities would help me fit in, for sure. Wrong. For several years prior, I'd learned to artfully play the violin and held the position of first chair. At my new school orchestra, I was disheartened when two other violinists beat me out of the prized first chair. I quit violin.

Since I was no longer in orchestra, I had extra time and I loved to sing. I joined chamber choir, thinking that in a bigger group I would blend in and be accepted for my musical contributions. You can imagine my horror when I was singled out for singing off-key. Another disgrace and defeat, yet I still had not hit the bottom of despair.

My mind flashed back to how I'd loved to dance. The dance classes were enjoyable and through this connection, I heard about the water ballet group. I joined in with synchronized swimming and loved how light I felt in the water. Unfortunately, after failing to grasp a new skill as fast as the rest of the group, I was told I couldn't participate in the competition.

The final blow was the failed sewing demonstration for 4-H home economics. After several months of preparing complicated sewing projects, combined with grueling practice of our public speech presentation, we were told our dresses were too short, our talk too simple and our content was incomplete. Another failure. These losses along with the memories of the comments of the ballet class groupies came back to haunt me once more. And now the lies were compounded by fresh wounds from students, teachers, 4-H judges, and Sunday school teachers. Of course, there is no way you can control what others may say or do to you but I didn't know how to process my negative thoughts about what had happened.

We are going to experience disappointments and discouragement and we're going to hear cruel and disparaging remarks throughout our lives. The comments I heard from other children in the ballet class, later were compounded by circumstances and grew from destructive criticism. These untruths I believed about myself. Through my decision to believe what God says is true about me, these lies are now tamed as I understand my identity in Christ. I share my lies here to offer you insight and direction. You might want to make a list of your own?

> Lie #1: "You are fat," translated into "You are not good enough." God's truth: "You are worth the life of my Son."
>
> Lie #2: "You are clumsy," translated into "You are not worthy." God's truth: "You get your identity from what I (God) have done for you."
>
> Lie #3: "You are boring," translated into "You are not popular." God's truth: "You get your identity from what I (God) say about you."

Lie #4: "You can't do anything right," translated into "You won't amount to anything." God's truth: "Your belief in what I (God) am capable of determines your behavior."

Like a hangman's noose, deception was enmeshed with false beliefs about myself, undermined my trust in God and almost choked my faith to death. These falsehoods had become my identity. I remember specifically, as an adolescent, wondering why God was holding out on me? I believed in God, but I didn't believe that He could be trusted. Can you relate? Has your identity been hampered by nicknames you've been called? If that's true for you, it helps to speak out your new identity over those scars and replace the lies with God's truth. Your mind will be renewed, and in time, you will believe what God says.

"Lie-knots" may increase in size as we harbor negative thoughts. They may even grow faster when fed by negative thoughts about a person or situation. My self-image and confidence had been altered for decades because of the lies I'd believed for so long. Maybe you have had a similar experience? You, like me, may have been victimized by lies that have pierced your emotions at a very young age. These lies tell us things that haunt us, affecting our self-talk and influencing our present-day decisions.

Through the years that followed, I learned how to cover up the snags, snares, and deceptions that had snarled me to a standstill. An emotional snag might not be noticed until it becomes deeply embedded, causing us intense pain. In my case, the trauma happened when I was very young. I didn't know how to defend myself or prevent lies from being rooted in my mind. The "lie-knot's" cords entangled me, bound me tightly, and held me back from maturity. I didn't want to face my past, but it was time to allow God to help me untangle the knots of the lies I believed. I had to look back, remember, and even feel the pain of a hurting history.

You Are Not Alone

Let's look at a foundational scripture about breaking free. "Therefore, since we are surrounded by such a great cloud of witnesses, *let us throw off everything that hinders and the sin that so easily entangles. And let us run with perseverance the race marked out for us*" (Hebrews 12:1). The imagery suggests the event to be an athletic contest taking place in an amphitheater. The *cloud of witnesses* are the Bible heroes mentioned in the beginning of the quoted verse: Abel, Enoch, Noah, and Abraham, each an example of persistence. Although these saints can't see or cheer on our progress from heaven, we can learn from them. David Guzik's commentary says, "…these witnesses are not witnessing us as we conduct our lives. Instead they are witnesses to us of faith and endurance."[2] The cloud of witnesses are our examples of how to move ahead despite something that may have kept us in knots.

The point of this book is to help you develop a plan. Do you see the warning found in the second half of the verse, "*and the sin that so easily entangles us*"? Let's look at the words "easily entangles" translated from the Greek word *euperistaton*, which can be interpreted four ways: 1. Effortlessly avoided (but are not); 2. Admired (must be set aside with intention); 3. Ensnaring (to the point of being trapped and unable to be freed); 4. Dangerous (ambushed and taken captive). This definition may make some of us feel overwhelmed already! Take a breath. Don't worry, you don't have to do everything at once. If you try, you may enthusiastically begin but because of delays or distractions, not finish. Or after several false starts, you run out of energy, burn out, and make your mind up that you have failed. Again. So why bother? Remember, we're discussing "lie-knots," emotional wounds or spiritual conflicts that may be the result of unconfessed or habitual sin. These lie-knots may be preventing us from moving forward. Also, there may be "lie-knots" that are not sin but are hindering us from running the race God has planned. Maybe the choice isn't between right and wrong, but is something we must choose to put down because it is weighing us down.

You may be wondering, so what does this mean for you and me? Interestingly, statistics show that seven in ten Christian women in the United States (72%) say religion is "very important" in their lives, compared with 62% of our country's Christian men.[3] In addition, women rank higher than men in their devotional habits. And 74% of women surveyed say they pray daily, compared to 60% of men. Then why do so many of us feel immobilized, jammed into a corner, and even overlooked by God? Others of us experience daily insecurity, and suffer weekly from anxiety or unexplainable fear?

May I offer a few insights?

How do we start the healing process? That's just it. You decided to find where a "lie-knot" began, that is, what is the root of the lie? Well done, you have just taken the first step. We can learn how to tell ourselves the truth.

To begin the process of untangling "lie-knots" we've believed about our past, we need to see the facts about what happened to us. That's how we find the end of the knot to begin to let God help us unravel it.

The second step is to believe God's Word and not our feelings. What events have happened to us or what lies have we believed about our Creator? Did you know behind every fear is a lie that needs to be uncovered? Untruth can trip us and we may become tangled to the point of immobilization, we don't know what we don't know. We are deceived. Proverbs 5:22-23 (NLT) says, "An evil man (woman) is held captive by his/her own sins, they are ropes that catch and hold him/her. He (she) will die for lack of self-control; he (she) will be lost because of his/her great foolishness." I've learned to pray, "Dear Lord, show me if there is any way or anywhere I am being deceived." It is necessary to find the root of the lie we've believed about ourselves.

The third step is to face our past. Sometimes it's easier to ignore it, especially if what happened long ago is painful or traumatic. We've buried it for so long, why bring it up now? Unfortunately, buried things tend to resurrect themselves. This may happen when we least expect it. Or if the past shows up, the symptoms can manifest in depression, discouragement, or despair.

We can learn to view our history through the grid of truth. The focus of this book is to ensure we process God's truth, not just as "head knowledge" but in our hearts. The most fundamental truth we need to know and act upon is our identity -- who we are in Christ. When you begin to connect the truth with your life, it will cut through any type of false belief we have about ourselves, other people, God or the future God has planned for us.

For me, the "lie-knot" started early as a result of the flippant comments others made to me in ballet class. During my early twenties as a pastor's wife, I found myself tied up in many knots. I needed a shortcut, but there was no alternate route around a season that lasted for six months. I was stuck. No matter what I tried, nothing loosened the tight knot. Trying and tangled times like my days of dark depression got my attention. Something needed to change. In many ways, the captivity I felt as a young pastor's wife and pregnant mother of a toddler was comparable to the time in my rebellious teen years when I'd been arrested for breaking the law. The feelings were fresh as I remember the confirmation of the truth—I was guilty. I was detained, handcuffed, and transported in the backseat of a sheriff's patrol car. I was humiliated and shamed. Once at the facility, my mug shot was taken and I was strip-searched, given a prison uniform, and placed in the stone-cold jail cell behind immovable steel bars. I remember the sound of the iron key in the keyhole as the dead bolt clicked shut. I was locked in. Like a hammer hitting an anvil, the sound stung my ears, signifying a final blow to my freedom.

My mind flashed and in seconds, I remembered how my poor choices led me there. I'd been raised in the church, yet I didn't know God as a loving Father. During my elementary school years, my family moved around a lot. Each time we relocated, I wanted to fit in. Belonging to the right group mattered more than anything else to me, so I decided to do whatever it took to be noticed by the popular kids. At the young age of twelve, I began smoking cigarettes, drinking alcohol, and using street drugs. By the time I was thirteen years old, I was a chain smoker, alcoholic, and drug addict. After running the streets of my town and others for several years, my addictive habits and unhealthy everyday life had caught up with me. I was caught, imprisoned, and now facing imminent punishment. Upon my release the next day, the outtake counselor confronted me with the reality of my lifestyle. I will never forget his words when he said, "If you don't make different choices, you will be locked up in prison the rest of your life or you will end up dead."

I was released from the detention facility, but for another year or so, the pattern of my choices repeated. I had more clashes with the law. Counseling, under the watch of a probation officer, accountability to a juvenile advocate, and attempts at rehabilitation were futile. Now at seventeen, I was careening deeper into drug addiction. I stayed high as much as possible, trying to fill the emptiness in my life with the highest high or the cutest guy while my need for affection only increased.

I couldn't wait to move out of my parents' home. My family pulled strings to get me a volunteer summer job at a Christian camp. The staff assigned me lists of chores, such as washing hundreds of dishes in the mess hall, raking piles of pine needles around the campgrounds, and even moving logs around the outdoor campfire ring.

Whenever I complained or threw fits over doing my chores or got caught smoking cigarettes and dope, the staff said, "Love covers over a multitude of sins" (I Peter 4:8). Their words, repeated over and over, penetrated my being for two weeks. The staff didn't tell me to change anything about my appearance, attitude, or addictions. Instead, they showed me what the invitation of love looked like. They were kind and offered the true love of God without forcing me to accept it.

This got me to thinking, isn't my sin too much for God to handle? That thought plagued me day and night. The staff's words, "love covers a multitude of sins," taken straight from scripture, began to penetrate my hard heart and foggy mind. I began to believe God's love could cover the things that held me captive to my addictions: drugs and alcohol, lying and stealing, promiscuity and drug dealing. It was finally clear—I didn't need to clean up my act before coming to God. He loved me passionately just the way I was. One night in my cabin, I submitted to the overwhelming love of God. He had reached out to me, and I, a most unlikely choice, finally grasped His hand. His abundant love did cover my multitude of sins. I accepted the invitation to live a new life. At that time I didn't know there was much more to finding wholeness and walking out the abundant life Christ promises. Maybe you can relate?

Who Are You?

I know. It seems like such an obvious question, one we should easily be able to answer. Don't reach for your driver's license or passport. I am wondering if you realize what "identity in Christ" means? And as believers in Christ, why does understanding your identity in Christ matter? Let me explain. You and I were made in "God's image" (Genesis 1:26), since God is spirit, we have a spiritual nature. Like Adam and Eve, our inner person is created in the image of God. Adam's core of his being, connected to his body means he was physically alive, like you and I. And now, for the most important part, Adam's spirit, connected to God meant he was spiritually alive, like us. God's design is for us to be connected to our physical body and our spirit is to be connected to God. It's in this spiritual connection God gave Adam and us three very important gifts:

Acceptance – Adam had an intimate relationship with God. He could talk to Him at any time and have His full attention.

Significance—Adam was given a purpose: to rule over the birds of the sky, the beasts of the field and the fish of the sea.

Security—He was totally safe and secure in God's presence. Everything he needed was provided for—food, shelter, companionship.

Dear one, you were created for that kind of life! In the beginning when God created the world, you were designed for complete acceptance by Him and other people, significance—a real purpose, and absolute security—no need to worry about a single thing.

Unfortunately, the world went terribly wrong when Adam and Eve disobeyed God's command, "But you must not eat from the tree of the knowledge of good and evil, for when you eat from it you will certainly die" (Genesis 2:17). Not only did they die spiritually, but the connection their spirits had to God was broken and they were separated from God. The acceptance they enjoyed and the close fellowship they had changed into a humiliating sense of rejection. The significance they appreciated was replaced by overwhelming guilt and shame. Their sense of security was given over to fear. So we are born into an environment that is not at all like what God originally designed for us. We want to find our way back to the acceptance, security, and significance we were meant to have.

Jesus came to restore our relationship with God. He came to earth not to judge, but as our Savior, to enable us to become spiritually alive again. "I have come that they may have life and have it to the full" (John 10:10).

When we become Christians, our spirit is reconnected to God's Spirit. If you are not a Christian, if you don't know Jesus as your personal Lord and Savior, please take a moment to flip to the back of this book to read a special message called *Love Letter to My Readers*. With Jesus Christ as Lord and Savior of our lives, we get back the life we were always meant to have with its acceptance, significance, and security. Eternal life is not just something you get when you die, it's a whole different quality of life right now.[4]

Envision the pleasure and contentment you'll feel as you work through family disagreements with love, patience, and kindness. Visualize your most important relationships growing closer and developing a deeper love for one another. Picture yourself rested, after decades of insomnia. You're finally able to get an entire eight hours of uninterrupted sleep. Imagine permanent relief from your nagging nicotine dependence. Can you foresee the gratifying results of losing that extra twenty-five pounds of weight? Abundant living can be a present state of being. Yes, we can benefit from a joy-filled, peace-abiding, grace-driven, victorious life.

Even though I had accepted Christ and experienced new life in Him, the season of my depression was a red flag for heart issues I hadn't dealt with. Like my jail time, I began to notice my emotional and spiritual imprisonment was one I'd crafted of my own making. As a defense mechanism, I'd become bitter and angry. I had decades of regret, shame, blame and unworthiness. Thinking I was protecting myself from further emotional damage, I denied my private emotional pain and misplaced truth. At the time, it seemed like a permanent condition. Every day my heart grew more hardened to spiritual things, all the while questioning God's love, goodness and grace, and wondering how I ended up in this restricted place.

I'd lost track of my days of anguish. I could not understand why I was so depressed. After all, I had a lot of reasons to be happy and even content with my life. Why wasn't I satisfied with those I had been given to love? A few years earlier, I had married my college sweetheart. Together we had a beautiful three-year-old daughter, and I was pregnant with our second child. We lived in my husband's hometown near family and were settling in to run a family business. Yet, every day I had a difficult time getting out of bed. I wondered why God was holding out on me. It felt like He had sent me to an isolated dungeon, locked me in, and abandoned me there to die.

The comfortable relationship with God I once enjoyed, when we walked closely and I shared honestly, now felt awkward and cold. He was distant. I questioned, did God hear my prayers? I'd been trying to serve God and live for Him for a few years. I was a graduate of a Bible college. I led prayer groups and Bible studies for teenage girls and my husband was a pastor. I knew how to believe God for other people. It seemed He was there to hand out answers and solutions for everyone else. I wondered, God, what about me? I began to be suspicious of God. I thought I had "kept short accounts" with Him. Yet I was stuck. I didn't know how to be released from the prison of my past. I couldn't get free. I'm a Christian and this doesn't happen to Christians. At least that's what I'd been told.

Maybe you can relate? You want peace. You long for a sound mind. You want your broken heart mended. You wonder if you will ever find the abundant life Jesus promises. You feel tangled up by your childhood hurts, past mistakes, or recent misunderstandings. We are products of our upbringing. How we respond to traumatic experiences in our past can be evidenced by choosing to believe something that might be keeping us emotionally, spiritually, or physically entangled in a lie of our own making

"Lie-Knots" Hold Fast

Dr. Ed Silvoso, best-selling author, founder and president of Harvest Evangelism and leader of the Transform Our World Network, says a stronghold is "a mind-set impregnated with hopelessness that causes us to accept as unchangeable situations that we know are contrary to the will of God."[5] When we are adopted into the family of God, no one erases the "hard drive" of our emotions, memories, or mistakes. We come into the relationship with our heavenly Father with false beliefs and coping mechanisms. When we listen to and believe the lies of the enemy, incorrect thinking patterns form. These patterns can trap us, and drive us into hopelessness and despair.

I've developed a list of life challenges and changes, which can begin with an emotional snag, a spiritual snare, and the beginnings of the entanglement of a "lie-knot." These are not all inclusive. If you don't find your current struggle listed, please feel free to add your own:

Disease: Lupus, fibromyalgia, cancer, and others.

Denial or Doubt: I want to believe God, but I just can't.

Depression: I can't get out of bed.

Destruction: 911 calls, a financial cliff, natural disasters, a shooting.

Despair: Why am I here?

Divorce: I wanted to stay married, but he did not.

Discouragement: I pray the same prayer over and over, but nothing changes.

Domestic violence: It's my secret; I am the silent sufferer.

Death: I never expected to bury him/her.

There is no denying these situations are grueling. We can choose to move through circumstances, chaos, confusion, and conflict without being deceived into thinking that difficulties happen because God doesn't love us. The option not to face the issue is never the answer. When we choose to believe God's truth, our new and perhaps unwelcome reality can be God's open door for us to walk through and even embrace the new adventures He has in store. God will not change His mind about His plans and purpose for us. We can be certain of His best as we trade our lies for the truth of His Word. How do we do this? Step two of the process is reading God's Word, getting wise counsel, and trusting dear friends.

Time to Unlearn

I didn't know how to explain "lie-knots," nor was I aware of them until I became so desperately entangled, I had no choice but to deal with them. One morning I woke up and couldn't get out of bed. "I just don't feel like doing anything today." And so I did absolutely nothing on day one. I stayed in bed all day. Day two, I felt the same. Not only was I unproductive, I was discouraged and overwhelmed with anxiety. Days melted into weeks and weeks into months. Before I knew it, six months had passed. This time was lost. I was stuck. I didn't know how to get out of the pit. I didn't know that strongholds prevent us from seeing what is true because of how they make us feel. I still had long-buried feelings of shame and I didn't think I deserved to be forgiven. I felt unforgiven, unloved, and ashamed.

I felt unworthy and condemned. These lies Satan fed me prevented me from believing God's truth about myself. I knew about the freedom and abundant life God offers us, but I thought it was for everyone else but me.

Through professional counseling and scripture, I found the truth about my depressed state. It was more than a physical issue; it was an emotional and spiritual tangled web where I was caught in the middle. I'd been burying the trauma of past events and the effects were depression, fear, anxiety, and self-deprecation. Maybe you too, are experiencing emotional, psychological and spiritual issues. Maybe you've begun to incorrectly reframe your view of major traumatic experiences.

Not Macramé

Knots can be and are useful for practical purposes and enhance our daily life. As a kindergartner, I discovered the value of double knots in my tennis shoelaces. In my teens, I understood the importance and usefulness of knots as I learned the craft of creating macramé plant hangers with square knots, spiral knots, and loop knots. Knots are functional and essential, especially when it comes to a luxurious Turkish carpet. At one hundred double-knotted threads per inch, the knots are what hold the elegant rug tight. Or a boating knot used to securely tie a line to a sturdy piling, rail, or post. Or a fisherman's knot used to secure a rope to a buoy or a line to any anchor. All of these types of physical knots are useful to us and we need them to perform their function.

"Lie-knots" are useful only to the enemy Satan, the accuser of the brethren; who wants us to feel worthless, helpless, and hopeless. His desire is to immobilize us into believing we are beyond God's help and God can't or won't forgive our sins. Because of our guilt and shame, we are not able to overcome and bear spiritual fruit. "He was a murderer from the beginning, not holding to the truth for there is no truth in him. When he lies, he speaks his native language, for he is a liar and the father of lies" (John 8:44).

When we become bound up in "lie-knots," we feel unable to free ourselves. Our problems seem larger than God and God seems distant and uncaring. We have believed the lie of "I have not." It seems as if God is holding out on us, even as if He is blessing everyone else but us. Others may give us well meaning advice or well intended counsel, yet these are not the tools necessary to cut the cords of deception, discouragement, despair, and free us from bondage. The only tool that will sever the bands holding us tight is the Word of God through the power of the Holy Spirit. Our circumstances may cause us to distrust God, but we have a choice about what or whom to believe.

Let me assure you, God wants to know all about what or who has hurt you. You've already taken one of the most important steps, and that is to begin the process of figuring out what to do. The next step is to talk to God about what or who has hurt you. If you are feeling any guilt or shame about your situation, please confess any sin you may have committed. David's restoration began when he confessed his moral failures before God. As he repented of his sins of deception, lying, committing adultery, and murder, he was restored into a right relationship with God. But more than that, his soul began the journey to healing. His prayer is found in Psalm 51:6, "Yet you desired faithfulness even in the womb; you taught me wisdom in that secret place."

Will you believe God's Word or your circumstances? We can change our belief system so that lies are replaced with the truth. What would your life be like if you had no fears? No guilt? No shame? No blame? You can be free from the ties that bind you and have kept you from moving ahead. God's ways may be different than our ways, and often His plans may seem strange or even harsh. ""For my thoughts are not your thoughts, neither are your ways my ways," declares the LORD" (Isaiah. 55:8). But God's ways can be trusted. We have the option of choosing. The choice to believe God is an act of faith involving trust.

Trusting God means we choose to cooperate with Him and implement His ways. We may have some unlearning to do. If we've repeatedly chosen our own ways and given place to sin, a stronghold will become entrenched. God invites us to see things from His perspective and that is my hope and prayer for you as you work through each chapter of this book. I am trusting you will feel God's arms of love around you and His welcoming tender presence. He will help you see what He sees about your past. And then He will help you loosen the knots. By claiming the truth and allowing Him to break down the strongholds you have believed, you will not have to live in fear, anxiety, and despair any longer. We will be discussing more about "identity in Christ" in chapter 2, but I am excited to share a few quotes from others who have experienced firsthand the freedom of understanding their identity in Christ.

> "God showed me the reasons why my life had taken the course it had. Any strongholds or chains that were attaching me to that negativity could be broken. And for me, that was incredible!"

> "The need to kind of please or do things for God to love me has completely gone. I no longer have the need to do things for God to love me. I just know that I am loved and I don't need to do anything for Him to approve of me or want me. And that has had such an effect on how I feel about myself and how happy I am."

"I am beginning to understand who I am in Christ, that I really am accepted, that I really am His child, that I really am adopted and that He will never let me go. It was a big deal. And that changed my life profoundly."

"I have truly learned to submit to God, to resist the devil and to know that he will flee from me, just like God says."[6]

In time, I hope you will add your own testimony to this list of those who have allowed God to untangle the "lie-knot" and help them find who they are in Christ. I wish I had discovered these tools before I became ensnared in a time of feeling hopeless. I am so excited to share these same tools with you.

Chapter 1: Knotted—How Did I Get Here?

Loosening the Lies

Individual or Group Study Questions and Guided Journal Opportunity

Thank you for taking the time to begin to unravel the "lie-knot." You might be thinking "I've believed so many lies, I can't decide which one to focus on first." Don't worry, God will help you. Together, with God's help, we can begin the process of "unraveling the lie-knot." Let's take the next step, based upon knowing the truth is found only in God's Word and trusting God to heal us. It's difficult to begin, but it happens by facing our failures, stepping forward by faith, and embracing our future. Jointly, we can allow the Holy Spirit to show us the end and where to begin to unravel the "lie-knot." Let me pray for you.

Dear Heavenly Father,

Thank You for my dear reader, who is coming to You for help. Lord, would You help her? Could You enable her to experience a deeper relationship with You? Help her to trust You to sever herself free from the lies she is used to believing. Liberate her to see herself as a woman who is healed, emotionally whole, and able to reach the full potential You have designed for her. Give her the abundant life she desires. I commit her to You. In Jesus' name. Amen.

Now it is your turn. Would you take just a moment to pray a prayer of commitment to the process?

Dear Heavenly Father,

Thank You for this opportunity to allow You to reveal areas of my past. The memories of my hurts and hang ups are exceedingly difficult to face, yet with Your help, we can begin. I commit to being open, honest, and vulnerable with You. I declare my dependence upon You. I choose to believe Your Word as truth. Dear Lord, show me if there is any way or anywhere, I am being deceived. Thank You for reminding me of Your faithfulness in the past, and Your presence with me now gives me peace. I ask for Your guidance and protection as I commit to do Your will. Thank You for giving me strength. In Jesus' name. Amen.

First, let's look to our acrostic using the word TRUTH.

T - Take time to pray through the acrostic. Give yourself permission to slow down, stop, and face the things you have been running from. It's time.

> Therefore, since we are surrounded by such a great cloud of witnesses, let us throw off everything that hinders, and the sin that so easily entangles. And let us run with perseverance the race marked out for us (Hebrews 12:1).

Dear Heavenly Father,

Would You show me the lies that have ensnared me?

R - Remember the facts — Determine to get to the root of what or who caused the first snag.

> I remember my affliction and my wandering, the bitterness and the gall (Lamentations 3:19).

Dear Heavenly Father,

Would You reveal the root of the lie? Please show me who or what caused the first snag.

U - Uncover your fear, "unravel the lie-knot" — Behind every fear is a lie that is believed.

> If we claim to have fellowship with him and yet walk in the darkness, we lie and do not live out the truth (1 John 1:6).

Dear Heavenly Father,

Would You show me the fear behind the lies I have believed?

T - Tell yourself the truth. Scripture spoken aloud ushers in healing and brings wholeness. This is how renewal takes place.

He has sent me to bind up the brokenhearted, to proclaim freedom for the captives and release from darkness for the prisoners (Isaiah 61:1).

Dear Heavenly Father,

I declare: You have shown me - You will bind up my broken heart.

You announce freedom for me, the captive, and You release me from darkness. Thank You.

H - Help is available by agreeing with God. Confess your sin, submit to God, declare the truth aloud over yourself. Let Jesus untie your bondage.

Jesus said to them, 'Loose him, and let him go' (John 11:44 KJV).

Dear Heavenly Father,

I confess my sin. I have sinned by (fill in the blank with your specific sin.)

I choose to submit to You. Thank You for cleansing me. I speak the truth over myself.

Jesus said to them, 'Loose (<u>fill in your name</u>) and let her go' (John 11:44 KJV).

Loosening the Lies

Individual or Group Study Questions and Guided Journal Opportunity

1. Describe the gifts God gave to Adam and Eve that were restored through the sacrifice of God's Son, Jesus Christ.

2. Can you think of ways you've been deceived and the untruths you've believed?

3. What has happened in your past to bring you to the point where you may have questioned "is God is holding out on me?"

4. Have any of these experiences caused you regret? Anguish? Anger? Other emotions?

5. Can you figure out if the areas you listed above might be a snare of entanglement for you? Why or Why Not?

6. If so, please take a moment and pray. Ask God to help you find the beginning of the "lie-knot." Write it down in the space below.

Dear Heavenly Father,

Please show me the end of the "lie-knot."

7. Ask God to help you learn how to begin to tell yourself the truth.

Dear Heavenly Father,

Thank You for the truth of Your Word. Help me find a truth tool that will begin to cut me free from the tangles of my "lie-knot."

8. Search out a Scripture verse or two from this chapter to help you counter lies you've believed about God. Write down the verse, reference, or page number here.

9. Ask God to show you how the lies you believed about Him affected your view of His provision, presence, and purposes for your life.

Dear Heavenly Father,

You are Lord of my life. Thank You for this time of reflection on Your goodness. Thank You for reminding me – yes, You can be trusted. I am grateful for Your work in my life. Thank You for restoring my acceptance, security, and significance through the finished work of Jesus Christ. Thank You for doing a new thing in me. In Jesus' name I pray. Amen.

10. Pray a prayer of commitment to the process

Dear Heavenly Father,

Thank You for Your commitment to me. Forgive me for trying to attempt overcoming my hurt and habits on my own. I see now, all along, Your plan was for me to do it in partnership with You. I am re-committing to Your provision, presence, and purposes for my life. Thank You, Lord, I don't have to go through this alone. I am strengthened through Your love, peace, and hope. Thank You for giving me a second chance. I am grateful and relieved. In Jesus' name. Amen.

Truth Tools

For the word of the Lord is right and true, he is faithful in all he does (Psalm 33:4).

God decided in advance to adopt us into his own family by bringing us to himself through Jesus Christ. That is what he wanted to do, and it gave him great pleasure (Ephesians 1:5 NLT).

Let perseverance finish its work so that you may be mature and complete, not lacking anything. If any of you lacks wisdom, you should ask God, who gives generously to all without finding fault, and it will be given to you. But when you ask, you must believe and not doubt, because the one who doubts is like a wave of the sea, blown and tossed by the wind. That person should not expect to receive anything from the Lord. Such a person is double-minded and unstable in all they do (James 1:4-8).

But when he, the Spirit of truth comes, he will guide you into all truth. He will not speak on his own; he will speak only what he hears and he will tell you what is yet to come (John 16:13).

The wicked have set a snare for me, but I have not strayed from your precepts (Psalm 119:110).

I am the (wo)man who has seen affliction by the rod of the Lord's wrath. I remember my affliction and my wandering, the bitterness and the gall. I well remember them, and my soul is downcast within me. Yet this I call to mind and therefore I have hope: because of the Lord's great love we are not consumed, for his compassions never fail. They are new every morning; great is your faithfulness. I say to myself, 'The Lord is my portion; therefore, I will wait for him.' The Lord is good to those whose hope is in him, to the one who seeks him (Lamentations 3:1, 19-25).

Freed by Faith

A prayer of adoration and devotion.

Dear Heavenly Father,

Thank You for Your goodness and faithfulness to show me any way or anywhere I have been deceived. Thank You for loving me enough to send Your Son, Jesus Christ, so I can know You in an intimate way. Thank You for my relationship with Jesus Christ, whose blood has covered all my sin. Thanks for Your gift of grace, which has enabled me to face my hurt and has helped be to trust You to find the end of the "lie-knot." Father, I am grateful for the increased opportunity to trust You. As You know, it's kind of scary, but I declare, "You are faithful in all You do" (Psalm 33:4). In Jesus' name. Amen.

We should be astonished at the goodness of God, stunned that He should bother to call us by name, our mouths wide open at His love, bewildered that at this very moment we are standing on holy ground.[1]

Brennan Manning

Chapter 2: Tangled - Where Are You God?

"I'm worthless. I'm not valuable. This has been true since childhood."

"I'm inadequate. I don't have what it takes – didn't then and don't now."

"People will always reject me just like my daddy did when I was four."

"No one will ever love me because I've made bad choices in my life."

"My first husband left me. I will never be unconditionally accepted."

These are a few of the statements that Erin Smalley (Focus on The Family's strategic spokesperson for the marriage ministry) has heard from women throughout the country. "I was shocked how cruel we women can be to ourselves" said Erin. "When I speak at marriage conferences, I pass out sticky notes and ask women to write down the negative self-talk they tell themselves. Looking at the long list, I realized the messages these women were telling themselves were lies. Every single one."[2]

What is at the root of this seemingly hopeless state? During trials and difficulties, half-truths, misguided guilt, undeserved blame, feeling stuck, depression, and anxiety, and other issues may surface. It may not seem or feel painful at the time, but eventually you realize there may be something unsettled in your life. You're not sure how or what issues need to be dealt with first. For some, the revelation of the importance of facing the untangling process may take years to happen. As was the case of my depression, any type of stress, adverse circumstances, or upsetting events often reveal our matted messes. The necklace unknotting principle is similar to the one we will learn as we discover God's answers for straightening out emotional or spiritual "lie-knots."

It goes like this. When we're adopted into the family of God, no one erases the "hard drive" of our emotions, memories, or mistakes. We have relied on the flesh for so long. Now we must reverse these flesh patterns and be taught how to depend on the Holy Spirit's guidance. Unfortunately, we come into a sweet relationship with our heavenly Father with false beliefs and dysfunctional coping mechanisms. We've been used to relying on ourselves and developing skills of coping through difficulties that may become flesh patterns. The good news is that it is possible to unlearn negative ways of thinking and tell ourselves the truth.

Dr. Neil T. Anderson, founder and president emeritus of Freedom In Christ Ministries says, "Strongholds are mental habit patterns of thought that are not consistent with God's Word."[3] These strongholds can be dealt with and we can live free from bondage to them. The step towards finding the solution to freedom takes trust and transparency. As we immerse ourselves in and apply God's Word to our lives, believe it to be the truth, how we view God and ourselves changes. It begins in our hearts.

Heart Matters

Jesus does a new thing in our heart when we respond to Him by faith. "I will give you a new heart and put a new spirit in you; I will remove from you your heart of stone and give you a heart of flesh" (Ezekiel 36:26). It helps to remind ourselves that the "old us" is gone, because we have a difficult time forgetting and forgiving ourselves of past mistakes. If we embrace this fact by application, it can result in heart transformation to activate our faith, trust, and hope in God's power. This truth helps us move forward. The renewed condition of our heart is a key component for us to break free from the control of our flesh and then begin to depend on the Holy Spirit. We can't live in lasting obedience to God without a change of heart. Once that change happens, we can trust and obey God wholeheartedly with assurance of results. Paul describes how our hearts become changed in Romans 6:17, "But thanks be to God that, though you used to be slaves to sin, you have come to obey from your heart the pattern of teaching that has now claimed your allegiance."

The second we become a Christian, everything changes. The decision to accept Christ as our Savior is the defining moment of our lives. The Bible says, "Therefore, if anyone is in Christ, the new creation has come; the old has gone, the new is here" (2 Corinthians 5:17). Can you be partly old or partly new? No! We've thought of ourselves as "a sinner saved by grace," which we are. But Romans 5:8 reminds us, "While we were still sinners, Christ died for us." It seems to imply that we are no longer sinners. The word "sinner" appears over 300 times in the New Testament and refers to those who are not yet Christians. The term does not refer to Christians unless it talks about who they used to be.[4]

Many of us have forgotten or have never known who we are in Christ. Instead of believing the lie that "God is distant and uncaring," we can remind ourselves in Christ that He is good. We may question God's goodness, especially when bad things happen, but His Word says that "His divine power has given us everything we need for a godly life through our knowledge of him who called us by his own glory and goodness" (2 Peter 1:3). Most of us wonder why there's so much tension between what we know God has given us and how we actually walk it out. Years after my conversion, I wondered why I felt frustrated and continued to fail in my efforts to forget my past. I knew Jesus as my Savior, yet I hadn't experienced the abundant life He promises.

Identity Matters

Adding to the tangled mess of adulthood, I got stuck in the devil's trap and allowed the ballet class nicknames to keep me ensnared. When depression surfaced two decades later, I was forced to pay attention to my emotions. I was a busy pastor's wife, weary mother of two young children, active PTA president, and community volunteer. I was hanging by a thread. If anyone asked how I was doing, I responded I'm fine. I was an actress. Not on the big screen or on Broadway, but I got quite efficient at pretending things were okay. I was dying inside.

In chapter one, we discussed that identity was not what you do or the roles you play. Identity in Christ is found in the position God has given us. I didn't know that strongholds prevented me from seeing what is true because of how they made me feel. I still had long-buried feelings of shame. I didn't think I deserved to be forgiven. I felt unforgiven, unloved, and ashamed. I felt unworthy and condemned. These lies Satan fed me prevented me from believing God's truth about myself. I knew about the freedom and abundant life God offers us, but I thought it was for everyone else but me.

I hadn't yet embraced the truth of my position in Christ found in Ephesians 1:18-21. "I pray that the eyes of your heart may be enlightened in order that you may know the hope to which he has called you, the riches of his glorious inheritance in his holy people, and his incomparably great power for us who believe. That power is the same as the mighty strength he exerted when he raised Christ from the dead and seated him at his right hand in the heavenly realms, far above all rule and authority, power and dominion, and every name that is invoked, not only in the present age but also in the one to come."

Once I understood this truth and let it soak into my spirit, it was as if the blinders came off. For two decades, I had tried to make myself feel hopeful. I did everything I could to gain my own approval. If I heard about a new self-help book, I'd buy it and read it. Or if I heard about a quick-fix seminar, I'd go. Or thinking how I looked or what I wore mattered, I'd dress in the current designer fashions. I would try the latest fad diet or exercise program only to feel ten times worse the next month when I'd gone off the programs and gained back the weight.

God wanted me to rest in the hope He provides, not in any hope I tried to make up. I made a choice to believe God and rely on His power, even when it felt hopeless. I chose not to trust my feelings. I thought about the power God exhibited when He raised Jesus from the dead. It stunned me to think that authority over death is mine to exert over my past. I let go of it and accepted the fact that the old me is dead. And now it was time for the new me to walk forward into an exciting and hopeful future.

Are you unaware of areas of deception? Are you depressed? Overly anxious? Is your mind filled with negative thoughts? Are you unable to sleep for more than an hour at a time? The symptoms I've listed may be the result of a "lie-knot" that is festering. These symptoms usually begin with a traumatic event that is processed incorrectly. The "lie-knot" we are discussing here is "I could not" and the deceptive concept is "God is distant and uncaring." When we feel like God can't be trusted, or doesn't have our best interests in mind, we question if He is good. We ask why should I trust God? It feels like He is distant, uncaring, absent. We look around, compare, contrast, and wonder why God seems so near to others and so far away from us. Often the lies that make us feel distant from God are deeply ingrained in our hearts. My heart was bruised, and my soul was damaged by the harsh comments dealt to me by those who wanted to make themselves seem more important. This was accomplished by making me look and feel small.

Is God Good?

God is held up before us as the standard of goodness, as described in scripture. Psalm 25:8 says "Good and upright is the LORD; therefore, he instructs sinners in his ways." God is the one who decides what is good and what is not. We don't. God has been accused of all kinds of evil—that His past actions may have been too harsh or that His words about what will take place at the final judgment are evil. We need to remember that God's works are good. Step-by-step as God created the world, He examined it and declared it to be good. In Genesis 1:9, 10, we see God's goodness magnified. "And God said, "Let the water under the sky be gathered to one place, and let dry ground appear." And it was so. God called the dry ground "land," and the gathered waters he called "seas." And God saw that it was good." He then surveyed the whole of creation, and said it was "very good."

The Psalmist said, "You are good, and what you do is good; teach me your decrees" (Psalm 119:68). God's gifts are good. God guarantees that for believers, "all things work together for good" and that even discipline is for our good. "Consider it pure joy, my brothers and sisters, whenever you face trials of many kinds, because you know that the testing of your faith produces perseverance. Let perseverance finish its work so that you may be mature and complete, not lacking anything" (James 1:2-4). Even in times of trial, disease, denial, doubt, depression, destruction, despair, divorce, discouragement, domestic violence, and death we can make the solid choice to believe what is true about God.

God's commands are good, and His laws are a reflection of His holy nature. His commandments are a revelation of His moral perfection. Our God-given goal is to become like God, and His laws are given for that very purpose "Be perfect, therefore, as your heavenly Father is perfect" (Matthew 5:48). God is the one who set the standard by which we measure goodness. No one truly knows goodness until they know God.

As a child, my heart became hardened by stressful events and others' evil actions toward me. It was time for me to unlearn the lies I believed about God. I now call Him my good, good Father.

The Heart of Me

I didn't trust God for decades. My heart had been hardened by the words of harsh people and horrific events. I didn't know the complexities of my own heart and the fact that it is much more than the "seat" of my emotions. The "heart" can be broken by loss, disappointment, or failure. The Bible explains that the heart imagines, considers, meditates, pours out and aches. Scripture also tells us to "set our hearts on things above." "Since, then, you have been raised with Christ, set your hearts on things above, where Christ is, seated at the right hand of God. Set your minds on things above, not on earthly things. For you died, and your life is now hidden with Christ in God" (Colossians 3:1-3).

In the Life Application Study Bible, the notes define this passage as "striving to put heaven's priorities into daily practice."[5] Why is this so hard to do? The human heart is the emotional axis of a human life. The heart is the center of our belief system. It mirrors what we hold to be true about ourselves, our circumstances, and God. We were made in God's image and in Genesis 1:26 we understand how God crafted us to be like Him. "Then God said, "Let us make mankind in our image, in our likeness, so that they may rule over the fish in the sea and the birds in the sky, over the livestock and all the wild animals, and over all the creatures that move along the ground.""

The following verses from God's Word may help you experience the process your heart feels as it's emotionally drawn to God in adoration.

- Love the Lord your God with all your heart, with all your soul and with all your mind (Matthew 22:37).

- As you lift up your praise in worship, "I will give thanks to you; Lord, with all my heart; I will tell of all your wonderful deeds" (Psalm 9:1).

- If you are confused with a decision, wavering from doubt to belief, "Teach me thy ways; O Lord, I will walk in thy truth. Unite my heart to fear thy name" (Psalm 86:11, KJV).

Embracing God's goodness, regardless of what is going on in our lives is an element of trusting Him that moves us to a deeper faith. It's in moving forward in faith we respond to God with an attitude of hope and submission to His ways with all of our hearts. How's your heart today?

Position's Purpose

In Christ, you have the tools to enable you to be free from your fears, depression, anxiety, discouragement and bitterness. The only solution we need is Jesus Christ. As you persevere and continue to step out in trust, God will meet you and heal your wounds. Some of us might want our healing from the past hurts, devastating losses, harmful wounds or irritating addictions to take place immediately. I get it. We want our deliverance. We want it now. We are used to accessing what we want in relatively short periods of waiting time. We can order groceries online and have them delivered to our doorstep. We can text our food or coffee order and have it brought to us within an hour.

God can provide immediate release from bondage. I have experienced it first-hand; God removed my desire to use street drugs the moment I received Jesus as my Lord and Savior. I wish I could say He did the same thing for my craving to smoke cigarettes. My release from my intense nicotine addiction was a process that took months. For other things, my deliverance has taken years. But I have not given up asking God to help me as I choose to die to my flesh and give more attention to living by the ways of the Spirit. This means I am devoted to reminding myself of truths such as, "For the word of God is alive and active. Sharper than any double-edged sword, it penetrates even to dividing soul and spirit, joints and marrow; it judges the thoughts and attitudes of the heart" (Hebrews 4:12). What do you want God to do for you?

Do you long for peace? Wonder what it would be like if positive thoughts came into our minds first, instead of negative ones? Need a break from worry and anxiety? I get it. It's been a process. I didn't know where to begin or what to do. Do you wonder if it's possible to be free? Let me assure you, it's not only possible, it is available. It begins with understanding who we are in Christ.

Remember, my identity is not the title that is listed on my driver's license or passport. My name is Sheryl Giesbrecht Turner. I am a woman, wife, mother, grandmother, daughter, employee, writer, speaker, friend, mentor, runner, and last but not least, avid dog-lover. These titles describe things I do and relationships I have but they do not describe who I really am. You may have heard of the word "saint," often referred to in the New Testament as a shorthand term for believers. In English, the word "saint" has been translated as "holy one." This means you and I are holy, set apart for God, special. We are "saints who sometimes sin." We are adopted into God's family. We are children of God. If we know who we are in Christ, we realize the victory has already been won. The battle is over. God's will is for us to let go of our past by trusting Him with all of our hurts and hang-ups. I've learned that we can't reach for anything new if our hands are still full of yesterday's junk. You are not saved by how you behave but by what you believe. When you begin to believe differently, your behavior will follow suit. If we apply this understanding of our identity in Christ, we begin to see how absolutely essential this knowledge is to live the victorious Christian life.

Instead of moving forward by faith into the abundant life God has for them, most Christians live their lives at a spiritual standstill, tied up in knots. In spite of the tangled web you may be trapped in, or how horrible you feel about yourself, the truth is, if you have accepted Jesus as your Savior, you can be free. Who you are in Christ is a fact because of the finished work of Jesus Christ. Who you are now is a fact and Satan cannot change it. But if he can get you to believe a lie about who you are, he can cripple your walk with God.[6]

What do I mean by "understanding our identity in Christ?" No matter what comes our way, in Christ we are secure. Our mistakes should not define us. God doesn't hold our sins, mistakes, or missteps against us. The real you is in your identity in Christ. Once we know what God says about us and believe it to be the truth, everything about how we view God and ourselves changes. Are there situations in your past that you need to acknowledge and be freed from? If you are a Christian, then the statements below are true of you.

Who I Am in Christ

I am accepted...

John 1:12 – I am God's child.

John 15:15 – As a disciple, I am a friend of Jesus Christ.

Romans 5:1 – I have been justified.

1 Corinthians 6:17 – I am united with the Lord, and I am one with Him in spirit.

1 Corinthians 6:19-20 – I have been bought with a price, and I belong to God.

1 Corinthians 12:27 – I am a member of Christ's body.

Ephesians 1:3-8 – I have been chosen by God and adopted as His child.

Colossians 1:13-14 – I have been redeemed and forgiven of all my sins.

Colossians 2:9-10 – I am complete in Christ.

Hebrews 4:14-16 – I have direct access to the throne of grace through Jesus Christ.

I am secure...

Romans 8:1-2 – I am free from condemnation.

Romans 8:28 – I am assured that God works for my good in all circumstances.

Romans 8:31-39 – I am free from any condemnation brought against me, and I cannot be separated from the love of God.

2 Corinthians 1:21-22 – I have been established, anointed, and sealed by God.

Colossians 3:1-4 – I am hidden with Christ in God.

Philippians 1:6 – I am confident that God will complete the good work he started in me.

Philippians 3:20 – I am a citizen of heaven.

2 Timothy 1:7 – I have not been given a spirit of fear but of power, love, and a sound mind.

1 John 5:18 – I am born of God and the evil one cannot touch me.

I am significant...

John 15:5 – I am a branch of Jesus Christ, the true vine, and a channel of His life.

John 15:16 – I have been chosen and appointed to bear fruit.

1 Corinthians 3:16 – I am God's temple.

2 Corinthians 5:17-21 –I am a minister of reconciliation for God.

Ephesians 2:6 – I am seated with Jesus Christ in the heavenly realm.

Ephesians 2:10 – I am God's workmanship.

Ephesians 3:12 – I may approach God with freedom and confidence.

Philippians 4:13 – I can do all things through Christ, who strengthens me.[7]

God's Truth Frees

God can release anyone from a painful past. It may take time, but the most important part of the process is when the individual chooses to begin allowing God to do their unraveling. Through submission to God, obedience to His Word and declaration of the truth, the process of deliverance is set in motion. We can ask God to show us any place in our lives where we are continually paying the consequences for something that needs to be broken. We can have truth in our minds, but it's not until we believe it and step into the course of trusting God to move us ahead that we discover true liberation.

God gives us the choice to take responsibility for what is ours. The baseline is God has given us the opportunity to know who we are in Christ. Each of us is a holy child of the living God who already has everything we require to be the woman God has created us to be. 2 Peter 1:3 says "His divine power has given us everything (not nearly everything) we need for a godly life." God has given us "every spiritual blessing" (Ephesians 1:3) He knew we would want. God has already done everything to enable us to walk in wholeness. It's up to us to make the daily choice to live as God intended or not.

The most defeated Christians give up and sit down without asking God to help them untie their "lie-knots." Others try to argue or reason their way through but are unable to make any progress. We can cut through the tangled mess as we obey the prompting of the Holy Spirit, and stay committed to obey the truth, no matter how we feel. Free will is important to God. Breaking free of our bondage is hard work but so worth every bit of effort. And we don't have to do it alone. "Walk by the Spirit, and you will not gratify the desires of the flesh" (Galatians. 5:16). The following is an amazing testimony of a woman who trusted God with her horrible childhood.

My parents were both very young when they got pregnant with me—around thirteen or fourteen years old. My grandmother was very young as well. Since my mom's pregnancy was unplanned and unwanted, she started feeding my mom turpentine, quinine and ginger root tea, old wives' tales for ways of getting rid of the baby. When she gave birth to me, she actually left me at the hospital. I had an issue with things like not being wanted, not being loved, and that carried on throughout my life.

I kind of established a way of putting a protection around myself, I tried to be good enough, pretty enough, and smart enough just to make people love me. Every time something traumatic happened in my life, it was like I was placing another brick on top of the wall. I was kidnapped at age four at gunpoint and was told by one set of the kidnappers, which was my biological family, (biological mother and grandmother) that they came and kidnapped me because my adoptive mom was going to kill me. And then I was kidnapped back by the adopted mom, who she told me that she came to get me because they were going to kill me.

So, each time a traumatic experience happened, it was like I was placing another brick on this wall I was building to supposedly protect myself from more injury, more hurt. And from that point, the molestation started, so that was further securing the lie that I wasn't loved, I wasn't wanted, I was rejected, I wasn't good enough. So, it led to a lot of failed relationships, and every time a relationship failed, another brick on the wall. And I had a friendship that broke up, another brick on my wall.

A couple of years ago, I was exposed to the *Freedom In Christ* message. I realized that I was already secure, and I was already significant, and I was already accepted by my Father God, and I was able to start breaking these walls down. So, every time I forgave someone, a brick came down. Every time I renounced the lie that I wasn't accepted, a brick came down. I chose to let the wall come down and I was able to experience the love of Christ in a way unlike anything I had ever experienced before.[8]

As you listened to this young woman's story maybe you, like me, felt a gamut of emotions? Horrified, saddened, shocked, and even questioning if justice would be served? My heart was shredded because of the generational sins committed against her. Only through Christ, was she able to heal from her abandonment issues, recover from the years of abuse, and overcome the decades of shame. I admire the courage she mustered to face her past, to find the end of her "lie-knot," and let God do her unraveling.

Negative self-talk really does influence our actions. We can rewire our brains to reflect the truth through our daily choice to think truth. God's truth. In response to Jesus by faith, He does a new thing in our hearts; the Holy Spirit's renewal is a key component to break the control of the flesh. As we stand in our position in Christ, depending on the finished work of the cross, our trust is renewed as He helps us find the end of our "lie-knot." We can invite Him to begin and have the confidence to let Him have His way.

The choice is yours. It takes a purposeful decision to think new thoughts. In doing so, you invite God to renew your mind and heal your hurts by the power of His Word. It's an "aha moment," to realize our belief system may not be in line with what God says is true in His Word. As we submit to God and give Him permission to bring to the surface any lies, we may have believed, we can examine each falsehood that is exposed, renounce the lie we have believed, and meditate on the truth from God's Word. If we make the decision to start the process, God will help us take the next steps. With His help, you can be transformed by the renewing of your mind. Come against the lies you have believed about yourself. Start telling yourself the truth. Now.

Chapter 2: Tangled – Where Are You God?

Loosening the Lies

Individual or Group Study Questions and Guided Journal Opportunity

Thank you for continuing the "unraveling lie-knot" discussion with me. In this chapter, *Tangled – Where Are You God,* we discussed the times when we feel like God is distant or uninterested. Thankfully, He is not the one who moves away, usually it is our choice to attempt to do things on our own that pushes Him out. Another possibility could be that our view of Him is clouded by our tragic circumstances or our unwillingness to agree with Him and let Him do things His way. Getting to the end of the snag of our "lie-knot" may take time. I know, wouldn't it be great if we could have quick relief? Yes, I agree, it would be wonderful. But usually it is not that quick or simple. Remember, we did not get into the place we are overnight. For some of us, myself included, we endured several decades without relief, which only caused us to become increasingly enmeshed. The process of "unraveling the lie-knot" may take time. And that is okay. Today, let me pray a prayer of commitment for you.

Dear Heavenly Father,

I pray for you, dear reader, from Ephesians 1:18, 19 " I pray that the eyes of your heart may be enlightened in order that you may know the hope to which he has called you, the riches of his glorious inheritance in his holy people, and his incomparably great power for us who believe." Thank You for the power and presence we find together by praying Your Word. In Jesus' name. Amen.

Now it's your turn. Here is your prayer of dedication to the process. Let's pray.

Dear Heavenly Father,

Thank You for the opportunity to ask, "Where are You, God?" Thank You for the gentle whisper of Your Holy Spirit, reminding me that even when I don't see it, You are working. Thank You for continuing to give me insight and revelation according to what Your plan is next. In Jesus' name. Amen.

Let's look to our acrostic using the word TRUTH.

T - Take time.

Let's pray through the acrostic using the T.R.U.T.H. statement. Give yourself space, time, permission to slow down, and let God show you His present involvement. Let Him reveal to you something new about His presence and your identity in Christ.

I've looked up two scriptures for you.

> His divine power has given us everything we need for a godly life through our knowledge of him who called us by his own glory and goodness (2 Peter 1:3).

> Praise be to the God and Father of our Lord Jesus Christ, who has blessed us in the heavenly realms with every spiritual blessing in Christ (Ephesians 1:3).

> *Dear Heavenly Father,*

> *Thank You for showing me something new about myself and my identity in Christ. In Jesus' name. Amen.*

Please speak aloud these two scriptures – 2 Peter 1:3 and Ephesians 1:3.

R - Remember the facts.

Do you remember what happened? Look back, recount, and review the course of your life events. It's time to replace the lies with truth. This is the process of how we cut free from the knots of deception. Holding close to truth is how we learn to take God at His Word.

You have renewed your pledge to devote yourself to search out and find truth. It is a choice to be dedicated to learning what God thinks about us. When we do this, the impact of the opinions and accusations of others will be diminished.[9] It helps to take control of our thoughts and say His Word out loud. The truth in Romans 8:1 breaks through guilt, shame, blame, and unworthiness,

Therefore, there is now no condemnation for those who are in Christ Jesus (Romans 8:1).

Let God defend you and free you through the power of His Word.

Dear Heavenly Father,
Thank You for giving me strength to remember the facts. In Jesus' name. Amen.

Declare aloud the truth of Romans 8:1.

U - Uncover your fear, unravel the "lie-knot."

Do you know why are you afraid? I know it is intimidating to face the truth, but that is where the healing begins. So, if you are able, please name the fear and replace it with truth. By doing so, you submit to God your decision to walk forward in faith. When we feel guilty, it is difficult to move forward. We don't have to be victimized by our past, held captive to our thoughts, or imprisoned by how others perceive us. Trusting God moves us ahead unhindered. Our progress becomes secure as we apply God's word to our circumstances and allow Him to move us from deception to truth.

Dear Heavenly Father,

Would You reveal to me my fears? Thank You, in Jesus' name, Amen.

T - Tell yourself the truth.

Scripture spoken and meditation is the way renewal takes place. It's a personal choice to claim the promises of God and allow them to become real. We can be "made new in our mind." Spiritual revitalization is available to each of us when we choose to allow God's Word to transform our minds by reading it, praying it, saying it, memorizing it, listening to it, and keeping it at hand.

Dear Heavenly Father,

Thank You for renewing my mind. Thank You for replacing lies with Your truth. In Jesus' name, Amen.

Declare this Scripture over yourself.

> Therefore, I urge you, brothers and sisters, in view of God's mercy, to offer your bodies as a living sacrifice, holy and pleasing to God—this is your true and proper worship. Do not conform to the pattern of this world but be transformed by the renewing of your mind. Then you will be able to test and approve what God's will is—his good, pleasing and perfect will (Romans 12:1,2).

H – Help is available by agreeing with God.

As we turn to God for help, that is where we find the answer for how to tell ourselves the truth.

> You were taught, with regard to your former way of life, to put off your old self, which is being corrupted by its deceitful desires; to be made new in the attitude of your minds; and to put on the new self, created to be like God in true righteousness and holiness (Ephesians 4:22-24).

Trusting God moves us ahead unhindered. Our progress becomes secure as we apply God's Word to our circumstances and allow Him to move us from deception to truth.

Dear Heavenly Father,

I come to You for help. I agree with You about my condition. Thank You for Your grace, mercy, and compassion. Thank You for Your support and presence. In Jesus' name, Amen.

Loosening the Lies

Individual or Group Study Questions and Guided Journal Opportunity

The Psalmist said, "You are good, and what you do is good; teach me your decrees" (Psalm 119:68). God's gifts are good. God guarantees that for believers, "all things work together for good" and even discipline is for our good. Sometimes this truth is difficult to accept or experience, so let's take a few more moments to process, okay?

1. Describe a time when you have felt distant from God or have questioned His goodness.

2. Explain your heart condition at that time and how it may have affected your choices.

3. If you have not already done so, please take a few moments to list several nicknames you were called as a child. (By the way, I am so sorry to ask you to go here, thank you.)

4. Are you aware of the lies behind the nicknames? (God is with you.)

5. As you remember, behind every fear is a lie you have believed. Can you determine the fear ("lie-knot") you believed?

6. Do you agree with this statement or not? "Who you are in Christ is a fact because of the finished work of Jesus Christ." Why or Why Not?

7. Yes, you can do it. Choose to "put off the old self," disown guilt, shame, and blame. Evict these things. They do not belong in you. Throw out these toxic attitudes by declaring God's Word over your life and your whole being.

Dear Heavenly Father,

Thank You for showing me how to allow You to cut away guilt, shame, and blame. Help me to claim at least one of the verses in the "Identity in Christ" statements of truth to come against the lie I have believed about myself, You, or my circumstance. Thank You. In Jesus' name, Amen.

8. Please take a few moments to go back to the "Identity In Christ" statements of truth. Speak them aloud over yourself.

9. Thank you for beginning the process to understand and own up to your identity in Christ. To experience our freedom in Christ and grow in the grace of God requires repentance, which literally means a change of mind. God will enable that process as we submit to Him and resist the devil.

> Resist the devil, and he will flee from you (James 4:7).

10. Share one scripture God has used to renew your mind and help you reclaim your identity in Christ. Pray a prayer of commitment to the process.

Dear Heavenly Father,

Thank You for helping me to begin the process of "unraveling the lie-knot" and showing me how to replace the lie with the truth found in Your Word. I am so incredibly grateful for Your goodness. Thank You for giving me renewed hope, peace, and strength in this time of renewal. It seems overwhelming sometimes, I feel like I have so far to go. Thank You for allowing me to take the time I need. In Jesus' name, Amen.

Truth Tools

The thief comes only to steal and kill and destroy; I have come that they may have life and have it to the full (John 10:10).

This is the confidence we have in approaching God: that if we ask anything according to his will, he hears us. And if we know that he hears us—whatever we ask—we know that we have what we asked of him (I John 5:14-15).

Yes, my soul, find rest in God; my hope comes from him (Psalm 62:5).

Ask and it will be given to you; seek and you will find; knock and the door will be opened to you. For everyone who asks receives; the one who seeks finds; and to the one who knocks, the door will be opened (Matthew 7:7-8).

Now to him who is able to do immeasurably more than all we ask or imagine, according to his power that is at work within us, to him be glory in the church and in Christ Jesus throughout all generations, for ever and ever! Amen (Ephesians 3:20-21).

 Devote yourselves to prayer, being watchful and thankful (Colossians 4:2).

Freed By Faith
A prayer of devotion and dedication.

Dear Heavenly Father,

Thank You for Your plan for my life. Thank You for helping to uncover my fears and begin to "unravel the lie-knot." Thank You for all You have done to show me how to accept the gifts of grace by understanding my identity in Christ. Thank You for restoring me into a relationship with You. Thank You for reminding me — I am accepted, I am secure, I am significant. I pray for myself — to remain committed to the process. I choose to remain dedicated to "ask and receive, seek and find out Your truth.' (Matthew 7:7-8) Thank You for revealing it to me. Thank You for the time we spent together today. I love You and thank You for keeping Your Word at the forefront of my mind. In Jesus' name, Amen.

The cruelest slavery is the slavery inflicted by ignorance of the truth.

Ed Silvoso[1]

Chapter 3: Snarled – Why Should I Trust You God?

Alexander the Great drew his sword high overhead. With one blow, the warrior sliced through the knee-high knotted mass as if it were a lump of soft butter. The legend was that the hero who performed the feat of untying the tangled knots attached to the ox-cart wagon's yoke would become ruler of all of Asia. Some questioned the method used. Not one to pass up a challenge or reward, the eager Alexander the Great was sure he would be the one to untie the Gordian knot. The general had pulled, pushed, and wrestled the ropes, only to make them constrict into more tightly bound knots. After several unsuccessful tries, he stepped away from the gnarly mess, and shouted, "It makes no difference how they are loosed." He drew his sword to slice the knot in half with a single stroke.[2] After all, the wagon's previous owner was thought to be Gordius; the father of Midas. The yoke's snarled mess was described by a Roman historian, "as several knots all so tightly entangled that it was impossible to see how they were fastened." The phrase "cutting the Gordian knot" is used to explain a creative solution to an overwhelming problem. Don't you wish it were that easy? Are you yearning for that one cut of a powerful weapon that could slash through your snarled "lie-knots?"

Find the End

It only took one slice of his powerful sword for Alexander the Great to solve the puzzle of the "Gordian knot." Like the mighty general, we can perform the same action spiritually with the sword of the Spirit—the Word of God. By noticing, paying attention, and making the choice to begin, God will help us through the process of untangling the "lie-knots" we've believed about our past. It's so hard to want to see the facts about what happened to us. Sometimes it's easier to ignore the past. We've buried it for so long, why bring it up now? God's Word promises that His divine power will move us forward into victory as we practice His methods. "The weapons we fight with are not the weapons of the world. On the contrary, they have divine power to demolish strongholds" (2 Corinthians 10:4). I wish I would have owned up to that truth during a time I'd felt especially melancholy.

Cut to the Chase

During my time of deep depression, I wasn't getting well as fast as my husband and I thought I should. I was stuck and unable to address the pain on my own, so we decided that I needed help. The day my husband, Paul, took me to see a psychologist, my thoughts and emotions bounced all over the place. I was hopeful, yet wary. We had visited other counselors as a couple without success and a few times I'd even gone on my own. I wondered, would God come through? He hadn't answered my prayers. Did He love me and want me better? Why would this counselor be any different?

Terrified, I entered the spacious office. We were welcomed as we settled into comfortable leather chairs. After a few moments of gathering background information, the counselor asked, "why are you here?" I began to sniff, trying to fight back the tears. Then I began to cry, weep, and finally, wail. I couldn't hold it together anymore. Doubled over, head to my knees, I covered my face with my hands and heaved, sobbing uncontrollably. Neither Paul nor the counselor moved toward me. The five or so minutes that passed seemed like an eternity, and then Dr. Dixon turned to me and said, "Tell me about your daily life." Through my sobs, I explained how Paul had asked me to take on more responsibilities with the business. I was now doing both excruciatingly, physical janitorial work, and mentally taxing bookkeeping, all while taking care of our three-year-old and preparing for the birth of our second child. These physical, mental, and emotional stressors made me tired and unable to cope. Surprisingly, the stress even began to reveal areas of spiritually unresolved conflict, much of which involved past illicit sexual experiences.

For more than two decades before that meeting, my hurt and hate of those who had wronged me lay buried alive. Now these painful and horrible recollections of people who had taken advantage of me, and my inability to defend myself were resurrected by multiple external pressures. In my weakened state I was vulnerable again. Could I finally come clean and be honest with myself? Would God use the situation not to my harm, but for my good? Author and speaker, Marilyn Meberg says, "You gotta feel it to heal it." I wasn't sure I wanted to hurt that good!

Unbeknownst to me, God was bringing to the surface issues from my reckless teen years, situations that I had emotionally blocked but that were still harming me from the inside. I didn't directly remember situations, people, or trauma that had robbed me of peace, but God was exposing this area and I was along for the ride. I didn't want to face or admit to the events that caused my past wounds. I thought these broken and bruised places in my life were better left alone. Buried. I was tired of feeling overwhelmed, anxious, and hopeless. I was through with letting my feelings determine my moods, find my friends, organize my schedule, and lie to me about my faith. God wanted to remove the sting of the countless times I had been victimized—to free me. I had difficulty separating my sin from what had been done to me. When I came to grips with the crimes committed against me and stopped owning them, and refused to shame myself for the things that happened without my consent, I began to sense freedom ahead. It was time to be straightforward.

If you've ever peeled an onion, you know there are several layers of "skin" before you get to the core. In psychology, the "presenting problem" is the one that takes the client in to see the doctor, but it is usually not why the client is there. "Therapy is the process of getting beyond the original complaint and digging deeper to find out if there are reasons even more significant than the presenting problem."[3] In addition to studying God's Word, and small group accountability, I sought out professional help to lead me through the valley of depression. It was essential for me to feel support, to know I was not alone. Do you need to know someone understands? You are not alone.

When You're Snarled to a Standstill

As long as we live on this earth, we will experience joy and endure trials. We can feel victorious one day and feel downcast the next. After setbacks and hindrances, discouragement may set in. Discouragement is the feeling of "a loss of confidence or enthusiasm, lost hope or confidence, a failure or difficulty that discourages someone." I believe discouragement, when properly handled, can be turned around. When you choose to tell yourself the truth from God's Word, encouragement returns. "I have told you these things, so that in me you may have peace. In the world you will have trouble. But tae heart! I have overcome the world" (John 16:33).

The enemy of our soul lies to us. God's Word tells us there is a limit to how the enemy can interfere in our lives. We have got to stop listening to the enemy's lies and learn how to tell ourselves the truth. Untangling a distorted mind-set about God, ourselves, and our responses to loss becomes complex if depression sets in. Freedom from depression begins with admitting the need for help, applying the choice to drive out lies, and then replacing the with the truth.

Only the truth will get us through the dark days, and this truth from God says we are not alone. He will never leave us nor forsake us. When we feel alone, we are not because even when we are by ourselves, Jesus is with us always. Neuropsychologist, Dr. Michelle Bengston, who suffered for years from severe depression said, "The problem with depression and anxiety is that we feel so alone. We're afraid to share our hurt and our pain because the stigma in society makes it so hard to tell people, because we are afraid of that potential rejection and abandonment."[4] Every day, I longed to be understood. I wanted to be known, to be accepted, to be included and for so many years had been afraid to share my true feelings. I dreaded rejection, again.

"The thief comes only to steal and kill and destroy; I have come that they may have life and have it to the full" (John 10:10). I didn't understand the weight of this verse until after I'd moved through my time of hopelessness. I couldn't recover the days, months, and years the enemy had stolen from me as I succumbed to depression. In the midst of it, I didn't know I was not alone. I didn't know I was among the approximately 23 million Americans who claim to struggle from anxiety disorders, the 17.5 million with clinical depression, the 530,000 who attempt suicide, and many others who endue the daily pain of fear and hopelessness.[5]

To help us understand how to begin to help ourselves or others be free from the tangles of depression, let's discuss the three different types. Most of us are familiar with clinical depression, and recognize it is much more than just a case of the blues. It is "a state of feeling sad, a serious medical condition where a person feels incredibly sad, hopeless, unimportant, and often is unable to live in a normal way. This condition is often accompanied by feelings of severe despondency and dejection."[6]

Clinical Depression is an umbrella for sub-types of depression such as postpartum depression, which is moderate to severe depression in a woman after she has given birth. It may occur soon after delivery or up to a year later. Most of the time, postpartum depression happens within the first three months after delivery. Exact causes of this depression are unknown but could be affected by changes in a woman's body from pregnancy and delivery or changes in work or social relationships. New mothers have less time and freedom for themselves, are sleep deprived, and worry about their ability to be a good mother. New mothers also have a higher chance of postpartum depression if they are under age 20, have an unplanned pregnancy, or mixed feelings about pregnancy. It's important to move toward treatment for postpartum depression, an obstetrician will usually prescribe medication and talk therapy.

The second type of Clinical Depression is Post Traumatic Stress Disorder (PTSD), often experienced by military veterans, and exhibited by a wide variety of symptoms. You might be surprised to know that Motor Vehicle Accidents (MVAs) are the leading cause of post-traumatic stress disorder (PTSD). Each year, there are an estimated six million MVAs in the United States, resulting in over 2.5 million injuries.[7] According to a National Institute of Mental Health (NIMH) study, 39.2% of MVA survivors develop PTSD. According to the PTSD Veterans Government, 7 out of every 100 people (7-8% of the population) will have PTSD at some point in their lives. And 10 out of every 100 women (10%) develop PTSD sometime in their lives compared with 4 of every 100 men (4 %).

It's no wonder those who have been involved in or have seen a terrible car or motorcycle accident have repercussions of shock and symptoms such as: feeling upset by things that remind you of what happened, having nightmares, vivid memories, or flashbacks of the event that make you imagine it is happening all over again; feeling emotionally cut off from others and feeling numb or losing interest in things you used to care about; and feeling constantly on guard, irritated or having angry outbursts, having difficulty sleeping, trouble concentrating, being jumpy, or easily startled. If you or a loved one has been in or witnessed a terrible car or motorcycle accident, treatment for PTSD is essential. It's beneficial to offer to go with your family member or friend to talk with a professional counselor or therapist to help thought processing, help them understand reactions, and provide ways to learn techniques to cope with challenging situations. Medications can also be used to help reduce tension or irritability and improve sleep.

The third type of clinical depression is despair. Our discussion on this specific point is wrapped up in our "lie-knot" "Why should I trust you, God?" Despair is "the complete loss or absence of hope. To no longer have any hope of belief that a situation will improve or change."[8] The state of being "in despair" is a choice. Choosing to despair is a choice to forget God. If e say there is no hope, we are essentially saying there is no God.

God is with us, He is for us, there is always hope. No matter what circumstances or situations come our way, we can see examples of truth throughout Scripture. Have you ever prayed a prayer that wasn't answered? Or when it was, it wasn't the answer you wanted? Of course, all of us have. When these circumstances surround us, despair is right in the middle. In the Bible, there are numerous examples of people who struggled with depression, discouragement, and despair. In John 11, Mary and Martha prayed a prayer that wasn't answered the way they had planned. Yet Jesus' plan prevailed

Jesus' Ministry of Unwrapping

Martha's hope was gone. In anguish, she ran to meet Jesus while grief-stricken Mary stayed home. Jesus was late. He'd heard His dear friend was sick but didn't make it in time. Upon His arrival, the short illness had claimed Lazarus' life. Caring and compassionate sisters, Martha and Mary, had done everything they knew to do. The top doctors had been called in and, they'd financed a strong course of medical treatments, but nothing helped.

The sisters sent an urgent plea to the rabbi-miracle worker, Jesus, "Lord, the one you love is sick" (John 11:3). The sisters believed in the Lord's ability to help because they had seen Jesus' miracles. They knew Jesus loved their family and hoped Jesus would hurry to get to Lazarus' side to restore him to health and bring the healing he needed. But Jesus was too late. Lazarus was dead.

When Jesus entered Bethany, Lazarus had been dead four days. As He made His way through the town, many thought He'd come to comfort the grieving sisters and, encourage friends and family who were shocked and saddened by their sudden loss. Imagine the gossip in the city that day. "I thought Jesus cared about this family. Didn't He stay with them a lot? But Jesus was late." "How could this be? Lazarus is dead." "God's glory, I don't see it, we want our brother and our friend back. Alive." "Lazarus, dead? I thought Jesus loved him?"

Martha's first words to greet Jesus were a scolding, "If you had been here, my brother would not have died. But I know that even now God will give you whatever you ask." Jesus said to her, "Your brother will rise again." Martha thought Jesus was talking about the resurrection at the last day. But Jesus asked Martha another question, "The one who believes in me will live, even though they die; and whoever lives by believing in me will never die. Do you believe this?" Her response revealed her faith during her suffering, "Yes, Lord, I believe that you are the Messiah, the Son of God, who is to come into the world." Martha ran to ask Mary to come meet Jesus and when Mary got to where Jesus was, she too said, "Lord, if you had been here my brother would not have died."

Jesus was deeply moved, "Where have you laid him?" Martha tried to discourage Jesus from going to Lazarus because of the stench of death and he had been dead four days. He'd begun to decompose. Yet, Martha, Mary and the grievers took Jesus to the tomb that held Lazarus' decaying body. Jesus' prayer in front of the cave-tomb after the seal was removed, "Father, I thank you that you have heard me, but I said this for the benefit of the people standing here, that they may believe that you sent me. When he had said this, Jesus called in a loud voice, "Lazarus, come out!""

The dead man came out. His hands and feet wrapped with strips of linen, and a cloth around his face. Jesus said to them, "Take off the grave clothes and let him go" (John 11:1-44). Lazarus was unloosed, freed from death, alive again.

Jesus showed us how to become "loosed." Stop, just a second. Put your name into the phrase our Lord used to bring Lazarus back to life. "_____, come out!" Envision for a moment, the scene: Jesus' gentle, yet authoritative command goes forth, "Take off the grave clothes and let her go." When asked, reliable Jesus will show you where to find the end. He knows where and how to begin the unwrapping, the unraveling, and the disentangling of your "lie-knots". You don't have to do it alone. The end is at the beginning of the place where He shows you. He will guide you as you submit, surrender, and put your "self" to death.

Jesus is willing to meet us in an up-close and personal way. His methods are always hands on. He is calling us forward into action and this involves His healing physical touch, tenderness, and compassion. He wants us to get beyond the stench of death. We've been bound up for so long, that we've started to reek. We cannot smell our own stench. We're "nose-blind" to the smell and the areas we've kept wrapped and hidden from the moment the wounds were inflicted. We wonder if our wounds are healed and we don't want to take the bandages off in case they're not. But, once the bandages fall to the ground, the healing starts. Jesus' specialty is to extend the ministry of untying, unwrapping, and unraveling the knots that bind us up.

Is Jesus beginning to loosen your bandages? Are you hesitant to let them go? Do you wonder how things might be without them? It's highly likely we notice the disgusting odor of someone else before our own stink. We can move beyond it and get involved to help these precious ones with their unwrapping. When we've experienced this type of freedom, we can jubilantly share the tools to help others become "loosed."

As women walking together, we trust God is using our hurts, habits, and hang-ups for His glory. We can generously offer others the freedom that awaits them. "The Spirit of the Sovereign Lord is on me, because the Lord has anointed me to proclaim good news to the poor. He has sent me to bind up the brokenhearted, to proclaim freedom for the captives and release from darkness for the prisoners" (Isaiah 61:1). Don't be afraid to let your unwrapping begin. It's time. You've waited long enough.

Cutting the Ties that Bind

The next time I returned for therapy, Dr. Dixon helped me to be brutally honest with myself. Years prior, I'd made a vow not to trust God with my life. "I will not trust God with my future or my loved ones." But since I was alone with the counselor, my urge to become whole was intensified. If it meant that I needed to be raw and honest, more than ever before, I was ready. I settled into the leather chair and anxiously gripped the arm. Dr. Dixon asked, "What happened?" I closed my eyes, wondering where to begin. In my mind's eye, it was like looking down a long hallway with lots of doors to closets that needed to be cleaned out. You know cleaning needs to be done, but which door do you open first?[9]

I started at the beginning, as far back as I could remember. It was my first ballet class incident and I cringed as I said the specific hurtful names aloud that day. "Fat-kins. Sausage. Clumsy." The names tumbled out of my mouth. One by one, these words continued to torment me and again brought me to tears. The doctor said, "Let it go." Finally, it was a relief to be rid of my burdensome emotional baggage. I felt lighter immediately.

A few weeks later, I returned to see Dr. Dixon. The Holy Spirit kindly stood next to another closet door. This was an area that needed deep cleaning. I waited as He flung the door open for me to view what was next. Although I had my eyes closed, God brought to mind numerous sexual encounters. It was as if I were watching a video of my activities. My stomach was sick, and my head pounded. The images were humiliating to think about, not to mention share with another human being. After all, I am a pastor's wife. Things became more real as I explained aloud to Dr. Dixon the details of each time I was victimized. I wasn't even sure if some of the encounters really happened. I thought they could have been dreams. Yet he encouraged me to remember, describe, and break the sexual bond I had with those involved.

A landmark turn of events was the day the doctor asked, "Was this consensual?" I said, "No." He said, "Then you need to recognize you were taken advantage of, you didn't give your permission. It doesn't matter if you were in the wrong place at the wrong time. If you didn't want this to happen, you were the victim." This was freeing news. I couldn't believe it. For so long, I thought these horrible encounters were my fault. Dr. Dixon helped me see which sins were other people's and which were mine. He encouraged me to receive the forgiveness offered to me through Jesus Christ. He also helped me to receive forgiveness from myself. "Jesus replied, 'Very truly I tell you, everyone who sins is a slave to sin. Now a slave has no permanent place in the family, but a son belongs to it forever. So, if the Son sets you free, you will be free indeed.'" (John 8:34-36)

All of us have things buried or lurking issues that God wishes to free us from. You may not have been sexually abused, but maybe you were harmed in other ways and have buried those painful memories and still live with the wounds. Those wounds may be festering. Those issues, though painful for you to face, are still there. God is waiting for you to let the light of truth free you. And you can be free. Jesus promises it.

Who Am I?

In 2015, Time Magazine's list of the top one hundred most influential people included author and theologian John Stott. Stott's remarks about self-talk are to be noted, "In practice, we should constantly be reminding ourselves who we are. It helps to speak aloud and ask ourselves, "Don't you know you are enslaved to God and are committed to his obedience?"[10] If we persevere, and stay in it to win it until we can reply, "Yes, I do know who I am. I am a new person in Christ." According to Romans 8:24, "Hope that is seen is no hope at all." The remedy is to focus on what God guarantees, we can find comfort and joy in what is true and reliable: the truth we find in God's Word brings forth hope. God's true biblical hope is explained in Hebrews 11:1 "Now faith is confidence in what we hope for and assurance about what we do not see." When we hope in God and fix our eyes on His promises, we can cling to the divine assurance of Scripture. Because God always keeps His promises, we can be confident our hope will never be disappointed. This Christ-centered hope must be the foundation of our being and when it is properly understood and applied, it affects every single area of our lives. Dr. Neil T. Anderson shares this evidence of how hope was restored in a desperate woman's choice not to give up when her pastor shared the truth statements related to her identity in Christ.[11]

> A lady in our church dropped by for counseling this week. She has been struggling in her relationship with her alcoholic husband. She was at her wits' end, feeling terribly defeated. She came to tell me she was calling it quits on their marriage. I pulled out the list of statements you shared with us declaring who we are in Christ. I said, "Here, read this aloud." She read about halfway through the list and began to cry. She said, "I never realized all this was true of me. I feel that maybe there is hope for me after all."

I had the same emotional reaction as I read the list aloud for the first time. I openly wept as I spoke the words from my lips. Yet inside I felt disbelief, shock, awe, wonder, and finally, turning my mind back to the realization, that each one of the statements of who I am in Christ are true. I've said the truths over and over so many times, now I walk by faith in the promise of God.

Pastor Mark Batterson, best-selling author of *The Circle Maker,* said "Half of spiritual growth is learning what we don't know. The other half is unlearning what we do know. And it is the failure to unlearn irrational fears and misconceptions that keeps us from becoming who God wants us to be." The process involves synaptogenesis, not just behavior modification, a literal rewiring of the human brain. I had to unlearn the senseless worries and misguided beliefs that had kept me tied up.[12] By cutting through the negative mindset, and focusing on scripture, I took that first step; I broke free from the "lie-knot" threatening to choke my spiritual life.

You, too, can be free. For two decades, I was unaware of my snarled state of the "lie-knot," "Why should I trust you?" I didn't know I harbored skeptical and faithless opinions about God. As I became pro-active, intentional about how I spent my time, and where I focused my mind, I found healing and wholeness. As I submitted myself and confessed the sin I participated in, God removed my depression and turned my despair into joy. "I will walk humbly all my years because of this anguish of my soul. Surely it was for my benefit that I suffered such anguish. In your love you kept me from the pit of destruction; you have put all my sins behind your back" (Isaiah 38:15, 17).

Free to Move

When we become entangled, snarled, bound up, and unable to move forward, remember what God's Word says. "In all this you greatly rejoice, though now for a little while you may have had to suffer grief in all kinds of trials. These have come so that the proven genuineness of your faith - of greater worth than gold, which perishes even though refined by fire - may result in praise, glory and honor when Jesus Chris is revealed" (I Peter 1:6-7). These truths offer release as we step out in faith and sink our prayers into the fertile soil of belief. Do you need help untangling something that's pulling you down? I know someone who can help. Our heavenly Father offers us good gifts, we may feel unworthy to receive them, but He is generously offering them in the place of our past mistakes. It is necessary to lay down our hurt, let go of our past, and trust the hand of God to use it all for our good and His glory.

You might be thinking, "This is so hard, I am not sure I can do this." And you are right, on your own, you can't do it. But God can help you. God has got this. God has got you. And He is with you in this process, at this very time, He is helping you through. I understand this is one of the most difficult processes to endure. You've heard what has happened to others who have laid down their hurt and let go of their past. In your heart, you've thought, "Someday, I will face my past mistakes." You've been putting it off for a while, now, haven't you? It's time. It takes work, but believe me, it is worth it. So, are you ready to be on your way? Let's ask God and let Him show you how to find the end of your "lie-knot." Please take a moment to pray this prayer of commitment to trust God:

Dear Heavenly Father,

Thank You for the blood of Jesus that covers over a multitude of my sins. (I Peter 4:8) Thank You that You have forgiven me and there is now no condemnation for those who are in Christ Jesus. (Romans 8:1) Thank You for helping me get rid of the knotted areas of my past mistakes, so I can walk forward in freedom and security. Thank You for not holding my past against me. Help me to let go of guilt and shame. I choose to grab onto grace and hope. Thank You for changing my mess into a masterpiece. Thank You for using me for an important work You have planned for me to do. (Ephesians 2:10) I choose to let go of the past so I can walk into the exciting future You have in store for me. In Jesus' Name, Amen.

If you've been interrupted by any voices other than those speaking truth, remind them whose you are and speak this prayer aloud:

Dear Heavenly Father,

Thank You for the precious shed blood of Jesus, who paid the price for my sins and forgave me. Thank You that in Christ I am made righteous. Thank You for protecting me with Your presence, Lord Jesus, by the power of the

Holy Spirit. Thank You for fighting this battle. I claim victory over the power of darkness. Bring the light and let me shine with Your truth. Thank You for freedom. In Jesus' Name, Amen.

Welcome to your new beginning!

Alexander the Great solved the problem by untying the Gordian knot. With one mighty slice of his sword, the knot was released. "For the word of God is alive and active. Sharper than any double-edged sword, it penetrates even to dividing soul and spirit, joints and marrow; it judges the thoughts and attitudes of the heart" (Hebrews 4:12). As we wield the Sword of the spirit—the Word of God, we too, can solve the puzzle, and God can loose us.

Chapter 3: Snarled – Why Should I Trust You, God?

Loosening the Lies

Individual or Group Study Questions and Guided Journal Opportunity

I am grateful you've prayed the prayers of recommitment and rededication today. If you haven't done so, now is your opportunity to do that. It only takes just a moment to act on your faith and make the choice to trust God. It may feel a little scary at first, but God will sustain you with His assurance and presence. His peace will come, and your confidence will grow. Here are the prayers:

Please take a moment to pray this prayer of commitment to trust God:

Dear Heavenly Father,

Thank You for the blood of Jesus that covers a multitude of my sins. (I Peter 4:8) Thank You that You have forgiven me and there is now no condemnation for those who are in Christ Jesus. (Romans 8:1) Thank You for helping me get rid of the knotted areas of my past mistakes, so I can walk forward in freedom and security. Thank You for not holding my past against me. Help me to let go of guilt and shame. I choose to grab onto grace and hope. Thank You for changing my mess into a masterpiece. Thank You for using me for an important work You have planned for me to do. (Ephesians 2:10) I choose to let go of the past so I can walk into the exciting future You have in store for me. In Jesus' name. Amen.

If you've been interrupted by any voices other than those speaking truth, remind them whose you are and speak this prayer aloud:

Dear Heavenly Father,

Thank You for the precious shed blood of Jesus, who paid the price for my sins and forgave me. Thank You that in Christ I am made righteous. Thank You for protecting me with Your presence, Lord Jesus, by the power of the Holy Spirit. Thank You for fighting this battle. I claim victory over the power of darkness. Bring the light and let me shine Your truth. Thank You for freedom. In Jesus' name. Amen.

T - Take time to pray through the acrostic using the truth statement.

I love those who love me, and those who seek me find me (Proverbs 8:17).

Dear Heavenly Father,

Would You show me the lies that have held me captive?

R - Remember the facts – Determine to get to the root of what or who caused the first snag.

Then they cried to the Lord in their trouble, he saved them from their distress. He sent forth his word and healed them; he rescued them from the grave (Psalm 107:19, 20).

Thank You, Heavenly Father,

For hearing and responding to my cry and by sending Your Word to heal me.

U - Uncover your fear, unravel the lie-knot – Behind every fear is a lie that is believed.

Yet I am always with you; you hold me by your right hand. You guide me with your counsel (Psalm 73:23, 24).

Dear Heavenly Father,

Would You reveal the root of the lie? Show me the fear that has kept me in bondage. Amen.

T - Tell yourself the truth. Scripture spoken aloud ushers in healing and brings wholeness.

My God whom I praise, do not remain silent. Psalm 109:1

Dear Heavenly Father,

Thank You for the power of praise. Thank You just thanking You and worshipping You brings peace, comfort, and hope into my snarled thoughts. Amen.

H - Help is available by agreeing with God. Confess your sin, submit to God, declare the truth aloud over yourself.

If you remain in me, and my words remain in you, ask whatever you wish, and it will be done for you. This is to my Father's glory, that you bear much fruit; showing yourselves to be my disciples. John 15:7-8

Dear Heavenly Father,

Thank You for the renewal I feel by agreeing with You. I submit to Your will and Your ways. Amen.

Loosening the Lies:

Individual or Group Study Questions and Guided Journal Opportunity

We heard about Alexander the Great's feat of cutting through the famous Gordian knot with one slice of his famous sword. Don't you wish it were that easy? Me too. The title of this book, *Unraveling the Lie-Knot*, incites action. It's an act of faith for us to be part of the process to allow God to do our untangling. God won't unravel our "lie-knots" for us, but He will unravel our "lie-knots" in cooperation with us, His Word, and the Holy Spirit. God holds us responsible to be part of the process by submitting to Him, confessing our sin, and declaring His Word. When we become entangled, snarled, bound up, and unable to move forward, remember what God's Word says.

> In all this you greatly rejoice, though now for a little while you may have had to suffer grief in all kinds of trials. These have come so that the genuineness of your faith - of greater worth than gold, which perishes even though refined by fire - may result in praise, glory and honor when Jesus Chris is revealed (1 Peter 1:6-7).

1. Do you agree that suffering may be part of the process of "unraveling the lie-knot?" Why or why not?

2. Describe situations when you have encountered suffering, or you have watched others suffer.

3. Have you thought you cannot trust God with your life or the lives of your loved ones?

4. Did you change any of your views on this subject by reading the chapter?

5. Can you relate to Mary and Martha's reaction to Jesus coming after Lazarus died?

6. Do you know anyone who is experiencing the symptoms of depression, discouragement, or despair?

7. Share a new concept you have learned about how to help someone experiencing depression, discouragement, or despair.

8. Can you think of a phrase or Scripture from this chapter that you might share with them to encourage them?

9. Has Jesus helped you "find the end" of your bandage to begin your "unwrapping"?

10. Write out an encouraging quote from this chapter.

Truth Tools

The fear of the Lord is the beginning of wisdom, and knowledge of the Holy One is understanding. For through wisdom your days will be many and years will be added to your life (Proverbs 9:10).

Draw near to God and he will draw near to you. Wash your hands, you sinners; and purify your hearts, you double-minded (James 4:8).

In the way of righteousness there is life, along that path is immorality (Proverbs 12:28).

For the eyes of the Lord range throughout the earth, to strengthen those whose hearts are fully committed to him (2 Chronicles 16:9).

Let us not become weary in doing good, for at the proper time we will reap if we do not give up (Galatians 6:9).

And my God will meet all your needs according to the riches of his glory in Christ Jesus (Philippians 4:19).

Freed by Faith
A prayer of adoration and devotion.

Dear Heavenly Father,

Thank You for revealing something new to me about Your compassion for me and my family. This concept has redefined my faith and strengthened my ability to trust You. Thank You for the opportunity to have confidence in You to care for them. I am choosing to draw near to You, I desire to commit them to You by prayer, and trust You because You know what is best. Thank You for keeping our needs in mind, keep our hearts loyal to You, You are so strong. Thank You for "supplying all of our needs." Thank You for Your power and purpose in all we do. In Jesus' name. Amen.

What comes into our minds when we think about God is the most important thing about us.[1]

AW Tozer

Chapter 4: Twisted - Why Didn't You Come Through?

"Everything you have believed about God is not true. To listen to our weekly hour long church service by phone, call this number." Click. The call to my cell phone abruptly ended. I sat in shock for a moment and remembered the four-day truth encounter I'd just attended. I flashed back to just five minutes before, as I walked to my car, my mind was quiet and peaceful. I felt guilt-free. I hadn't entertained a self-condemning thought for at least an hour. I felt as if I could conquer anything. And now, this phone call? I was rattled. In essence, the message I heard the voice say was "the truth is false."

I recognized the interruption as a spiritual attack. Remembering what I had been taught, I spoke aloud, "In the name of Jesus, I rebuke you. There is no weapon formed against me that will prosper. Greater is He who is in me than He who is in the world. Thank you, Lord Jesus, that You have not given me a spirit of fear, but of power, love and of sound mind. I renounce this spirit of fear. I want to live by faith in You and in the power of the Holy Spirit. In Jesus' name, Amen."

After courageously vocalizing my prayer, I broke down in tears of relief. I had dodged the enemy's sneaky trap, passed the testing of my faith by implementing the truth and speaking out the Word of God. The uninvited phone call that came to me that day was very real. My self-image and confidence had been altered for decades because of the lies I'd believed for so long. Maybe you can relate? You, like me, may be victimized by lies that pierced your emotions at a very young age. They tell us things that haunt us, affecting our self-talk and influencing our present-day decisions.

One of the lies I'd finally surrendered to the truth was "you don't fit in." That unusual phone call had threatened to trip my trust as, I questioned, "Is there a place for me in the family of God?"

The Need to Belong Theory

God created us with a requirement to belong. Human beings share an emotional need to be joined with others. The Coronavirus pandemic we experienced disrupted lives around the world and affected every people group. Social distancing, quarantine, shelter-in-place, senior shopping times, challenges, and chaos were the result of the war on the unseen COVID-19 enemy. Feelings of isolation, separation, and despair resulted in increased depression, despair, anguish, substance abuse, and suicide. Those were interesting times, weren't they? "Nearly half (45%) of adults in the United States reported that their mental health had been negatively impacted due to worry and stress over the virus." Though the measures taken were necessary to slow the spread of the virus, these situations were linked to poor mental health outcomes, such as isolation and job loss. Additionally, feelings of anxiety were increasingly common, as people were fearful that they or their loved ones would fall ill. They were also uncertain of the repercussions of the pandemic.[2]

God specifically created each of us with a need for security and a unique place in humanity. A study was conducted within a series of clinical trials, to prove human beings are created with a need to belong. Scientists placed participants into a Magnetic Resonance Imaging (MRI) machine and asked them to remember a recent rejection. As they recalled their emotional pain of feeling left out, ignored, dismissed, or fired, the MRI machines registered surprising results. The researchers found the same areas of our brains were activated when we experienced rejection as when we endured physical pain.[3] "It's in Christ that we find out who we are and what we are living for" (Ephesians 1:11 MSG). God created us for fellowship with Himself. Rejection hurts because it is usually self-inflicted. When our self-esteem is hurting most, we often go and damage it even further. Our brains are wired to respond that way.

Emotional pain is only one of the ways rejections impact our wellbeing. Rejections damage our mood and our self-esteem. They may cause anger, aggression, and destabilize our need to belong. But, we were on His mind from the beginning of time. Henri M. Nouwen reminds us, "Self-rejection is the greatest enemy of the spiritual life because it contradicts the Sacred Voice that calls us the beloved."[4]

What difference does it make that we belong to God? This simple truth can transform our lives. We better understand our self-worth. We matter to God – this gives order to our lives. When we first understand our identity in Christ, how we live in other roles as a mother, daughter, friend, and worker are all secondary. The fact is we belong to God first. If we truly believe God and accept ourselves the way He has accepted us, we can cut through the twisted "lie-knots." We can tell our feelings to bow down to the truth, and we can overcome the pain of facing rejection, rebuffs, and even refusals.

Last to Be Chosen

I remember a time on the elementary school playground where I waited for what seemed like an eternity to be chosen for the girls' softball team. Everyone else's name had been called except mine. I was the last person to be invited to join. It felt good to finally be included. My feelings of belonging, of being part of the team, and involved, were short-lived as I sat on the bench most of the season. Although I wasn't put in the game, I still hoped to be accepted by the group of girl athletes. It never happened. They didn't talk to me or include me and I felt invisible.

Have you experienced a similar situation? In a report published in Health Affairs shows that Americans spend over $200 billion a year on methods promising to help them loosen the knot of insecurity.[5] Why does rejection bother us so much? Have you ever felt distanced by people who used to be friends with you? Something happened and you're still not sure exactly what it was you did or said, but you've realized family members or friends haven't invited you for the holidays. I can relate.

During the four-day truth encounter, God asked me to trust Him. I chose to submit. I followed God's ways and decided to renounce these lies. Once I did this, I could again be centered to believe the truth. Empowered, refreshed, and reaffirmed in ministry, I couldn't wait to see what God would do next.

Instead of feeling overpowered by a phone call, I was empowered by the Holy Spirit. The help He gave me through the time of testing validated His presence in my life.

What is Real

How do we know what's real and what's counterfeit? Federal agents who are trained to identify counterfeit money learn to do so by studying genuine money. Each bill printed is identified by certain characteristics. The approach to distinguish a genuine bill from a counterfeit bill is "touch, tilt, look at, and look through."[6] All of us have faith in something, or someone and the choices we make come down to what we believe. Faith is choosing to believe what is already true. Hebrews 13:8 says, "Jesus Christ is the same yesterday and today and forever." That's why He is the one person we can put our faith in who will never fail us. He has never failed to be and do all that He said He would be and do. He never changes.[7] In the same way, we can rely on what God's Word tells us about ourselves, believe the Bible as absolute truth, and rely on it as if our lives depended on it. Because they do.

I rebuked the cult telemarketer's phone call that day in a tangible way. I spoke the truth of God's Word aloud. It was like distinguishing and exposing a counterfeit bill. In the same way, we must recognize and rebuke the lies of deception each day. Through the power of God's Word, "we can extinguish the lure of every seed from the world that has been sown into us so it cannot grow. When we learn to silence every voice that is not of Jesus Christ that speaks error into our hearts, we grow stronger in our ability to discern the truth."[8] The culture bombards us with ideas contrary to Scripture. This carnal mind-set is of the flesh. The tension of the flesh versus the Spirit is very real. We can unlearn past coping methods and refuse to buy into what the culture is selling by taking every thought captive.

If we respond with the Word of God, we can renounce misguided ideas of human reasoning and arguments that falsely denounce Christ and tame every rebellious thought. "For though we live in the world, we do not wage war as the world does. The weapons we fight with are not the weapons of the world. On the contrary, they have divine power to demolish strongholds. We demolish arguments and every pretension that sets itself up against the knowledge of God, and we take captive every thought to make it obedient to Christ" (2 Corinthians 10:3-5).

With this knowledge, I was able to abide with God-confidence that all my wrongs were now covered by the blood of the Lamb. I could stand firm, confident, and strengthened. In my authority in Jesus, I was secure in my Lord's complete acceptance of me. Finally I could accept myself as a "saint who sometimes sins." The occult offers us immediate false answers. We can be sucked in unless we know the truth of God's Word. By knowing the truth, we can counter the occult offerings with God's Word. In the days before the phone call, God had begun working in me so I understood how to come against the lies of the enemy.

Why Are More Women than Men Attracted to the Occult?

Attraction. Magnetism. Draw. We're curious. Inquiring minds want to know, don't we? We long to know if we will be successful in our careers. Who will we marry? How many children will we have? We are tempted by the bait that promises we can see what will happen in the days ahead. Every occult practice relates to the mind or the future. If we have unmet needs, we're more open to investigating tarot cards, observing astrology, consulting horoscopes or practicing transcendental meditation. Maybe we're disappointed in God, or someone we love and thought we could always depend on let us down. We want to talk to anyone who can help us instantly feel better about ourselves. The bottom line: we want control. We think if we know what our future holds, we can manipulate the outcome. Or at least that's what we would like to see happen. We look for someone or something to give us a quick fix.

Women are drawn to spiritual experiences. "An estimated 83.4 % of women around the world identify with a faith group, compared with 79.9% of men." A December 12, 2018 statistic from Telegraph News said, "1.5 million American women now identify as witches."[9]

Surprised? Me too. We may have stumbled into occult practices accidentally. Perhaps someone bought us a ticket to see a psychic performance and we thought we would go just "for fun." We innocently watched horror movies or read horoscopes or tarot cards with our girlfriends at teenage sleepovers. Now we're having nightmares about the bloody images and murderous chase scenes we witnessed. Little did we know the after effects would haunt us and make us hungry for additional similar encounters?

In a recent Charisma News article I read, Patriots quarterback Tom Brady was quoted giving thanks to his wife, Gisele Bundchen, for their latest Super Bowl win. Specifically, he credits the former Victoria's Secret angel's witchcraft."Gisele said,"You're lucky you married a witch—I'm just a good witch,"" Brady said of his wife's spirituality. Brady told reporters that he believes the Patriots' win over the Rams was derived from the work the couple does spiritually."I have these little special stones, healing stones, protection stones and she has me wear a necklace, take these drops she makes, say all these mantras."[10] There is no such thing as a "good witch." It makes no difference if they say they are "good" – they all have the same master, his name is Satan.

Why do women choose to seek answers in the occult: séances, tarot cards, crystals, New Age practices, or spirit guides? You, like me have probably noticed that we live in an age of chaos. Why? Chaos offers an escape, an adrenaline rush, which unfortunately negatively fuels social media, athletic events, and entertainment. In the blockbuster movie Avengers: Infinity War, the Hulk becomes fearful and runs scared when the evil Thanos comes to take his revenge. In past episodes, the Hulk has witnessed the damage Thanos caused and how powerful he is. The entire group of Avengers is in disarray, so the Hulk gets caught up with what's happened in the past and tries to get them to understand how much danger they are facing which causes even more confusion.[11] The scene is much like the children's story Chicken Little, looking up at the sky, running around in circles yelling "The sky is falling, the sky is falling." At least that's what we read in the headlines of social media and the highlights of a government that seems out of control.

New Twists to New Age

In his bestselling book, The Bondage Breaker, Dr. Neil T. Anderson states that "over the past four decades, people in the West have begun to think there is more to life than what science can explain and what they can discern with their five senses. Instead of turning to Christ and His church, they are filling their spiritual voice with old-fashioned occultism dressed in the modern garb of parapsychology, holistic health, Eastern mysticism, and numerous cults. Satan has deceived these people into thinking they are serving themselves when, in fact, they are serving the world, the flesh and the devil."[12] "The thief comes only to steal and kill and destroy; I (Jesus) have come that they may have life, and have it to the full" (John 10:10). Satan, the enemy of our souls, uses the occult: the myriad of counterfeit offerings, to ensnare, trip up and trap whoever will take the bait.

As believers in Christ, I suppose we don't intentionally try to serve anyone or anything but God, but when we do, we've been deceived by the enemy. He is an angel of light, looking for ways to draw our attention away from God. In 2 Corinthians 11:15 (MSG), we find that "Satan does it all the time, dressing up as a beautiful angel of light. So it shouldn't surprise us when his servants masquerade as servants of God. But they're not getting by with anything. They'll pay for it in the end." Satan knows how to get to us, he can't read our minds, but has our habits memorized. And so, he appeals to us as an angel of light, flattering us, appearing gentle and innocent. His goal is the same, to lead us, to lead anyone into destruction. "He (Satan) was a murderer from the beginning, not holding to the truth, for there is no truth in him. When he lies, he speaks his native language, for he is a liar and the father of lies" (John 8:44). Satan will attack wherever people are weak. We can learn his methods and choose to let God strengthen our will and make us stronger in character, as we purify our minds and choose to abide in Christ.

Unraveling Lies with Truth

To know the future, you don't have to consult a fortune teller or medium. What lies ahead has already been predicted in scripture. Matthew 24:10-14 says, "At that time many will turn away from the faith and will betray and hate each other, and many false prophets will appear and deceive many people. Because of the increase of wickedness, the love of most will grow cold, but the one who stands firm to the end will be saved. And this gospel of the kingdom will be preached in the whole world as a testimony to all nations, and then the end will come." In context, this verse discusses the persecution of the early church, but these same principles can be applied today. It's happening now, but we can expect a further escalation of deception, a rise in spiritual attack, and an increase in counterfeit signs.

A lifestyle blogger commented about the numbers of women being sucked into the occult. She writes "The ritualistic nature of the occult, as well as its emphasis on femininity has drawn the modern woman in. In a society where masculine energy has a higher value, women often adapt by silencing their feminine energy."[13]

Women, may I have your attention?! In Christ, we are not silenced. "It's in Christ we find out who we are and what we are living for." In Ephesians 1:12 (MSG) Paul states that in Christ we are fully alive. "He had his eye on us, had designs on us for glorious living" In Christ we have the solution and the tools we need to decipher what is counterfeit and what is real. We can learn to tell ourselves the truth. I don't know about you, but this scripture, I would like to shout from the nearest rooftop. It always helps me to speak to Jesus and rehearse the truth of scriptures aloud. It's eye-opening to verbally state what is already true about me. As I choose to believe and act upon what is already true about God, my faith is strengthened and my trust grows stronger.

If a woman finds herself frustrated with her faith in God, her view of God's power could be blocked. She may seek answers through her external environment, what's easily available, or what seems to be helpful at the time. Webster defines "occult" as an adjective: 1) not revealed (secret); 2) not easily understood (mystery); and 3) hidden from view (concealed). As a noun, "occult" means, "matters regarded as involving the action or influence of the supernatural or supernormal powers or some secret knowledge of them."[14] The definition explains why we need to be wary because of the things that are shrouded in darkness. In Christ the counterfeit is revealed and it can't be hidden any longer. The shadows are diminished by the light of God's Word. The truth of the battle is found in Ephesians 6:12. "For our struggle is not against flesh and blood, but against the rulers, against the authorities, against the powers of this dark world and against the spiritual forces of evil in the heavenly realms." If we understand our struggle is not of this world, but happens in the spiritual realm, we also may want to examine why we process or avoid dealing with issues the way we do. Understanding the way our personal worldview was developed and how we processed our circumstances (or not) helps us to find the end of our "lie-knot." And then we can allow God to help us start the unwrapping.

Worldview Matters

The culture or system we grew up in and live in is "the world." Satan is the ruler of the world and works through it but uses three main tactics to divert us from the truth. We were created to have the kind of life Adam had; that is one hundred percent accepted by God, the highest level of significance and perfect security. "Christian worldview must be derived from Scripture, culture, or personal experiences which are too limited in scope and time," said Neil Anderson. However, the life we were born into did not have the spiritual connection we were meant to have. Each of us were created with the built-in need for acceptance, significance, and security. Our connection with God would have fulfilled this need. As we grew up, we began searching to fulfill the needs for acceptance, significance, and security. The world entered in and offered us the solutions. The world has handed us false formulas:

Performance + accomplishments = significance

Status + recognition = security

Appearance + admiration = acceptance

Each one of these proposed answers is a lie. However, in the absence of a spiritual connection to God, we fall for them. I'm sure you've experienced how this works—the world makes us feel insignificant, insecure, and that no one likes us. Of course, the world's solution to our feelings of inadequacy is to make us think by dressing in the latest name brand labels, being buddies with well-known business leaders or pastors, earning secondary degrees, making notable achievements, or obtaining a six-figure profession will fix our problems. Most of these things on this list are not bad in themselves. It's just when we believe they will fix our problems, that's when we buy into a lie. The more we buy into the world's lies and act on them, the more unhelpful patterns of thinking become established in our minds, which become default ways of behaving. The world gives us a distorted view of reality but serves it to us as if it is the real thing. We are influenced by our family, our schooling, our friends, and the media. Without realizing it, we develop a way of looking at reality that is not true. If our worldview is faulty, it will lead to faulty judgment about what happens in our lives.[15]

We can know the difference between the trustworthy voice of God and the evil intended falsehoods of the enemy. Martin Wells Knapp, co-founder of the Wesleyan Church best explains this when he quotes from Hannah W. Smith's book *Impressions: From God or Satan, How to Know the Difference*. Writing at the end of the 19th century, Knapp attempts to distinguish between the lies of Satan and the leading of the Holy Spirit with the inspirational words from Smith:

There are the voices of evil and deceiving spirits who lie in wait to entrap every traveler entering the higher regions of spiritual life. In the same epistle that tells us we are seated in heavenly places in Christ, we are also told that we will have to fight with spiritual enemies. These spiritual enemies, whoever or whatever they may be, must necessarily communicate with us by means of our spiritual faculties. And their voices, as the voice of God, are an inward impression made upon our spirit. Therefore, just as the Holy Spirit may tell us by impressions what the will of God is concerning us, so also will these spiritual enemies tell us by impression what is their will concerning us, though not of course giving it their name.[16]

Have you, like me, wondered if the conversation in your head is your own reasoning or God's voice? We can be assured as we walk forward in faith that God does share His plans with us. This happens through our choice to know His voice as our shepherd. In John 10:3-4, we find how the sheep listen to His voice. "The gatekeeper opens the gate for him, and the sheep listen to his voice. He calls his own sheep by name and leads them out. When he has brought out all his own, he goes on ahead of them, and his sheep follow him because they know his voice." When we spend time in prayer, we know His quiet nudges and His loud directions. We determine which path to take as we observe peace and guidance through the Holy Spirit. Life change, through spiritual transformation is possible only with a supernatural encounter with God's truth. Pho Mihn found out first-hand about a truth encounter when her eastern world view was changed to a biblical world view.

Transformed by Truth

Pho Mihn experienced trauma when she was a young girl in the poverty-stricken country of Mauritius. Years later, Pho heard the truth of the gospel in college, found the love of God irresistible, and replaced the eastern worldview with which she'd been raised.

My parents gave me away because they were very poor. They gave me to the high priestess of the Buddhist temple in Mauritius, so I was brought up there. We used to do all sorts of things like bowing down to idols. We used to eat food sacrificed to idols and we used to do horoscopes. We used to do a lot of things that involved spiritual manifestations, so as a child, I was quite frightened by them. I knew there was good and I knew there was evil. I thought the good was the gods I worshipped and I had to pacify them. But I also thought that each group had their own gods, and you had to stick to your own gods. And as long as the Chinese people worshipped their own gods, and the white people worshipped their own gods, and the Hindus worshipped their gods, there would be peace in the world. That was the worldview

I was brought up into. Then I went to university and became a Christian. I found out that Jesus was for everybody. He wasn't just for the white people. When I became a Christian, I acknowledged Him as King of Kings and Lord of Lords. I acknowledged Him as my Redeemer and my Savior. At the back of my mind, I still thought there were lots of other gods, who had equal power as Jesus. To me, the enemy was still powerful and Jesus was this equally powerful god. Sometimes He wins and sometimes He doesn't. And it was only when Steve mentioned that Satan had no power over us because we are in Christ and Christ has all authority and all power that something just clicked. I remember that first night, being really afraid, thinking, "What if God really doesn't help me?" "What if I am actually on my own?" "What if He doesn't meet me?" I was prepared to take that step of faith and I remember proclaiming that verse where it says, "the evil one cannot harm me because I am born of God and Jesus protects me." And I literally kept saying it over and over again out loud, proclaiming it, trying not to show the fear. And it worked! I don't have to be afraid. I don't have to be afraid of the enemy. I don't have to be afraid of the dark. I am seated in Christ, in the heavenly realms next to the Father. I am. And it's a fact.[17]

As I listened to Pho express the account of early childhood trauma, I was appalled by the ways she suffered through abandonment, poverty, feeling overlooked, and abused. Pho was able to break free from a few "lie-knots" through a *Steps to Freedom In Christ* appointment. She began a life-long process by submitting to Jesus in repentance according to God's truth as revealed in Scripture. She had a personal, spiritual encounter with the heavenly Father and she dealt honestly before God with every issue God brought to her mind. I am sure, like me, you were amazed by her encounter with God's love and her choice to embrace God's truth. Maybe you or someone you know will be next?

Freedom for Pharisees and Psychics

Earlier in this chapter we discussed how Federal agents are trained to identify counterfeit money. They learn to do so by studying genuine money. In the same way, when we depend fully on what God's Word tells us about ourselves and believe it as absolute truth, we can unveil the falsehoods around us. The "spiritual counterfeit versus real" controversy has been around for many years. The apostle Paul talked about it in his letter to the Corinthian church. "Therefore, since through God's mercy we have this ministry, we do not lose heart. Rather we have renounced secret and shameful ways; we do not use deception, nor do we distort the word of God" (2 Corinthians 4:1, 2). Our Lord Jesus also discussed this tension with counterfeit versus real with His disciples. He said to the Pharisees and Sadducees, "A wicked and adulterous generation looks for a sign" (Matthew 16:4).

A sign only points to something and should never be considered an end in itself, just like knowledge is not an end in itself, which is the problem of legalism. Righteousness is the ultimate test of orthodoxy. Just be aware that the devil can and does perform signs and wonders. To illustrate, Neil Anderson shares the following e-mail from a former psychic:

> I just finished your DVD based on The Bondage Breaker, in which you discuss deception and the lure of knowledge and power. As a former channeler let me share how psychics work. They only know what they are told by demons, and demons only know that which they have observed or what has been spoken out. For example, if my husband and I were talking about going to Hawaii for a vacation and I went to see a psychic, they might say something like, "I see you on vacation somewhere warm. There is a beach and sand. You're with a tall dark man - your husband. I believe it is Hawaii."

Of course anyone would be impressed (deceived) by that apparent knowledge of the unknown. I worked as a psychic and ran in circles with those who were very "gifted" in that area. I got hooked at an early age. They were always able to tell me what had been spoken out and even some things that looked like they might happen. For example, I have always been a writer (and musician) and they would tell me that I was talented and would succeed in both areas, but everyone (even non-channelers) told me that because of my passion for writing. It was an obvious gift and I was persistent. So, of course, I would naturally find ways to get published and eventually that happened. It did not happen in the time frame they predicted, because that was unknown to them - so they bluffed their way through. Some of their future predictions happened and some of them didn't. What I did notice was that a psychic could give intimate details about a person's past, but not their future. That was always vague and often untrue in the unfolding events.

The key to becoming a good psychic is submitting to "the spirit," which I was constantly told. I had the "gift," but it would be stronger/better if I'd only submit more. I was told I was rebelling from my "gift" when I resisted. God is gracious and merciful. There was always something (the Lord no doubt) that held me back to fully committing, and even though I was not a believer I eventually saw the inconsistency and deception, and slowly stepped away. After becoming a believer and going through your Steps to Freedom I was set free from my involvement in these areas and saw the entire deception clearly.[18]

Let's take a little time to evaluate ourselves. Ask yourself who you are submitting to? Have you trusted a counterfeit? I am proud of you for taking some time for a fierce moral and spiritual inventory. You see, if you make the decision to start the process to come against the enemy's lies and deception and focus on the truth, God will help you take the next steps. "The mind governed by the flesh is death, but the mind governed by the Spirit is life and peace" (Romans 8:6). With God's help, you can be transformed by the renewing of your mind. Come against the lies you have believed about yourself. Start telling yourself the truth. Now.

Chapter 4: Twisted—Why Didn't You Come Through?

Loosening the Lies

Individual or Group Study Questions and Guided Journal Opportunity

Maybe you don't think the occult is a big deal. You've never intentionally played an innocent game of Ouija Board, paid for a palm reading, or attended an entertainment event with a hypnotist. However, in today's culture, the occult is a big deal. Satan is disguised as an angel of light. In 2 Corinthians 11:3-4, the apostle Paul gives words of caution to Corinthian church,

> But I am afraid that just as Eve was deceived by the serpent's cunning, your minds may somehow be led astray from your sincere and pure devotion to Christ. For if someone comes to you and preaches a Jesus other than the Jesus we preached, or if you receive a different spirit from the Spirit you received, or a different gospel from the one you accepted, you put up with it easily enough (2 Corinthians 11:1-4).

Did you get that? The opposite of the Holy Spirit is a different spirit. The contrast of the Gospel of Jesus Christ is a different gospel. Watch out, counterfeits are awaiting to ensnare and entrap you and your family.

In the next section, 2 Corinthians 11:12-15, Paul describes how spiritual warfare works.

> And I will keep on doing what I am doing in order to cut the ground from under those who want an opportunity to be considered equal with us in the things they boast about. For such people are false apostles, deceitful workers, masquerading as apostles of Christ. And no wonder, for Satan himself masquerades as an angel of light. It is not surprising, then, if his servants also masquerade as servants of righteousness. Their end will be what their actions deserve."

In this portion, please prayerfully consider whether you have been exposed to any occult or occultic activity.

Dear Heavenly Father,

Please show me any areas I've been involved either knowingly or unknowingly in activities of the darkness. Reveal to me, by the light of Your Word, circumstances, or alliances I have made that need to be confessed, renounced, and declared to be cut off. Thank You, in Jesus' name. Amen.

Let's process using the TRUTH acrostic.

T - Take time to pray through the acrostic using the T.R.U.T.H. statement.

I will set my face against anyone who turns to mediums and spiritists to prostitute themselves by following them, and I will cut them off from their people (Leviticus 20:6).

Dear Heavenly Father,

Thank You for revealing to me areas I've been involved in activities of the evil one.

R - Remember the facts — Determine to get to the root of what or who caused the first snag.

I am writing these things to you about those who are trying to lead you astray. As for you, the anointing you received from him remains in you, and you do not need anyone to teach you. But as his anointing teaches you about all things and as that anointing is real, not counterfeit—just as it has taught you, remain in him (1 John 2:26, 27).

Dear Heavenly Father,

Thank You for showing me the truth behind the counterfeits I have used to cope with the stress and struggles in my life. I renounce each one of them. I choose to accept Your Holy Spirit as the only spirit who is worthy of trusting with my life.

U - Uncover your fear, unravel the lie-knot – Behind every fear is a lie that is believed.

> But you have an anointing from the Holy One, and all of you know the truth. I do not write to you because you do not know the truth, but because you do know it and because no lie comes from the truth. Who is the liar? It is whoever denies that Jesus is the Christ. Such a person is the antichrist—denying the Father and the Son (1 John 2:20-22).

Dear Heavenly Father,

Show me the fears behind the lies I've believed.

T - Tell yourself the truth. Scripture spoken aloud ushers in healing and brings wholeness.

> Then you will know the truth, and the truth will set you free (John 8:32).

Dear Heavenly Father,

Thank You for the truth. Thank You for replacing the counterfeits with the truth.

H - Help is available by agreeing with God. Confess your sin, submit to God, declare the truth aloud over yourself.

> Then I acknowledged my sin to you and did not cover up my iniquity. I said, "I will confess my transgressions to the LORD." And you forgave the guilt of my sin (Psalm 32:5).

Loosening the Lies

Individual or Group Study Questions and Guided Journal Opportunity

1. Why are women drawn to the occult?

   Now fear the LORD and serve him with all faithfulness. Throw away the gods your ancestors worshiped beyond the Euphrates River and in Egypt and serve the LORD. But if serving the LORD seems undesirable to you, then choose for yourselves this day whom you will serve, whether the gods your ancestors served beyond the Euphrates, or the gods of the Amorites, in whose land you are living. But as for me and my household, we will serve the LORD (Joshua 24:14, 15).

   Dear Heavenly Father,

   Show me why women are drawn to the occult.

2. Do you agree with the "need to belong theory?" Why or Why Not?

3. List opportunities society presents us to connect with the supposed knowledge the occult offers.

4. Describe any unusual supernatural experiences you have had. Please list them here.

Dear Heavenly Father,

Bring to my mind any unusual supernatural experiences.

5. Do you know if you have experienced any connection with the occult? Please list those here.

    Dear Heavenly Father,

    Bring to my mind any connection with the occult.

6. Please take a moment to pray.

    Dear Heavenly Father,

    I confess I have attempted to depend on counterfeits such as (fill in the blank). I renounce them here. I ask for You to cancel any ground the enemy has gained in my life. Thank You I can declare the truth of Your Word. Your Word says, "The Spirit himself testifies with our spirit that we are God's children" (Romans 8:16). As God's child, I will walk in the light. In Jesus' name. Amen.

7. What roles are you playing to cover up your true self?

Dear Heavenly Father,

Bring to my mind any way I am being deceived.

8. How do you plan to begin to tell yourself the truth?

Dear Heavenly Father,

Show me what Scriptures to use to tell myself the truth.

9. Describe how you feel better equipped to deal with uncovering counterfeits.

10. Pray a prayer of commitment to the process.

Dear Heavenly Father,

Thank You for Your commitment to me. Thank You for truth. Thank You for showing me that I can't be partly light and partly dark. Thank You for shining Your light of truth over every area of darkness I've opened myself up to. Thank You for helping me close each door. Thank You for cancelling the ground that was gained by the enemy. Thank You for the victory You have won. Lord, "Never take your word of truth from my mouth, for I have put my hope in your laws" (Psalm 119:43). Thank You for helping me to see in Christ, I have the authority to win any battle I must face. I give You all the praise and glory. In Jesus' name. Amen.

Truth Tools

You shall have no other gods before me (Exodus 20:3).

Whoever conceals their sins does not prosper, but the one who confesses and renounces them finds mercy (Proverbs 28:13).

I prayed to the LORD my God and confessed: 'Lord, the great and awesome God, who keeps his covenant of love with those who love him and keep his commandments.' (Daniel 9:4)

Nevertheless, God's solid foundation stands firm, sealed with this inscription: 'The Lord knows those who are his,' and, 'Everyone who confesses the name of the Lord must turn away from wickedness.' (2 Timothy 2:19)

At that time many will turn away from the faith and will betray and hate each other, and many false prophets will appear and deceive many people. Because of the increase of wickedness, the love of most will grow cold (Matthew 24:10-12).

The LORD is near to all who call on him, to all who call on him in truth (Psalm 145:18).

Freed by Faith

A prayer of adoration and devotion.

Dear Heavenly Father,

Thank You for turning on the light in the areas I've tried to hide from You. Thank You for not allowing me to go any further into the occult or be deceived by the liar. Thank You for showing me the areas I needed to confess, renounce, and resolve to declare truth. Thank You for the power You have given me to use the Truth Tools here and many other resources I have available. Thank You for reminding me You are Truth. I love this from John 1:17, "For the law was given through Moses; grace and truth came through Jesus Christ." I choose to remain in Your truth. In Jesus' name. Amen.

Not that I am (I think) in much danger of ceasing to believe in God. The real danger is of coming to believe such dreadful things about Him. The conclusion I dread is not ,"So there's no God after all," but, "So this is what God's really like. Deceive yourself no longer."[1]

C. S. Lewis

Chapter 5: Snagged - Does My Life Matter?

On June 13, 1978, a group of energetic middle school students aimed to set a Guinness World Record for the largest tug of war game ever played. Many of us used to play tug of war at recess in grade school. But tug of war is now celebrated as much more than just a game. It's widely used to bring groups together through team building, cooperation, and unity. It has become an important part of community events around the world.[2] Miriam-Webster defines tug of war as "a struggle for supremacy or control usually involving two antagonists."[3] Wikipedia explains that, tug of war "is a sport that pits two teams against each other in a test of strength: teams pull on opposite ends of a rope, with the goal being to bring the rope a certain distance in one direction against the force of the opposing team's pull."[4]

Ancient Egyptians, Chinese warriors, and Greek athletes documented tug of war's positive virtues. British sailors formally introduced the activity in the late 1880s, and not too much later, it became an official spectator sport. It was included as an Olympic game in 1900. In a typical tug of war contest, there is a massive amount of tension that builds up. The proper rope must be used, or the tension can cause recoil like a slingshot and, thousands of pounds of stored energy could be released causing injury or even death.

Unfortunately, the Pennsylvania suburb middle schoolers were unaware of the dangers ahead when the rope they used for their contest was the wrong kind. Only twenty minutes into the event, the 2,000 foot-long-braided nylon rope snapped and catapulted away from the team's grasp. Nearly 200 students were wounded, many with second-degree burns, and several with severed fingers.

In 1988, a 59 year old retiree from Nova Scotia decided to participate in his home county's annual tug of war event. As the match ensued, the man saw a loop in the rope and decided to grab it to get a better grip. He had just put his hand into a slipknot as thirty people pulled with all of their strength on each side of the rope. There was no way he could get his hand out and by the time the game was stopped, he had lost four fingers.[5]

The two "tug of war" accidents highlight vivid imagery providing a powerful illustration about "lie knots." We are in a spiritual tug of war. We may be unaware of the dangers of our own "lie knots." These chokeholds may be the noose that strangles our spiritual or emotional vitality, putting into our minds that we are permanently maimed for life and our hope for ministry destroyed. When we take time to study what God's Word tells us about our enemy, Satan, we can understand his methods and thwart his attacks by speaking the truth. Let's see how it works.

Fit to Be Tied

Our fierce spiritual encounter —a sacred tug of war, if you will, is a very real conflict between truth and lies. It takes place not on the playing field but in the battlefield of our minds. I'm sure you have felt the inner turmoil, the mental struggle, and a tangible clash between fact and falsehood. Paul describes this battle in Romans 7:15 – 18, "I do not understand what I do. For what I want to do I do not do, but what I hate I do. And if I do what I do not want to do, I agree that the law is good. As it is, it is no longer I myself who do it, but it is sin living in me. For I know that good itself does not dwell in me, that is, in my sinful nature. For I have the desire to do what is good, but I cannot carry it out."

Jesus Christ has defeated the enemy. He has already won the victory over Satan. We don't have to add anything to this truth. By faith, we accept the truth and believe. At the cross, Jesus took away Satan's authority over us. In Colossians 2:15, we see how He did this. "And having disarmed the powers and authorities, he made a public spectacle of them, triumphing over them by the cross." Our actions evidence what we believe. The Christian faith is true and therefore we can choose to believe it or not. The enemy wants to keep us from believing God's Word, thus trapping us into defeat, depression, and despair.

In the previous chapter, we discussed the subtle ways we may become intertwined with the occult, even roped in because of unmet needs or the desire to feel a sense of belonging. In this chapter, we will further discuss the tension between the flesh and the spirit. We will delve deeper into God's passion for us and His intentional desires to bless his children. We will see exciting results as we share what we have learned and how we can invest in the lives of the saints. We will discuss the tactics of our enemy, Satan. It is essential for us to discover what God's Word tells us about the enemy. "The one who does what is sinful is of the devil, because the devil has been sinning from the beginning. The reason the Son of God appeared was to destroy the devil's work" (1 John 3:8). By understanding Satan's tricks, traps, and temptations, we can ready ourselves for battle through studying God's Word.

Did you know you don't have to believe every thought that comes into your head? Think of your mind as an airfield landing strip and you're the air traffic controller. You can hold each thought up against truth and choose to accept or reject it. You can choose which thoughts you allow to "land" in your mind. The issue is not where the thought came from, but whether or not it is true. In 2 Corinthians 10:5, we are told to take every thought captive. "We demolish arguments and every pretension that sets itself up against the knowledge of God, and we take captive every thought to make it obedient to Christ." We are instructed that through Him, we have the power and the authority, because of our position in Christ, to focus on the negative thought (lie) and replace it with God's truth. Remember when we talked about how bank tellers are trained to recognize forgery by studying the real thing? We need not be stressed, fearful or overly confident about dealing with the enemy's tricks but be aware of how Satan works to defeat us, through temptation, deception, and accusation.

Untwisting the Loop

God has a plan for your life and so does Satan. If we could see the traps being laid by the enemy, we would most certainly side step the snares meant to trip us and bring us down. Great news! You can learn how the enemy works and through Christ, have victory over his tactics. Let me explain. The enemy tries to get us into sin and keep us there by trapping us in negative patterns of thought like "I am hopeless" or "I will never be able to." He wants us to think we can work things out on our own. Some over analyze things and hope they can get free by merely thinking more positively. Defeated Christians believe the lies and give up. Others try to argue or reason with their thoughts. Victorious Christians ignore negative thoughts after they have taken every thought captive to the obedience of Christ. "We demolish arguments and every pretension that sets itself up against the knowledge of God, and we take captive every thought to make it obedient to Christ" (2 Corinthians 10:5). In Christ's power, we have what we need to win our victory; however, it helps to understand why the battle continues to rage.

Let's step back to the beginning of history to help us understand how the spiritual tug of war began. Spiritual darkness came over humanity because of Adam and Eve's one wrong choice. The only thing God told them not to do, they did. The couple ate of the tree of the knowledge of good and evil (Genesis 2:16, 17; 3:6). The enemy's deception entangled them in a snare that changed their future and ours, too. "Then the eyes of both of them were opened, and they realized they were naked; so they sewed fig leaves together and made coverings for themselves" (Genesis. 3:7). Adam and Eve's sin alienated them from God. Because of this separation, strife in human relationships was introduced, innocence was replaced by shame and guilt, and dominion was replaced by weakness and helplessness.[6] Adam and Eve's first reaction when God sought them out was fear, "I heard you in the garden and I was afraid because I was naked, so I hid" (Genesis 3:10).

Satan is a cunning, active enemy who delights in setting up clever ways to snag us with deception. His best devices are to set up decoys in the shadows, prepare traps in the corners, and stay disguised until he can pounce and catch us in his net. In this section, we will take note of the devil's tactics. Some of his methods are putting thoughts into our minds, like the "fear of missing out." And he likes to convince us to pretend like we are doing fine (when we are not). Or he may attempt to wear us down by constant temptation or accusation. We cannot fight the enemy on our own. "For the weapons of our warfare are not physical (weapons of flesh and blood), but they are mighty before God for the overthrow and destruction of strongholds" (2 Corinthians 10:4 AMPC). Throughout Jesus' life and ministry, He showed us how to trust in God, depend on Him, and make disciples. He also taught us how to do battle with our enemy, Satan.

During the forty days of temptation in the wilderness, Jesus spoke only scripture in response to the devil's lies. In Matthew 4:1-11, we find how the enemy tried to tempt Jesus. "Then Jesus was led by the Spirit into the wilderness to be tempted by the devil. After fasting forty days and forty nights, he was hungry. The tempter came to him and said, "If you are the Son of God, tell these stones to become bread." Jesus answered, "It is written: "Man shall not live on bread alone, but on every word that comes from the mouth of God." Then the devil took him to the holy city and had him stand on the highest point of the temple. "If you are the Son of God," he said, "throw yourself down. For it is written: "'He will command his angels concerning you, and they will lift you up in their hands, so that you will not strike your foot against a stone.'" Jesus answered him, "It is also written: "Do not put the Lord your God to the test." Again, the devil took him to a very high mountain and showed him all the kingdoms of the world and their splendor. "All this I will give you," he said, "if you will bow down and worship me." Jesus said to him, "Away from me, Satan! For it is written: "Worship the Lord your God and serve him only. " Then the devil left Him, and angels came and attended him."

Like Jesus, we can have the Word of God on the tip of our tongues, in our hearts, and on our minds. God's Word is the answer to combating the lies of the enemy. The next time you notice your thoughts are snagged up into a knot, choose to untangle them with the truth of God's Word. The more we know His Word, give the Holy Spirit permission for it to sink deep into our heart, mind, and soul; we can break free in every area. It's our choice to keep our thoughts centered on the only One who can help. Psalm 25:15 reminds us, "My eyes are ever on the LORD, for only he will release my feet from the snare." It takes practice to choose to keep our minds' eye on God's plan, but when we do so, we will confirm the truth and be released from the "lie-knot". In this next section, we will discuss how the enemy works against God's plans. It is valuable to be aware of how our enemy may attempt to set decoys to distract us and to be on the lookout for the specific ways the devil may ensnare us.

Fear of Missing Out

The cunning serpent tricked Adam and Eve by mixing up their reasoning. They mistakenly thought they were missing out on something good. This is the first type of temptation we will discuss…Fear of Missing Out. You may have seen it used in texting abbreviations: FOMO. Adam and Eve believed that God was holding out on them, they felt like they deserved more than what they had. Remember, when you are deceived, you don't know it. The FOMO type of temptation begins with "if only" statements. If only my kids were obedient. If only my husband treated me better. If only I wouldn't have gotten into drugs or alcohol. If only I wouldn't have picked up that first cigarette. If we decide to think differently, instead of saying "if only," we can choose to say, "but God."

Consider how a change in your mindset might alter the way you see yourself or view your future. Earlier, I gave you an example from my own life "I suffered from addiction as a teenager, but God has given me victory over tobacco, alcohol, and drug abuse. He has delivered me from chemical dependence." Won't you think through a few "but God" statements for your own life? It could be something like, "I've always looked at my past as a curse, but God has a plan for my future and that gives me hope" (Jeremiah 29:11). Or "I've worried, fretted, and felt anxious about not being in control of my family, I'm fearful of what might happen. But God has given me peace, power, love and a sound mind" (2 Timothy 1:7).

Pretending or Hiding

The second type of temptation the enemy entangles us with is by tricking us into coping by pretending or hiding. It can happen when we don't want to face the truth, so we may procrastinate or postpone dealing with our issues by using this method. If we make believe we are someone we are not, we conceal the actual person we are. Adam and Eve lost the complete acceptance and intimacy with God "Then the eyes of both of them were opened, and they realized they were naked; so they sewed fig leaves together and made coverings for themselves" (Genesis 3:7). They were ashamed of their nakedness and the conditions of guilt and shame entered as they hid from God. Adam pretended nothing had happened. We may be afraid to reveal the truth of who we are to others, and possibly to our Lord.

If we have been wounded by people or are broken in our soul, we may still be struggling to break free of the trap of feeling defined by what someone said or what happened to us. This concept of seeing ourselves as damaged goods circles back to our discussion in chapter two about our identity in Christ. We are who God says we are, as He tells us in His Word. It may have happened if we took a risk and showed our true self to others, only to have them reject us. We mull over the bait of the accuser, "If you reveal who you are, they won't like you. Why don't you pretend to be someone else?" We accept Satan's invitation to conceal our real selves, and to perform like we are someone other than who we are.

We may choose to dress another way than we prefer, talk differently than we would approve of, or act like we favor something when we don't. Pretending is a form of hiding. In chapter two, we discussed the importance of living in our identity in Christ. Joyce Meyer says, "If we are going to have our souls healed and walk in wholeness, we need to realize that our true identity is not found in what we do, how we dress, or how we speak, or what we pretend to like, but we need to know we are accepted, valued and loved by God and free to be the unique individual He made us to be."[7]

Enter Jesus into the world. Jesus Christ is the only solution that can restore our relationship to God. Only His redeeming love can cut through the web of a sin-scarred world. In chapter 1, we discussed how the Son of God fulfilled the prophesy found in Isaiah 58:6, "to loose the chains of injustice and untie the cords of the yoke, to set the oppressed free and break every yoke." Jesus came to give us the choice to follow Him or not. Walking in the freedom Jesus offers is a life that is not just resuscitated.

No. It's a resurrection. Jesus was raised from earthly death into eternal life, just as he did for Lazarus. In Christ, it is a brand new, fresh life, and an abundant existence that is resurrected. The benefits are out of this world.

Moving Ahead Unhindered

Our Christian walk is lived by faith in God's Word and according to what God says is true. The biblical response to truth is faith. We cannot rely on whether or not we feel it's true. "It is for freedom that Christ has set us free. Stand firm, then, and do not let yourselves be burdened again by a yoke of slavery." (Galatians 5:1) Martin Luther King Jr said, "Take the first step in faith. You don't have to see the whole staircase, just take the first step."[8] That's the hardest part.

We are to turn away from lying, deceiving, or stretching of the truth, or anything else connected with false reports. Believing lies will keep us in bondage. It's essential to understand behind every fear is a lie we have believed to be truth. How do we practically "take every thought captive?" It happens through our choice to submit, repent, confess, and declare the truth.

It's amazing what happens when we renounce the lies and declare the truth. If you haven't already done so, I encourage you to take time to verbally speak out the affirmations of truth on your own as you cancel the enemy's lies and declare God's truth. It's not about chanting, saying the right combination of words, or speaking an empty liturgy.[9] The declarations are words of truth, from God's Word, the Bible. You are merely speaking them aloud to remind yourself that what He says about you is the truth. You are cancelling the enemy's lies and replacing deceptive thoughts with statements of truth. It works.

I can't wait to share the story of Julia Ochoa; a pastor's wife, who struggled to overcome anxiety and insecurity. Julia was raised in a family where adultery and affairs were acceptable and expected. In her marriage to a pastor, Julia anticipated she would experience her husband's unfaithfulness because he regularly counseled women. Julia also thought she would be unfaithful to her husband, defaulting to her parents' methods of coping with each others' adulterous affairs. As you read her story, make it a point to notice how she made the conscious choice to focus on declaring the truth over her past. She chose to rely on the Bible's teachings and the Holy Spirit's help to cut through the deception of her upbringing.

> I knew the Bible, I went to seminary, but somehow I couldn't connect the truth with the daily struggles I had. In my upbringing, we were not Christians, so infidelity was a common thing. I saw it all around in my family. I felt like the same thing that happened to my mother was going to happen to me. It's inevitable. It's a matter of time. He (my husband) works as a pastor and, he deals with women all the time. I would be so overwhelmed, dealing with all these thoughts and thinking it's only a matter of time till infidelity will happen, and my marriage will be broken. Before the Freedom In Christ teaching, I didn't know what was happening. Now I understand that these are lies versus the truth

in the Bible. I began to understand God is there, He's sovereign, He's almighty, and He's my loving Father. Over time, I began to keep fighting these wrong thoughts and kept on putting them with the scriptures. And I would say after a year or so, my husband said, "You have changed." I wasn't that nervous wreck and so insecure and anxious. It changed me. I am secure, I am dearly loved by God, I'm a child of God. God is there and I just need to rest, rest in His sovereignty. And even if anything should happen, I am still okay because I am a child of God.[10]

In Julia's upbringing, the sin of infidelity was an ordinary part of a marriage relationship, condoned and embraced as a common practice. As Julia grew in her faith, she learned what God's Word teaches about sexual intimacy. She understood God gave it to mankind for procreation and a gift to enjoy within the boundaries of marriage. Since these concepts were new to her, she also had to choose to submit to God's Word, confess her sin of infidelity, and accept God's forgiveness for being unfaithful to her husband. Julia learned to claim God's truth as her own, she believed God's Word for her future, and allowed her past to be covered by the blood of Jesus. Julia's story and many others are a testimony of the precious grace of God. I love the fact that when Julia trusted God by confessing her past sin, she allowed God to heal the broken and bruised places in her past. In this conscious choice, she saw herself the way God saw her: dearly loved, secure, and a child of God. She received God's gifts of peace, security, and a new beginning. I believe you are next. Are you ready?

Untangled Thinking

Every spiritual battle is won or lost at the threshold of the mind. We can unlearn negative self-talk and learn how to speak truth to ourselves. We can learn to recognize the enemy's lies quickly, reject them completely, and replace them with God's truth. How do we tell ourselves the truth? First, we can choose to "put off the old self," and move away from guilt, shame and blame. It takes courage to see guilt as something we take on as a feeling of condemnation. It takes wisdom to understand we don't have to feel guilt, be disgraced by shame, or take the brunt of responsibility by blaming ourselves. We can learn to disown all of these things. These toxic emotions don't belong in you. We can evict these poisonous attitudes towards ourselves by declaring God's Word over our lives and our future.

This happens by understanding and owning up to our identity in Christ. No matter what comes our way, in Christ we are secure. Even though, like Julia, we may suspect our own life patterns will be the same as the way we were brought up, through Christ, we can change the future. The mistakes of our ancestors or our childhood do not render a way to define us. God doesn't hold our sins, mistakes, or missteps against us. "He (Satan) was a murderer from the beginning, not holding to the truth, for there is no truth in him. When he lies, he speaks his native language, for he is a liar and the father of lies" (John 8:44).

Satan is Powerless

Adam and Eve's act of sin is called "the fall." Not only did they fall from God's grace and lost their place in the Garden of Eden, they landed in the trap the enemy had set for them. Adam and Eve handed their right to rule the world over to Satan.[11] Unfortunately, the trade they expected to bring them freedom ushered in slavery to sin for them and all of mankind. Jesus referred to Satan as "the prince (or ruler) of this world" (John 12:31). Satan is also called "the ruler of the kingdom of the air" (Ephesians 2:2) and "the whole world is under the control of the evil one" (1 John 5:19). Does that mean Satan is more powerful than Jesus? No. God and Satan are not equal. Satan is a created being. "Through him all things were made" (John 1:3). Unlike God, Satan can only be one place at a time, yet rules this world through "rulers, authorities, the powers of this dark world, and spiritual forces of evil in the heavenly realms" (Ephesians 6:12). Jesus completely disarmed Satan at the cross and he can only operate within the boundaries God sets for him. "And the angels who did not keep their positions of authority but abandoned their proper dwelling—these he has kept in darkness, bound with everlasting chains for judgment on the great Day" (Jude 1:6). Satan's authority and power do not compare to God's – they are not equal power sources. Satan works by putting thoughts into our mind and more often than not, they sound like our own voice.[12]

Free at Last

Do you struggle with shame, blame or feelings of unworthiness? Do you think your sin is too much for God to forgive and forget? I get it. For twenty years, I was tangled to a standstill in a noose of shame, blame, and unworthiness. I couldn't forgive myself for the wrong that I had done nor could I forgive others for what they had done to me. I thought the victimization was my fault. I found out I was wrongly holding myself responsible. The devil had ensnared me in a web of "lie knots" and unfortunately, the decades of entrapment were nearly my spiritual demise.

Let me remind you again, when God forgives us, He will not use our past against us. There is no sin that is not forgiven. Psalm 103:12 says, "as far as the east is from the west, so far has he removed our transgressions from us." Not only has God removed our sin, through Jesus Christ, we have become the righteousness of God. In his book, Daily With My Lord, Rev. W. Glyn Evans, former professor of Practical Theology at Wheaton College Graduate School said, "The accusations of Satan hit me in a most vulnerable spot: my sinful past. He is fully aware of the life I have lived and like a dog with a buried bone, he continually digs up what I have long confessed to God. Not that Satan can undo my salvation, not at all. But he functions like a moral pest whose chief delight is to unsettle the mind by simply pointing to acts and facts of which I am aware."[13] In 2 Corinthians 5:21, we find that "God made him who had no sin to be sin for us, so that in him we might become the righteousness of God." Be encouraged, through the sacrifice of His son Jesus Christ, God has forgiven your sin. God has chosen not to remember your sin. God will not ever bring up your sin and use it against you. Never. And that, my friend, is great news!

Once we know who we are in Christ, how is it possible that we are "made new in our mind?" It is entirely available to each of us when we choose to allow God's Word to transform our minds by reading it, praying it, saying it, memorizing it, listening to it and keeping it at hand. "Therefore, I urge you, brothers and sisters, in view of God's mercy, to offer your bodies as a living sacrifice, holy and pleasing to God—this is your true and proper worship. Do not conform to the pattern of this world, but be transformed by the renewing of your mind. Then you will be able to test and approve what God's will is—his good, pleasing and perfect will" (Romans 12:1, 2).

The choice is yours—you don't have to accept every negative thought that comes to mind. As we meditate on God's Word, our mind is transformed, and elevated to focus on what pleases God. This practice allows God to renew our minds and heals our hurts by the power of His Word. This takes time. As in Julia's case, the process took up to a year. Often it takes less time, sometimes, more, but the bottom line is we have to begin the process. That is the hardest part.

I think it's important that you turn back to chapter 2 and declare aloud the "Who I Am in Christ" statements. We discussed owning our identity in Christ, but the daily "putting on of our new self" happens most effectively when we choose to live in the truth by renewing our minds with the truth. Now we have learned the mind is the control center, now we will discuss how the heart is the seat of emotions. Let's move ahead to discover how the condition of our hearts adds to our kingdom contribution. Yes, that's right. God has a plan and a purpose for your past.

Cut Free

We may not perceive how entangled we are until we ask God to show us areas where we are being deceived. If we want to be spiritually healthy, with God's blessings over our lives and ministry, it helps to participate in a regular spiritual heart check-up. It's really like taking a fierce spiritual inventory; when we stop and give God permission to sever away the negative attitudes and deceptive thoughts. Like signing a medical release to give a surgeon permission to remove a tumor, it's our choice to give God the scalpel and submit to His methods of cutting through the lies we have believed. Ezekiel 36:26 reminds us, "I will give you a new heart and put a new spirit in you; I will remove from you your heart of stone and give you a heart of flesh."

After years of embarrassment and hiding my hurt, I've found it helpful to take emotional risks and share how God has helped me heal. When appropriate, I divulge areas of new growth release from the pesky "lie-knots" from which I've been freed. I share with my husband, intimate friends, and those going through similar "heart surgery," I invite them to be part of the "heart solution." In my discipleship classes, I pray about who God wants me ask, and invite them to help me maintain spiritual accountability. Without others in the body of Christ who are praying, understanding, and holding us responsible, we can become ensnared, hard-hearted and calloused toward God and life lessons. Or we might believe Satan's lies and become deceived to not believe God. "Those who live according to the flesh have their minds set on what that flesh desires; but those who live in accordance with the Spirit have their minds set on what the Spirit desires" (Romans 8:5). When this happens, we might even stop following the living God.

Our hearts become tough toward God and our ability to hear His voice decreases. The result: our spiritual senses are dulled as our heart chases after sin. We begin to desire things, allow impure thoughts, and eventually act out in behaviors we despise, all because we haven't checked our hearts. In Matthew 22:37 "Jesus replied: "Love the Lord your God with all your heart and with all your soul and with all your mind.""

When we learn how to examine our own hearts in confession; then we agree with God about our condition. This comes by first deciding to submit to God, resist the devil, and close the door. The last action of closing the door, involves three things – when all bondages are broken, all mental strongholds have been torn down and all sources that feed the problem have been cut off. Jesus has freed us with His Word: the key of the truth. It's with His strength that we close the door on past bondages. As we move ahead in our faith journey, you might notice other areas God is revealing to you, areas where you might feel stuck or ensnared. In the upcoming chapters, I look forward to sharing additional tools about how to uncover lies we've believed.

Psalm 37:3 reminds us, "Trust in the Lord and do good." Trusting is an action verb that involves us choosing to do things God's way and not ours. This means by faith we submit to God's ways and His timing, although we may not agree with His direction. Most of us spend time waiting. We hate to wait. Waiting is hard, but I've learned a secret. May I share it with you? If we invite God into the places where we are waiting on Him to work, the time is well spent. We may grow weary in the waiting. We want our healing to take place fast, and we want a quick fix. In the natural world, when something breaks down, we are relieved to phone or text someone to make an appointment for the repairs. We may be disappointed when we can't get our repairs done the same day. Quick fixes, we think, are the best way to go.

Are you ready for God to fix a situation or do a work in your life before He is ready to do it? Satan tricks us by causing us to think God is holding out on us. We are deceived to think our lives or our pain doesn't matter to God. You can resist the temptation to be frustrated and instead, try asking God what you can learn from the situation or how you can grow spiritually while you wait. It's in the time of waiting, as we patiently invite God to work in us, that He does a deeper work in our hearts.

Freed to Serve

Things change when we decide to trust God and do good for others. I've experienced first-hand, if we do things God's way, marvelous things can happen in and through us. Fifteen years ago, I said yes to an invitation to teach a class at our local women's homeless shelter. The women who live there are court-ordered placements or women who lived on the streets and willingly entered the one-year discipleship program. Many of these precious ones are drug addicts, felons, victims of domestic violence, and prostitutes. Some have lost their homes, families, and children. At first, I wasn't sure if it was a good fit for me, but as I stepped into the opportunity, God broke my heart for them. We've grown so fond of each other. Through the years, I've met many women who have entered the program, and some have exited the program before they completed it. And yet others, I've seen graduate, been honored to mentor, and remain teacher's assistants in my weekly classes or help in our street ministry. I've watched God restore families, rebuild lives, and renew priorities for life. God has continued to use my story to help hundreds of residents and rescue mission staff. I'm humbled, honored, and amazed God could use my past hurt, covered by the healing blood of Jesus, to encourage others. He wants to do the same for them. And He wants to do the same for you. At first, it seems surprising, but God gets all the glory. It's His work in us. What are you waiting for?

When we take our eyes off ourselves, we can actively focus on God's work in our life. Francis Frangipane, who is an international pastor, a best-selling author, and the founder of River of Life Ministries, said, "What is perhaps most wonderful about serving the Lord is that, even when we fall short, He remains true to His purpose with us. Although His hands wound, they also heal. His correction is not rejection."[14] It's exciting to pay attention to how far we have come, as we have allowed God to cut us free from the snare of our hurt. In serving others, instead of expecting to be served, God can use our story to encourage others to trust God to help them move forward in freedom.

We don't have to let every thought we think take root in our minds. We can choose to think about what we think about. This takes practice and determination. The transformation only happens when we make it a point to renew our mind by the power of His Word. Philippians 4:6-7 reminds us, "Do not be anxious about anything but in every situation, by prayer and supplication with thanksgiving present your requests to God. And the peace of God, which transcends all understanding, will guard your hearts and minds in Christ Jesus." You wonder, how does this help?

If I feel overwhelmed by my issues or wonder how long God will take before I can see His victory in my life, it's futile to look back with regret and yearn for what could have been. We can choose to keep ourselves encouraged by "setting our minds on the things above, not on earthly things." (Colossians 3:2) Additionally, Philippians 4:8-9, discusses how thinking about truth works for our benefit, "Finally, brothers and sisters, whatever is true, whatever is noble, whatever is right, whatever is pure, whatever is lovely, whatever is admirable—if anything is excellent or praiseworthy—think about such things. Whatever you have learned or received or heard from me, or seen in me—put it into practice. And the God of peace will be with you." God's healing work in a person's heart, mind, and soul is remarkable.

Maybe you feel as if you are losing the tug of war with the enemy. Has he dragged you over a bottomless pit and you are spiraling downward? Or are you are in a raw and rugged place right now? Sometimes the ache in your soul can be so intense you wonder if you are of any value to God or anyone else? You wonder, can I even get through the day?

Let me encourage you, your life matters. And so does your healing. Someday, if you are willing to share it, God will use your unique story to help someone else in the same place. Your contributions to God's kingdom make a difference. Do you know, when God heals your soul, He heals it completely? I am trusting God to do the work on your behalf, to heal your soul for a great kingdom contribution. God and I want this for you. Even when we are on the road to healing, if we choose to share how God is working and step out to take that risk, our need to belong is met.

I believe God can use anything in our past for His glory. May I propose that there is someone in God's kingdom that is waiting to hear how God has healed you? As you continue to cooperate with God by submitting yourself to His plan, and trusting Him with the hurt of your past, He will remove every twinge of pain you have felt. James 1:4 says, "Let perseverance finish its work so that you may be mature and complete, not lacking anything." I am cheering you on to the finish line. There is no one else with your experiences, your personality and your history, who may offer what you have to offer, except you. If someone provides a testimony in court, they provide evidence about what has happened from personal experience. It's through your personal experience with the challenges you have faced, you can speak of the lessons God has taught you. Because of that credibility, God will minister to someone who needs to hear.

You and I are surely not set out to win any world records in the tug of war with our "lie-knots." We want to be cut loose and set free, once and for all. Not to be ensnared again. And we can be. The shepherd boy, David learned to do battle by praising God. He prayed as he watched his sheep. Psalm 21:13, "Be exalted, O Lord, in your strength; we will sing and praise your might." David slew Goliath, the Philistine giant, proving God's power, and David's dependence on God's strength. David the shepherd boy became David the Giant Slayer. "So David triumphed over the Philistine with a sling and a stone; without a sword in his hand he struck down the Philistine and killed him" (1 Samuel 17:50). Years later, King David was terrorized and chased by jealous Saul and his enemies. He was on the run more often than not. His prayer against being deceived, ensnared, or entangled is recorded in Psalm 31:4; "Keep me free from the trap that is set for me, for you are my refuge." And that, my friend, is a prayer God wants to hear from us.

Chapter 5: Snagged—Does My Life Matter?

Loosening the Lies

Individual or Group Study Questions and Guided Journal Opportunity

Satan's aim in tempting us is to destroy our will power. Jesus' temptation in the wilderness was the enemy's first attempt to destroy Him. (Matthew 4:1-11). Remember, this test happened immediately after Jesus' baptism. Satan attempted to entangle Jesus with three carefully planned temptations, each meant to entrap Jesus' dedication and resolve, preventing Him from fulfilling His Father's will. Jesus showed us how to discern the truth, by cutting through the enemy's lies. We can meet Satan head-on. As we reaffirm our commitment to rely on God's power, we will receive the victory. Let's see how it works.

T - Take time to pray through the acrostic using the truth statement.

Be alert and of sober mind. Your enemy the devil prowls around like a roaring lion looking for someone to devour (1 Peter 5:8).

Dear Heavenly Father,

Give me a new revelation of Your truth.

R - Remember the facts – Determine to get to the root of what or who caused the first snag.

The Word became flesh and made his dwelling among us. We have seen his glory, the glory of the one and only Son, who came from the Father, full of grace and truth (John 1:14).

Dear Heavenly Father,

Would You show me any way I am being deceived?

U - Uncover your fear, unravel the lie-knot – Behind every fear is a lie that is believed.

For the Spirit God gave us does not make us timid, but gives us power, love and self-discipline (2 Timothy 1:7).

Dear Heavenly Father,

Help me to face my fears, reveal to me the lies I've believed.

T - Tell yourself the truth. Scripture spoken aloud ushers in healing and brings wholeness.

And you also were included in Christ when you heard the message of truth, the gospel of your salvation. When you believed, you were marked in him with a seal, the promised Holy Spirit… (Ephesians 1:13).

Dear Heavenly Father,

As Your Word says, I am "In Christ." Thank You for reminding me — I am included. I am sealed by the Holy Spirit. Your Word is truth.

H - Help is available by agreeing with God. Confess your sin, submit to God, declare the truth aloud over yourself.

Rather, we have renounced secret and shameful ways; we do not use deception, nor do we distort the word of God. On the contrary, by setting forth the truth plainly we commend ourselves to everyone's conscience in the sight of God (2 Corinthians 4:2).

Dear Heavenly Father,

I renounce my secret sins of (fill in the blank).

I renounce my shameful ways (fill in the blank).

I declare these are cancelled by the shed blood of Jesus Christ. I commit to renewing my mind by "setting forth the truth" found in Your Word.

Thank You for the opportunity to allow You to cut through the lies of deception and set me free to live by truth. In Jesus' name. Amen.

Loosening the Lies:

Individual or Group Study Questions and Guided Journal Opportunity

1. Describe a new concept you learned from the sacred "tug of war" discussion.

2. Do you agree with this statement? "Our Christian walk is lived by faith in God's Word and according to what God says is true. The biblical response to truth is faith. We cannot rely on whether or not we feel it's true." Why or Why Not?

3. Explain times you may have responded to someone or a certain situation because of strong feelings you had about it.

Dear Heavenly Father,

Please bring to my mind circumstances when I reacted from feelings instead of facts.

4. How did that work out for you?

5. Can you relate to the Apostle Paul's lament in Romans 7:15-18?

"I do not understand what I do. For what I want to do I do not do, but what I hate I do. And if I do what I do not want to do, I agree that the law is good. As it is, it is no longer I, myself who do it, but it is sin living in me. For I know that good itself does not dwell in me, that is, in my sinful nature. For I have the desire to do what is good, but I cannot carry it out" (Romans 7:15-18).

Dear Heavenly Father,

Show me how I can say "No" to the flesh. Help me to do what my new "spiritual" nature empowers me to do.

6. Clarify the concept and why it is important to not allow every thought to land.

Dear Heavenly Father,

Help me to take note of those thoughts that are not true. Show me the ways I am being deceived. Help me to find just the right "truth tool" to enable You to renew my mind.

7. Give details on the three ways Satan may lay a snare of temptation for us. Write out the verses, references, or page number here.

8. Clarify aspects of how to recognize temptation.

9. Share your own feelings of blame, shame, guilt, and unworthiness.

Dear Heavenly Father,

You are Lord of my life. Thank You for this time of discussion about the "spiritual tug-of-war." Thank You for the reminder that You have already won the victory. In Jesus' name, Amen.

10. Describe ways to avoid becoming ensnared in sin.

Truth Tools

Your will be done (Matthew 26:42).

You were running a good race. Who cut in on you to keep you from obeying the truth? (Galatians 5:7)

Instead, speaking the truth in love, we will grow to become in every respect the mature body of him who is the head, that is, Christ (Ephesians 4:15).

Stand firm then, with the belt of truth buckled around your waist, with the breastplate of righteousness in place... (Ephesians 6:14)

Do your best to present yourself to God as one approved, a worker who does not need to be ashamed and who correctly handles the word of truth (2 Timothy 2:15).

They triumphed over him by the blood of the Lamb and by the word of their testimony; they did not love their lives so much as to shrink from death"(Revelation 12:11).

Freed by Faith

A prayer of adoration and devotion.

Dear Heavenly Father,

Thank You for Your gracious gifts of restoration and renewal. Thank You for showing me ways I have been deceived by the world. Thank You for revealing to me methods I have used to deceive myself. Thank You for exposing techniques I have used to wrongly defend myself. I ask for Your forgiveness. I choose to agree with You by confessing and renouncing these ways of coping or not coping with my hurt, habits, and hang ups. By faith, I turn to You for help. I trust You to defend me. I have confidence in You to protect me. Thank You for renewing my mind and restoring my hope. In Jesus' name. Amen.

Unraveling the Lie-Knot

Forgiveness is not about removing someone else's liability, but about setting our own hearts free.[1]

Shelia Walsh

Chapter 6: Enmeshed - Are My Sins Forgiven?

Craftsman Skip Hipp found himself tied up. Literally. As a boy, he fell in love with knots. It was a memorable day when his mother taught him to tie his shoelaces. Then he watched his grandmother braid her waist-length hair and she showed him how to braid. More than three decades later, Skip Hipp, the master knotter, has fine-tuned the skill of tying more than 500 varied types of knots. Featured in Knotheads Worldwide and the Knottyer's Forum, Hipps' dream is to earn a spot in the *Guinness Book of World Records*.[2]

Hipp has logged over 1,000 hours, averaging eight hours a day, to tie up the title of creating the largest knot in the world. He said, "It's approximately 22 inches across and 6 foot 7 inches long. There are 650 strands. Every strand is tucked 650 times for a total of 422,500 tucks." The International Guild of Knot Tyers must verify the number of strands and confirm there are no mistakes before the *Guinness Book of World Records* will publish his accomplishments. "This knot is so outrageously big," Hipp marveled, "It's a Matthew Walker knot made from 30,000 feet of polyester cord commonly used in mini blinds. Each line, one at a time, is tucked in underneath all the other lines between those two layers." The craftsman goes on to explain, "It takes hours to do this type of work, no machine can do it. People have lost patience for this type of detailed work." Through his years in the Navy in the early 1980s, Hipp was often commissioned to make gifts for admirals and captains.

Skip Hipp set out to make a title for himself in the *Guinness Book of World Records* for creating the largest knot in the world. Hipp painstakingly practiced tying the details of the Matthew Walker knot and said, "I savor the start of the project, when the main sennit (braided straw, hemp, or fibrous material used in making hats) comes into form and everything feels right. I find great satisfaction at the last knot, when I can stand back and just look at the whole thing, without a mistake."[3]

In the same way, I picture Satan finding great satisfaction in standing back to observe his evil deed when we are snarled to a standstill. Using the snare of doubt and the noose of unbelief, he lures us away from God's truth and successfully keeps us tied up in spiritual knots.

In this chapter we are going to uncover subtle ways Satan may use to trap us, such as unforgiveness, bitterness, and anger. He wants us to be so enmeshed in feeling we didn't deserve to be mistreated or wronged that we think it's impossible for us to break free. The imagery of Hipps' attempt to create the largest knot in the world gives a tangible illustration of Satan's plan to bind us up into a mangled mess. If we haven't forgiven those who have wronged us, our belief system is twisted into believing our situation is too difficult for God to untangle. I imagine Satan gloats with glee when he sees us trapped in a web of shame, blame, and unworthiness as we struggle against our "lie-knots."

Bound Up

If we can't make spiritual progress to trust God's Word and depend on God's power, it may be because we haven't forgiven those who have wronged us. I get it. Some of us have been genuinely mistreated and others think they have been mistreated but were not. We will discuss both challenging situations since we encounter them daily. To find complete freedom in Christ, we can unlearn what we have been taught about what forgiveness is and what it isn't. Satan's primary strategy to prevent us from becoming fruitful disciples is to keep us tangled up in the trap of unforgiveness. We can learn to accept God's forgiveness and relate to others in the same way God relates to us. Let's get started.

The story of a familiar and well-loved Old Testament character helps us understand how forgiveness works when it is the fiber of a life of faith. At seventeen, Joseph was the eleventh of twelve sons and his father Jacob's favorite. Unfortunately, Jacob didn't hide his intense love and favoritism toward Joseph. Not only did Jacob lavish Joseph with adoration and attention, he gave him expensive gifts, including an elaborately decorated ornamental robe. Joseph's brothers burned with jealousy and coveted their father's interest for themselves. Joseph was naturally self-assured, somewhat egotistical, and overly confident of God's plans for his future. God gave Joseph two dreams, which were both a foretelling of things to come. The first dream was about bound sheaves in a field, Joseph's sheaf stood upright, while his brother's sheaves bowed down to it. In the second dream, the sun, moon, and eleven stars (standing for his father, mother, and brothers) bowed down to him. Joseph shared these dreams with his brothers, and they hated him even more. In time, Joseph's presence became unbearable to his ten older brothers.

One day, the ten brothers were tending their flocks, and saw Joseph approaching. In Genesis 37:19, 20, we learn of their scheme to get rid of Joseph. "Here comes that dreamer," they said to each other. "Come now, let's kill him and throw him into one of these cisterns and say that a ferocious animal devoured him. Then we'll see what comes of his dreams." Reuben, to save Joseph, suggested they throw him into a well. Fearing his father's wrath, Reuben privately devised a plan to go back to rescue him. With Joseph at the bottom of the well, the brothers discussed their options. Now Joseph was their captive and even though the brothers felt somewhat better, they decided against killing him.

Midianite merchants passed by, the brothers saw an opportunity to get rid of Joseph and sold him into slavery. Although the brothers didn't kill him, they didn't expect Joseph to survive as a slave. In the NIV Study Bible the situation is summarized so clearly, "They were quite willing to let cruel slave traders do their dirty work for them. Joseph faced a 30-day journey through the desert, probably chained and on foot. He would be treated like baggage, and once in Egypt, he would be sold, like a piece of merchandise."[4] The Midianites took Joseph to Egypt and sold him to Potiphar, one of Pharaoh's officials.

Joseph knew he could do nothing to change his brother's jealousy and hatred. He was not surprised about how his brothers planned and carried out his kidnapping, holding him prisoner, and selling him into slavery. He had endured years of bullying and hatred throughout his childhood. Daily, Joseph learned to forgive his brothers for the constant abuse they dealt to him. Now he was given additional opportunities to choose to forgive or not. Joseph chose to forgive his brothers for selling him into slavery.

Tied Down

Joseph was stripped of the ornamental robe given to him by his earthly father, yet no one's destructive actions or evil intentions could remove the favor of the heavenly Father. The Lord gave Joseph success in everything he did. Potiphar, his Egyptian master, noticed Joseph was trustworthy, capable, and served with honor. Joseph was given responsibility for the household. Potiphar trusted him and "So Potiphar left everything he had in Joseph's care; with Joseph in charge, he did not concern himself with anything except the food he ate" (Genesis 39:6).

Joseph was an upright young man, well built, and handsome. Potiphar noticed Joseph for his management skills, but Potiphar's wife lusted after how Joseph might satisfy her sexually. When Joseph refused her advances, she created a false narrative to spite his rebuff and hide her feelings of being rejected. In Genesis 39:16-18, we see how this false narrative played out. Potiphar's wife "kept his cloak beside her until his master came home. Then she told him this story: "That Hebrew slave you brought us came to me to make sport of me. But as soon as I screamed for help, he left his cloak beside me and ran out of the house." Potiphar sent Joseph to the king's prison. Joseph had another opportunity to choose to forgive or not. Joseph's relationship with God gave him hope amid a hopeless situation. He embraced his time in prison with a positive attitude, diligence, and did his best with each small task he was given. Joseph forgave Potiphar's wife for lying about his advances and forgave his former boss for sending him to prison for something he didn't do.

Joseph was in prison. The Lord showed him kindness and granted him favor in the eyes of the prison warden. The warden put Joseph in charge of all the prisoners and everything that happened in the prison. The Lord continued to give Joseph success in everything he did.

Two of Pharaoh's servants, the cup bearer and the baker were sent to prison. The warden assigned Joseph to care for them. Later, both the cup bearer and the baker had a dream on the same night. Joseph noticed they were upset by their dreams and asked them to tell him their dreams. Joseph explained the dreams, "Do not interpretations belong to God?" (Genesis 40:8) Joseph interpreted the cup bearer's dream and then the baker's dream. Joseph asked them to remember to mention his interpretations to Pharaoh. Soon after, as Joseph predicted, Pharaoh restored the chief cup bearer to his position, but he hanged the chief baker. Unfortunately, the chief cup bearer forgot about Joseph and did not mention him to the king. Joseph chose to forgive the cupbearer for not remembering him.

Unwinding Truth

Pharaoh had two dreams. He was disturbed by the dreams and asked the Egyptian wise men and magicians to interpret them. No one knew what the dreams meant. The chief cup bearer overheard the discussion and remembered Joseph's interpretation of his dreams. He then told Pharaoh about Joseph. Pharaoh summoned Joseph. When Joseph was asked if he could tell Pharaoh what the dream meant, he said, "I cannot do it, but God will give Pharaoh the answer he desires" (Genesis 41:16). Joseph gave credit to God for interpreting the dreams for Pharaoh. The dreams were of seven good cows, seven heads of grain, followed by seven lean ugly cows and seven worthless heads of grain. They were a foreshadowing of seven years of plenty, followed by seven years of famine.

In addition to interpreting the dreams, Joseph gave the king a survival plan for the next fourteen years. The Hebrew suggested Pharaoh find a discerning and wise man and put him in charge of Egypt. When Pharaoh asked his officials who this person could be, he said to Joseph, "Since God has made all of this known to you, there is no one so discerning and wise as you. You shall be in charge of my palace, and all my people are to submit to your orders. Only with respect to the throne will I be greater than you" (Genesis 41:39-40).

Joseph refused to keep score of the wrongs done to him. The favor of God continued to rest on him, and he was thirty years old when he became governor of Egypt. Pharaoh gave Joseph an Egyptian wife; two sons were born to them before the years of famine. Joseph named the first-born Manasseh, "It is because God has made me forget all my trouble and my father's household." The second son he named Ephraim, "It is because God has made me fruitful in the land of my suffering"" (Genesis 41:51-52). God gave Joseph supernatural ability to manage the years of plenty, so there would be ample resources for the years of famine.

The famine reached far and wide, all the way to Joseph's home country of Canaan, affecting his father, Jacob, his brothers, and his extended family. Jacob heard there was grain in Egypt, so he sent his sons to find out how to buy what they needed. Joseph recognized his brothers, but they did not know him. He remembered his childhood dreams about his brothers bowing down to him. He regretted being boastful to them; but as God ordained, he now understood the dreams he had were coming true.

Joseph didn't hold a grudge against his brothers for selling him into slavery, but he wondered if they had changed their evil ways. He put them through a few tests to see if they were as cruel to his favorite brother, Benjamin, as they had been to him. Joseph found out his brothers had dramatically changed for the better. Joseph chose to forgive his brothers for the wrongs they had done to him.

Unwrapping Lies

Joseph's excellent management of Egypt's years of plenty and planning for the years of famine saved lives. His actions prepared the way for the beginning of the nation of Israel. When Joseph revealed himself to his brothers, they too, understood God's plan for him and for themselves. "I am your brother Joseph, the one you sold into Egypt! And now do not be distressed and do not be angry with yourselves for selling me here, because it was to save lives that God sent me ahead of you" (Genesis 45:4-5). Upon Joseph's invitation, their fragile father, Jacob, and the whole family relocated from Canaan to Egypt. Jacob was thrilled to see his favorite son Joseph alive and well. He not only got to see his son, but also meet Joseph's sons. Jacob died and at his request, the family buried him in Canaan. His brothers feared their day of judgment was coming, but Joseph had already forgiven them for their past offenses toward him and their father. Genesis 50:19-21 says, "But Joseph said to them, 'Don't be afraid, Am I in the place of God? You intended to harm me, but God intended it for good to accomplish what is now being done, the saving of many lives. So then, don't be afraid. I will provide for you and your children.' And he reassured them and spoke kindly to them." Through thirteen years of trouble, Joseph made many tough choices to forgive. He chose not to hold onto his hurt, anger, bitterness, and hate against those who wronged him. Joseph did a thorough job. He kept short accounts. Joseph didn't keep lists of the wrongs done against him.

Joseph forgave his jealous brothers, the slave-trading Midianites, his gullible master Potiphar and his conniving wife. He forgave the prison warden, the forgetful chief cup bearer, and the powerful ruler, Pharaoh. I am sure there were others Joseph chose to forgive that are not listed. Remarkably, Joseph stayed free from offense, bitterness, anger, and hate. The plan of God was established in his life and the lives of his brothers, affecting future generations for the Israelites and the prosperity of Egypt.

Joseph understood his identity in Christ and knew God had big plans for his future. What a great example Joseph's story gives us in times of trouble. We must not forget who God has called us to be. Although Joseph didn't know or understand what God's plans were, he trusted Him anyway. He kept moving ahead by faith. Joseph desired the favor of God more than anything else. God was with him in the pit, in the prison, and in the palace. God showed him kindness and granted him favor. Joseph developed greater endurance, confident hope, and an increased awareness of God's presence. Maybe you are wondering how was Joseph able to forgive? I am so glad you asked.

Untangling Hurt

You can experience freedom and break free from the tangles of the "lie-knot." Let's define what forgiveness is and what it is not. Forgiveness is agreeing to live with another person's sin. The choice to forgive others means no one really forgives without bearing the consequences of the other person's sin. This doesn't mean we condone the sin, but we forgive the sinner. The act of forgiveness is application of the act of substitution Christ offered to His heavenly Father for us. God required His Son, Jesus Christ to give Himself up as a sacrifice for our sins. God has granted us substitutionary forgiveness. The Old Testament records God's stipulation for the blood of a lamb to satisfy the substitutionary requirement. In Hebrews 9:22 (NCV) we see the concept of an innocent life in payment for the sin of a human being; "The law says that almost everything must be made clean by blood, and sins cannot be forgiven without blood to show death." The Lord Jesus is our substitute, literally becoming sin for us. "Look, the Lamb of God, who takes away the sin of the world" (John 1:29). Jesus's crucifixion wounds belonged to us; He was punished in our place to satisfy God's requirement. His sacrifice provided for our righteousness.

"Christ had no sin, but God made him become sin so that in Christ we could become right with God" (2 Corinthians 5:21 NCV). We can learn to relate to others the way God relates to us. God gave us a way to keep the lines of communication open between Him and us. We can learn to forgive completely.

Unforgiveness can be used by the enemy as a "lie-knot" so we cannot move ahead in our Christian walk. (God has a plan for your life, and so does Satan.) Bitterness, anger, and hate are by-products of unforgiveness, but these snares can be cut away as we choose to forgive our offenders. Through God's Word, our minds are renewed, and we can be trained not to use the past against those who have wronged us. Each of us will have opportunities to forgive but some of us will have many opportunities. "Anyone you forgive, I also forgive. And what I have forgiven – if there was anything to forgive – I have forgiven in the sight of Christ for your sake, in order that Satan might not outwit us. For we are not unaware of his schemes" (2 Corinthians 2:10, 11). Not forgiving those who have wronged us gives Satan more cord to add to the "lie-knot."

Forgiveness is a choice; it's a decision, a crisis of the will. Jesus reminds us to "Be merciful, just as your Father is merciful" (Luke 6:36). Although it is still our choice to forgive or not, if we want mercy, we are commanded to be merciful to those who have wronged us, through forgiveness. Forgiveness is a supernatural process. Complete forgiveness can only take place as we submit to our heavenly Father through repentance, trust the unwavering love of God, and have complete dependence on the power of the Holy Spirit. It happens through our choice to submit, repent, confess, and declare using "*The Steps to Freedom In Christ.*" You will find information about how to obtain this resource in the Freedom In Christ Resources section.

Finding the End of the Knot

Early in our years of ministry, my first husband, Pastor Paul and I were spending a quiet Saturday afternoon at home when we received a phone call that forever changed our lives. I'd just put a pan of brownies in the oven to bake. We were startled when the telephone rang. We'd planned on spending the evening of fellowship and dessert with our senior pastor and his family at their home. When Paul answered the phone, I could hear the pastor say in a very stern voice, "Paul, don't bother coming over tonight, I'd like you to turn in your job resignation." For no Biblical or ethical reason, my husband was fired from his pastoral position.

It made us wonder if this was what a divorce must be like. This rejection was a sudden and harsh disconnection from the church. The departure was not our choice, but we had no recourse. We were told what to do and how to act and we were to leave the congregation. Although we didn't move out of town, we parted ways and severed plans with friends, youth group families, and partners in ministry. There was an emotional ripping and tearing as we alienated ourselves from those we had grown to love. Not only did my husband lose a job, we lost our church family. With only my part-time day care job, I became the sole financial supporter of our little family of four. I remember wondering, How could this happen in a church? Why was my husband fired? I vowed, I would never forgive the people who hurt me and my family.

Months later, Paul and I were increasingly spiritually intertwined from his expulsion. Our anxiety level was higher than it had ever been. We didn't trust any Christians and we noticed we'd become tense and angry whenever we discussed the situation. Remembering the way things were handled or mishandled by the church board, we didn't agree with how his dismissal had played out and even considered a libel suit. Soon we found out the entire episode was planned to secure a place on the staff for the senior pastor's good friend. We'd already questioned the ethics and integrity of the leadership and now we questioned their honesty. And this was a church staff?

Days and months passed while we continued to nurture our hurt and our hate. We were extremely angry and increasingly bitter. Our participation in this unproductive mindset only added "more cord to our lie-knot." The result was -- a knotted and mangled mess of emotion. I wonder if Satan stood by admiring his work. I imagine he stood back and gloated over our spiritual struggle. We did not recognize the damage we were doing to ourselves or the devastating entrapment of the snarled spiritual battle. My husband and I knew we needed to do something to get over our grudge, but we just weren't exactly sure what. We grew more irritable and increasingly annoyed with each other and the church. We had forgotten what peace felt like. We had no joy or enthusiasm about God or ministry. We didn't know it at the time, but God's plan to cut us free was coming—and in His own perfect timing.

Entangled by Grudges

We think we are in control when we cling to grievances and keep track of wrongs against us. We feel we have a right to be angry or keep our distance from someone who has been hurtful to us. Offenses may seem harmless, but even gossip or misunderstandings can deeply wound us. Holding onto grudges is self-deception. We believe we can control situations by refusing to let go. This doesn't damage the person we are "begrudging" as much as it damages us. Best-selling author and pastor Max Lucado said, "Grudges are the cocaine of anger, they require more and more hate to keep it alive."[5] Resentments are like a cancer. They multiply and intrude on our mental health, relationships, and sound sleep. That kind of holding on can become an addiction.

We are fearfully and wonderfully made by our masterful Creator God. Our emotions are like the red warning light on our car dashboard. The light is there to warn us of a potentially serious problem in the engine. Steve Goss, Director of Freedom In Christ International said, "Our natural reaction when a painful emotion appears can be to ignore it – but that's like taking a piece of tape to cover the warning light – 'no problem, the light's gone away.' Consciously ignoring our feelings or choosing not to deal with them is unhealthy. It's like trying to bury a live mole. It will eventually tunnel its way to the surface, usually in some other unhealthy way – maybe in the form of an illness."[6] God has designed us not to keep lists of anything that has hurt, angered, offended, or wronged us. It's only through God's power that this is possible.

Letting God cut us free of the emotional noose of offense is good for our physical and spiritual health. Refusing to release our resentments increases tension and stress, depletes energy, causes isolation, and prevents old wounds from healing. Grudges steal joy, disrupt sleep, and harden hearts and arteries. Such bitter emotions can even get in the way of prayers. In 1 Corinthians 13:5 we find that "Love keeps no record of wrongs." Resentment and anger keep us tied up in knots unless we recognize it as bitterness. If we choose God's way of forgiving our offenders, by giving up the grudge and our right to get even, we will gain peace, a sound mind, and restful sleep. We can train our minds to refuse to keep score of the wrongs others have committed against us through the power of God's Word.

Choosing to forgive is to trust God with the outcome. Forgiving others is an act of obedience. It's like finding the very end of the knot. Once we give the end to God, He does the rest of the untying. International author, speaker, and television personality Joyce Meyer said, "Who are you helping most when you forgive the person who hurt you? You're helping yourself more than the other person. And we are also helping the other person by releasing them so God can do what only He can do. If I'm in the way—trying to take revenge or take control of the situation myself—God has no obligation to deal with that person. However, if we trust God and choose to forgive, He will take care of the rest. He is faithful to bring a harvest of blessing to us one way or another."[7] That is a promise to cling to.

Offenses such as robbery, divorce, molestation, murder, and rape can cause us to feel justified to hold onto our pain. We are angry at the events and want revenge on the perpetrators. Humorist, author, and speaker Karen Scalf Linamen said, "A grudge usually has a legitimate beginning, someone we trust—an acquaintance, friend, or family member—does something that causes us to feel hurt. But here's where that logic goes awry. Too often, we conclude: If I have a right to feel hurt, then I must have a right to feel hurt for a very, very long time."[8] Wrongs done against us are exceedingly difficult to overcome.

In chapter two, I shared my painful journey through depression, the emotional warning light that God used to alert me that it was time to face my teenage sexual victimization. God showed me how to forgive those who took advantage of me. It's never easy to face our hurt and hate. It's only possible through God's supernatural strength. To illustrate how God can heal anyone from any hurt, I'm honored to share the testimony of Lucinda Schatt who forgave the murderer of her only child.

> To lose a child it feels like you have lost a part of yourself basically. Rekiah was 22 years old when she died. She'd met a guy at work who'd come into her work, where she worked at Harvey Norman at the time and he got her number through social media. And they started dating. We started noticing bruises on her which we questioned her

about. It had gone on for quite some time and we prompted her to leave the area so that he couldn't find her. But he kept looking her up and basically stalking her. And then one day we had the police come and tell us that he had killed her. After the trial was done, we had to have a plea hearing before the sentencing, and we had the opportunity to submit a victim impact statement. And I spent a long time doing the statement. I wanted to reflect the forgiveness God had given us. In my victim impact statement, I faced him and told him that I forgave him and that I didn't hold any grudges against his parents either.

During the Freedom In Christ session on forgiveness, we had the opportunity to write down people's names that we needed to forgive, and I kept feeling prompted to write his name down. So, I wrote his name down, took it up to the front and tore up that piece of paper and there was a sense of real release that was coming from the heart. That peace, I think, is just I know it's not humanly possible, but with God's Holy Spirit within us it's possible. There are still difficult times, I won't minimize that and say it's easy to forgive. It's for your own sake, basically, it's you. When you forgive, you don't carry around that bitterness and rage inside you. People say it gets easier, I guess it does in a sense. But it's always there and you have to live with knowing that your daughter is not here anymore. Though it makes it easier knowing that she did accept Jesus into her life. So, I will see her again one day.[9]

Lucinda's story about the murder of her only child is heart-wrenching. You may have wondered how she was able to forgive? The answer is found in her quote, "When you forgive, you don't carry around that bitterness and rage inside you." You can let it go. You can give it all over to God. The issue of forgiveness is between us and God. We are commanded to forgive because God knows bitterness will cause us to miss out on the abundant life, He has for us. When we are ready to forgive those who have wronged us, God is ready to help us fulfill His command. It's only through God's strength that we can forgive. Forgiveness is to set the captive free and realize you were the captive. Galatians 5:1 reminds us, "It is for freedom that Christ has set us free. Stand firm, then, and do not let yourselves be burdened again by a yoke of slavery." The yoke of slavery is returning to our former ways of coping with hurt and hate through score keeping, revenge, and punishment. God will help us forgive and only through the completed work of Jesus Christ on the cross can our freedom in Christ be maintained. Let's find out how this works.

Untwisting Hate

Forgiveness is not forgetting. Pastor Paul and I still felt stuck and struggled against the bands of bitterness because of the wrong deeds done against us. These emotions were like a lasso that held us captive. We became tense and argumentative when we talked over the situation with each other. The church elder board instructed us not to discuss the outcome with anyone. We felt abandoned and ignored.

Interestingly, our new church was hosting a training conference taught by a man we'd never heard of. Dr. Neil T. Anderson was speaking about *Resolving Personal and Spiritual Conflicts*. We signed up to attend and God met us there with tools to help us cut through our bondage. Dr. Anderson shared testimonies of the power of finding freedom through submitting to God and declaring His truth. In the two-day seminar, he gave us sound Biblical teaching on the principles of forgiveness and how to apply God's Word to areas of deception. Homework was assigned to implement those principles. It was recommended we each make a list of people we needed to forgive. I shuddered at the thought but knew it was time. The names flew from my pen onto the paper when I first sat down to make my list. The obvious came easily but the more difficult ones I didn't want to release. After considerable struggle, I decided I wanted to be completely honest with God.

The list of those God asked me to forgive spanned nearly twenty-five years, encompassing seventy-five people. It took God and me an excruciating two hours to pray through them. Allowing forgiveness to visit the core of my emotions proved liberating. Now I was restored to walk in the freedom of forgiveness. I went through that list, and I forgave the people who had fired my husband and taken the joy of life away from our family. I took the offenders off my hook and put them on God's. I knew God wanted me to grant them forgiveness, although I didn't think they deserved it. His forgiveness preceded mine. Now it was my turn. I allowed God to have His way in the situation, although I might not ever see it resolved here on earth. I forgave them and was now free to move on with my life.

God offers us compassion, understanding, and forgiveness. For our emotional health, He wants us to offer the same mercy and grace to all who offend us. I found the first step to find the end of the "lie-knot" was to forgive those who wronged me, my husband, and my family. It was so hard. It was impossible without God revealing to me what I needed to do. As I submitted to God's plan, read aloud God's Word, confessed my sin, declared truth over each lie I believed, I felt peace, comfort, and hope. Through the supernatural intervention of the Holy Spirit the trappings of my bondage were cut free. The most difficult thing was to give God permission to do whatever He wanted with me and my offenders. I choose forgiveness instead of bitterness. This is one of the most difficult steps of faith I've ever taken. Martin Luther King Jr. said, "Forgiveness is not an occasional act, it is a permanent attitude."[10] Forgiveness should begin at the time of the offense. Forgiveness is the only way to follow God in faith.

Severed to Soar

To tie-up the title and create new a world's record with a humongous 6-foot 7-inch knot, Skip Hipp, invested over 1,000 hours of knotting. He developed a simple system to keep the cord from tangling as he looped the cords into each other over 650 times and accomplish the feat of documenting a grand total of 422,500 tucks. When he was done, it's no wonder he stepped back to admire his finished work. Upon Pastor Paul's firing from the church, I added more cord to increase the size of my "lie-knot," by harboring bitterness, hate, and keeping long lists of my unmet needs. I wondered if my pain would ever stop, I thought I could win an award for the devastating abuse we'd experienced because of church leadership. I was not trying to break a world's record, but because of my unwillingness to forgive, my spiritual walk had snarled to a standstill.

Releasing unforgiveness cuts us free from the snares of bitterness, anger, hurt, and hate and sets us free from the enemy's plans to prevent us from enjoying the abundant life Jesus died to give us. John 10:10 says, "The thief comes only to steal and kill and destroy; I have come that they may have life and have it to the full." Founder of Messengers International and best-selling author John Bevere said, "If you stay free from offense you will stay in God's will. If you have become offended, you will be taken captive by the enemy to fulfill his own purpose and will. Take your pick. It is much more beneficial to stay free from offense."[11]

I am forever grateful for the Spirit-filled, Bible-founded teaching on how to find freedom through forgiveness. If it were not for the timing of the conference and our application of the truth from God's Word, I would not be in ministry today. I learned how to cooperate with God through believing the blood of Jesus covers all my sins. Because of the finished work of Jesus Christ, I can accept God's gift of grace and give it away to anyone who has offended me. Forgiveness was the last act Jesus did on the cross. Jesus' dying words from Luke 23:34 were, "Father, forgive them, for they don't know what they are doing." As the Father has forgiven us, we can forgive ourselves and our offenders. And that, my friend, is a finished work to be admired. Step back and be in awe of God's grace to you.

Chapter 6: Enmeshed – Are My Sins Forgiven?

Loosening the Lies

Individual or Group Study Questions and Guided Journal Opportunity

In the Old Testament, the people of God lived under the Old Covenant. To be forgiven of sin, the person who sinned had to present a perfect animal sacrifice to God. The sacrifices could be any of these livestock – a turtledove, a lamb, a pigeon, a calf, or a goat. When the sacrifice was brought to the priest, either the person or the priest laid his hands on the animal's head, confessed the sin, and acknowledged his guilt. The animal was viewed as a substitute for the person who sinned. The animal was put to death, the animal's blood was accepted as a sacrifice, so the person's sin would be covered.

When Jesus came to Earth, the Old Covenant sacrificial system was well understood. John the Baptist explained the concept in John 1:29,

> Look, the Lamb of God, who takes away the sin of the world!

People understood. Generations had passed when people had sacrificed lambs as substitutes for their sins. Now, because of the finished work of Jesus Christ on the cross, His blood has covered all our sin. He became the sacrifice for our sin.

> He did not enter by means of the blood of goats and calves; but he entered the Most Holy Place once for all by his own blood, thus obtaining eternal redemption (Hebrews 9:12).

Now, it's your turn. No matter what you have done, you are forgiven. You don't have to carry any guilt, shame, or blame any longer. Jesus' blood has paid for your sin, completely. You are forgiven. Would you take a moment to pray a prayer of commitment?

Dear Heavenly Father,

Thank You for the sacrifice of Your Son, Jesus. I submit to Your plan and the process of confession. I do this by agreeing with You about my condition. Thank You for Your Word that says in 1 John 1:9, "If we confess our sins, he is faithful and just and will forgive our sins and purify us from all unrighteousness." I ask for your forgiveness. Thank you that You no longer hold my sin against me. In Christ, I am forgiven. In Jesus' name, Amen.

Let's look at our acrostic using the word TRUTH.

T - Take time to pray through the acrostic using the T.R.U.T.H. statement.

Get rid of all bitterness, rage and anger, brawling and slander, along with every form of malice (Ephesians 4:31).

Ask God to bring to your mind people you need to forgive.

Dear Heavenly Father,

Thank You for forgiving my sins. I confess I have tried unsuccessfully to control others and manage situations by holding onto resentment, misunderstanding, and unforgiveness. I don't have the power to even want to forgive those who have hurt me or my family. Yet, I choose to forgive them because You know what is best. Please bring them to my mind. Thank you, in Jesus' name. Amen.

R-Remember the facts – Determine to get to the root of what or who caused the first snag.

Anyone you forgive, I also forgive. And what I have forgiven - if there was anything to forgive - I have forgiven in the sight of Christ for your sake, in order that Satan might not outwit us. For we are not unaware of his schemes (2 Corinthians 2:10-11).

For each person and circumstance on your list, please pray this prayer,

Dear Heavenly Father,

I choose to forgive (name the person) for (what they did or failed to do), because it made me feel (share the painful feelings, for example, rejected, dirty, worthless or inferior).

After you have forgiven every person for every painful memory, then pray as follows:

Dear Heavenly Father,

I choose not to hold onto my resentment. I relinquish my right to seek revenge and ask You to heal my damaged emotions. Thank You for setting me free from the bondage of my bitterness. I now ask You to bless those who have hurt me. In Jesus' name, I pray. Amen.[12]

U - Uncover your fear, unravel the lie-knot – Behind every fear is a lie that is believed.

> Then you will know the truth, and the truth will set you free. So, if the Son sets you free, you will be free indeed (John 8:32, 36).

Ask God to show you anyone you have forgotten. You have felt like you are unable to forgive because of unmet needs, unfulfilled wants, or unrealistic expectations. Go back to the previous step and pray the prayer of forgiveness.

T - Tell yourself the truth. Scripture spoken aloud ushers in healing and brings wholeness.

> God made him who had no sin to be sin for us, so that in him we might become the righteousness of God (2 Corinthians 5:21).

Dear Heavenly Father,

Thank You, for sending Your Son to restore me into a relationship with You. Thank You for showing me how to let go of my hurt and hate. I receive the forgiveness You offer me. Would You heal the broken and bruised places in my damaged emotions so I can share with others the same truth? Thank You, In Jesus' name. Amen.

H - Help is available by agreeing with God. Confess your sin, submit to God, declare the truth aloud over yourself.

> In whom we have redemption, the forgiveness of sins (Colossians 1:14).

Dear Heavenly Father,

Thank You for Your design of submission to You, and confession to You. I am so grateful for the process. I declare the truth of my redemption in You. And the forgiveness of sins. In Jesus' name. Amen.

Loosening the Lies

Individual or Group Study Questions and Guided Journal Opportunity

1. At the beginning of the chapter, I made this statement, "I imagine Satan gloats with glee when he sees us trapped in a web of shame, blame, and unworthiness as we struggle against our "lie-knots." Do you agree? Why or Why Not?

2. Joseph suffered unjust treatment from his own family. Describe a new truth you learned during Joseph's journey from the pit to the palace.

3. Do you have any questions about the events that happened in Joseph's life?

4. How does Joseph's story encourage you in your faith?

5. Can you relate to Pastor Paul and Sheryl's dishonorable discharge from the church position?

6. Clarify the concept of holding onto a grudge.

7. Why is it important to let go of bitterness, hate, and anger?

8. Define what forgiveness is. Explain what forgiveness is not.

9. Do you think it is possible to implement the act of forgiveness at the time of the offense?

10. Describe any new opportunities God has given you to trust Him by forgiving others, yourself, and God.

Truth Tools

Therefore, I tell you, whatever you ask for in prayer, believe that you have received it, and it will be yours. And when you stand praying, if you hold anything against anyone, forgive them, so that your Father in heaven may forgive you your sins (Mark 11:24, 25).

As far as the east is from the west, so far has he removed our transgressions from us (Psalm 103:12).

In him we have redemption through his blood, the forgiveness of sins, in accordance with the riches of God's grace (Ephesians 1:7).

For he has rescued us from the dominion of darkness and brought us into the kingdom of the Son he loves, in whom we have redemption, the forgiveness of sins (Colossians 1:13, 14).

Their sins and lawless acts, I will remember no more (Hebrews 10:17).

And where these have been forgiven, sacrifice for sin is no longer necessary (Hebrews 10:18).

Freed by Faith

A prayer of adoration and devotion.

Dear Heavenly Father,

Thank You that Your lovingkindness has led me to repentance. Thank You for revealing people and situations from my past, especially those that caused me distress. Thank You for helping me to apply Your Word, as it has shown me how to find freedom through forgiveness. I choose to forgive them, and I choose not to hold their mistakes against them. Please heal my damaged emotions, replace my hate with Your love. Thank You, In Jesus' name. Amen.

God must do everything for us. Our part is to yield and trust.[1]

AW Tozer

Chapter 7: Warped - I Don't Want Anyone to Tell Me What To Do!

Expecting to draw attention to his unusual acts, escape artist Harry Houdini searched for fame by producing shock and awe. His goal was to make a name for himself and to earn huge amounts of cold cash to fill his empty pockets. He set out to create the most spectacular escape acts. He toyed with danger, and put himself into life-and-death situations. He said, "Give 'em a hint of danger, perhaps of death—and you have them packing in to see you!"

Houdini's humble beginnings as an unsuccessful magician turned wannabe stuntman led him to attempt a dramatic exploit no one had ever done before. He would escape from thick ropes knotted tightly around his wrists and ankles, all the while securely tied to the back of a running horse. After making arrangements for the use of a horse, he wanted to ensure the newspapers would give him the publicity he craved, so he notified reporters to witness and headline his newsworthy feat. Houdini could overhear the excitement of the crowd as they assembled. The volume indicated the audience's anticipation and eagerness for the show to begin. He climbed onto the horse's back, his hands tied securely behind him and then his feet were firmly bound up underneath the horse's belly.

Suddenly, a loud noise spooked the horse and, it began bucking. The pair took off at a gallop and Houdini couldn't stop the horse and he couldn't be thrown off of the horse. Since the horse was bucking so wildly, he was unable to free himself from the bands on his ankles and wrists. After the horse galloped a few miles, the animal was exhausted and finally stopped. Houdini was able to loosen the knots, remove the bands, and free himself. He completed his escape. Unfortunately, his feat didn't quite work out the way he had planned. There was no audience to witness it, nor reporters to record it. That day, he learned to anticipate unforeseen obstacles or the possibility of error. Because of this dangerous lesson, Harry Houdini learned the value of planning ahead and practicing every act before he performed it.[2]

I can only think of a few things scarier than being on the back of a run-away bucking bronco with my wrists and ankles tied up. I wonder if any thoughts crossed Houdini's mind like, "Whose idea was this anyway?" or "I never liked horses, after all." The horse ran until it was tired and stopped. Houdini could not control him because his wrists and ankles were tied together. Spiritually, you and I may inadvertently bind ourselves up with attitudes that are contrary to Scripture but culturally acceptable. In this chapter, we will discuss the "lie-knot" behind the attitude of "I don't want anyone to tell me what to do." As we explore this attitude, it helps to renew our definition of what submission is and what it is not. It also helps to define rebellion. Did the hair on the back of your neck stand up? I know. Before you tune me out, please keep reading and listen to my heart. I am coming alongside of you. I've found peace in learning how to pray against a rebellious spirit. I'm teaching myself to pray, "Lord, show me any area I've been deceived." I am praying this prayer for you now.

Entangled by Enemy Exploits

What's the opposite of submission? Rebellion. None of us plan to be rebellious. Innocent newborns scream and yell to get their needs met. They grow into toddlers who throw tantrums to get their way. These youngsters become active elementary age students, who tease, pull hair, and compare each other's parents -- "My dad is better than your dad." If you've overheard them talk about what they want to be when they grow up, you probably won't hear them say, "When I grow up, I want to be a heroin addict?" or "I plan to be a life-time criminal and spend my years in the federal penitentiary." No, I don't believe they would. In addition to discussing rebellion versus submission, we will go over the difficult spiritual task of allowing our will to be molded to God's will. The concept is termed submission. We will define what rebellion is and what it isn't. We will discuss and reveal the truth behind these lies: "I don't want to submit. I don't want anyone to tell me what to do. I don't want to lose my freedom." We will learn the Biblical definition of submission. By depending on the truth of God's Word, we can begin to cut ourselves free. This happens as we understand that submission is obedience. And, with obedience to God, comes great blessing and reward.

Unfortunately, the results of Adam and Eve's choice to believe the enemy's lies in the Garden of Eden still affects us today. When they ate of the tree of the knowledge of good and evil, the connection their spirits had to God was broken and they were separated from Him. And now, all of their descendants, (that's us!), are born physically alive, but spiritually dead. We've previously discussed the loss of relationship that occurred. We lost the acceptance, the significance, and our security with God. God's plan was for all of humanity to have intimate fellowship with Him and not have to worry about a single thing. Jesus Christ is God's solution to re-establishing our relationship with Him. God wanted us to become spiritually alive again, and restore our fellowship with Him.

The first couple bought into the enemy's lie that they could do a better job than God and set out to take charge of their own lives. Nancy Leigh DeMoss Wohlgemuth, best-selling author and founder of the nationally syndicated radio ministry, Revive Our Hearts, said, "The real war is a battle for control. To surrender to the Creator's control is not onerous or burdensome; it is, in fact, the place of blessing, fullness, and peace. The first blip on this perfect screen came when one of God's created beings – already a rebel himself— approached the happy couple and challenged God's created order. Until that point, there had never been any question about who was in charge and who was taking direction. Now the suggestion was made that the man and woman could oversee their own lives, that they didn't have to take direction from anyone else. You don't have to live a surrendered life, you can be in control, the tempter implied."[3] The purpose of our discussion is how to renew our minds with God's truth and align our will with God's Word by relinquishing control to Him.

A rebellious spirit affects our attitude toward God, ourselves, and leaders we don't agree with. The word "submission," may cause concern or even anxiety. It might make us feel tethered and held back from the freedom of being ourselves. Some of us may be unintentionally tangled up and securely bound to a runaway bucking bronco of rebellion. We are bound with cords of judgment, criticism, and jealousy, and unknowingly headed in an unproductive path.

It's important to see what God says about how rebellion is a subtle way the enemy can warp us into thinking we don't need to obey leaders in our civil government, in our churches, in our families (husband or wife), or God. Proverbs 12:8 reminds us, "A person is praised according to their prudence, but one with a warped minds is despised." In His Word, God shares a powerful truth about how generous He has been to offer us the opportunity to willingly submit to Him. The Old Testament provides a notable account of the well-known Bible character, Daniel, who teaches us how to navigate our faith even under evil and unjust leadership.

Babylon Bondage

The story of Daniel shows us a powerful example of submission. The evil Babylonian King Nebuchadnezzar's army had conquered and pillaged Jerusalem. The wicked ruler was feared throughout the world and when his army invaded a country, there was certain defeat. After gathering up the spoils from the conquered land, the enemies took the most talented and useful people back to Babylonia. The poor and feeble were left behind to fend for themselves. Great loyalty was fostered from conquered lands and the enemy had a constant supply of wise and talented people for civil service.[4]

The children of Israel had been taken captive into Babylon and were held as prisoners. The king ordered his officials to choose a few young Israelite men who were physically flawless, good looking, quick learners, knowledgeable, disciplined, and competent to serve in the king's palace. The plan was for them to learn the country's current language, Aramaic, and also the ancient Babylonian tongue so they could be tutored in mathematics, astronomy, history, science, and magic. The training would take three years. The palace officials were instructed to give them food to eat and wine to drink from the king's table. In an effort to make them Babylonian, King Nebuchadnezzar changed their names, thinking this would help them assimilate into the culture.

Daniel didn't reject the new name he had been given, nor did he argue with the terms and conditions the king handed down. Except one. Daniel was very intentional about what he and his friends submitted to and chose not to submit to. "But Daniel resolved not to defile himself with the royal food and wine, and he asked the chief official for permission not to defile himself this way" (Daniel 1:8). Daniel determined not to eat the king's food or drink the king's wine. It could have been because the meat may have been a food forbidden by Jewish law. We don't know the details, but Daniel was unwavering in his commitment to do what was right, even in the midst of circumstances where he had been wronged. Dr. Neil T. Anderson highlights this powerful example of Daniel's submission in his book *Discipleship Counseling*:

> It could be argued that King Nebuchadnezzar overstepped his authority by requiring Daniel and his people do something that went against their faith. Notice how Daniel responded. He showed respect to the king and those who carried out the king's commands. Nebuchadnezzar wanted those who were in his service to eat the food he chose. Daniel did not want to defile himself with the king's food, so he sought permission from his immediate superior to eat as God required, as long as he remained healthy enough to be a servant of the king, which is all the king really wanted. Because he was neither defiant nor disrespectful, "Now God had caused the official to show favor and compassion to Daniel" (Daniel 1:9). Daniel offered a creative alternative that allowed the commander to save face in the sight of the king and also to fulfill the wishes of the king to have wise and healthy servants.[5]

Daniel had pledged his allegiance to God, first, and he kept his commitment. Daniel understood how to live under authority. He knew he was under God's authority first. God allowed him to be taken to Babylon as a prisoner, but that didn't change his allegiance to God. Daniel embraced his identity in Christ and although his name had been changed, his position in Christ had not. Daniel recognized the king's official had risked his life to appeal to the king and God showed favor to Daniel and his friends. Daniel trusted in God's protection and provision throughout his training and preparation for the king's service.

For decades, Daniel dutifully and faithfully served under the rule of three Babylonian kings: Nebuchadnezzar, Belshazzar, and Darius. Under King Darius, Daniel had shown exceptional leadership skills, combined with supernatural wisdom and grace. He was trustworthy, honest, and diligent. King Darius planned to promote Daniel to the number two position in the kingdom of Babylon. The king's administrators and executives were jealous of his prominence and coveted his position. Daniel had made enemies by doing an excellent job. The resentful officials couldn't find any fault with Daniel, so they attacked his belief in God. Daniel trusted in God when the king listened to the officials and agreed with their suggestion to give an edict, "issue an edict and enforce the decree that anyone who prays to any god or human being during the next thirty days, except to you, your Majesty, shall be thrown into the lion's den" (Daniel 6:7). Daniel continued to pray three times a day as was his custom. Daniel did not hide his daily prayer routine from his enemies in government, although he knew he would be disobeying the new law. Daniel needed guidance, peace, and strength. He knew the Lord his God would provide all he needed.

Daniel demonstrated his faithful devotion to God. When the king's edict was implemented into law, it could not be repealed. Daniel was arrested and thrown into the lion's den. "At the first light of dawn, the king got up and hurried to the lions' den. When he came near the den, he called to Daniel in an anguished voice, "Daniel, servant of the living God, has your God, who you serve continually, been able to rescue you from the lions?" Daniel answered, "May the king live forever! My God sent his angel and he shut the mouths of the lions. They have not hurt me because I was found innocent in his sight. Nor have I ever done any wrong before you, your Majesty." The king was overjoyed and gave orders to lift Daniel out of the den. And when Daniel was lifted from the den, no wound was found on him, because he had trusted in his God" (Daniel 6:19-23).

Early in his training, Daniel offered an alternative to eating the king's food. Daniel's offer was accepted. Decades later, Daniel's allegiance to his God was tested when he would not pray to King Darius' idol. Daniel continued to pray to the Lord God. Daniel endured the consequences, and to God's glory. As Daniel encountered opportunities to compromise, you and I may also be presented with similar instances. These are tests that invite us to choose to submit to God, by honoring His ways, and trust Him or not. It may be tempting to want to appease our manager, if we are asked to lie, cheat, or steal, we can kindly offer alternatives without being disrespectful.

Daniel had maintained a steadfast allegiance to God and didn't allow the culture to influence his core beliefs. If we choose to trust God and submit to God's ways, He will come through for us, too.

Snarled by Submission

Word Association is a popular word game involving an exchange of words often associated together. The game is based on the noun phrase word association, meaning "stimulation of an associative pattern by a word."[6] At the mention of the word submission, we may immediately associate obedience by duty, be overcome by power, or admit defeat. You may be cringing right now, and rightly so, if you have had past experiences with abusive leaders or legalistic parents, teachers, or other authority figures. I am so sorry for those painful memories. Let me remind you, these situations can be ways the enemy might use to snag you up into a "lie-knot." Let's take a look at a Biblical definition of submission as it relates to faith in God. We discussed our constant spiritual tug of war with understanding truth over deception. We examined God's plan for us to accept His forgiveness for our sins, receive His grace over our past mistakes, and offer mercy to ourselves, our history, and those who have wronged us.

Vine's Expository Dictionary of New Testament Words defines the word submit as, "to yield."[7] James 4:7 explains, "Submit yourselves, then, to God. Resist the devil and he will flee from you." In this passage, James gives us insight into how to cut the cords of deception that are keeping us tied up as we "out truth" our defeated enemy. We can overcome when we gladly submit or respectfully yield to God's will. That's what ushers in His power. As we surrender to God's authority and His will, we commit our life to Him and His control. Voluntarily, we can make the choice to follow Him.

In the 1800s, Pastor Andrew Murray, travelling preacher, teacher, and prolific writer of over 240 books and tracts said, "A soul cannot seek close fellowship with God, or attain the abiding consciousness of waiting on Him all the day, without a very honest and entire surrender to all His will." Tragedy struck when Murray became ill and lost his voice. He named this difficult season "two silent years." This period of time caused Murray to surrender everything to God. He came to a place of deep humility, as well as a love for God and others.[8] Murray heeded the sound advice offered to us in Proverbs 11:2 "When pride comes, then comes disgrace but with humility comes wisdom." Not only is it wise to trust God, and freely give control of our lives to Him, it's our Creator's best plan for us.

We can refuse to go along with Satan's plan. We can decline his offer, and reject the temptation. As we give God control, the Holy Spirit has permission to respond and we can draw nearer to God. He helps us step over the trap the enemy has laid for us and we can victoriously avoid being entangled. As long as you are submitting to God when you resist the devil he has no choice but to flee. This applies to every Christian no matter how weak or frail they feel, or how long or how short a time they have been a Christian. However, even though Satan is defeated, he still "prowls around, like a roaring lion looking for someone to devour" (I Peter 5:8). Every believer has the same authority and power in Christ over the spiritual world.[9]

Promotion of Position and Authority

It helps to visualize what Jesus has already done for us, and what He is doing now. By doing this, we can acknowledge the truth of our status as a saint whose position has been claimed because of the finished work of Christ. When we accept Jesus Christ as our Savior, we can rest assured our eternal reservation has been made in heaven. We are reminded of this in John 14:2, 3, "My Father's house has many rooms; if that were not so, would I have told you that I am going there to prepare a place for you? And if I go and prepare a place for you, I will come back and take you to be with me that you also may be where I am." This promise is comforting, isn't it?

Until the day we are promoted to our heavenly home, there is great spiritual strength in seeing ourselves raised up in the heavenly places. Jesus is seated at God's right hand, the ultimate seat of power and authority. In Ephesians 1:18-22, we see just what God has planned for us. "I pray that the eyes of your heart may be enlightened in order that you may know the hope to which he has called you, the riches of his glorious inheritance in his holy people, and his incomparably great power for us who believe.

That power is the same as the mighty strength he exerted when he raised Christ from the dead and seated him at his right hand in the heavenly realms, far above all rule and authority, power and dominion, and every name that is invoked, not only in the present age but also in the one to come. And God placed all things under his feet and appointed him to be head over everything for the church." Here, we are told Jesus is head over everything. As we turn over the control of our lives to God, the core issue is do we believe God is trustworthy? Do we believe God's Word? Do we think God has our best interests in mind? Let me assure you, He does.

Reminding ourselves that the battle takes place in the heavenly realms is crucial to overcoming the enemy. "For our struggle is not against flesh and blood, but against the rulers, against the authorities, against the powers of this dark world and against the spiritual forces of evil in the heavenly realms" (Ephesians 6:12). When an eagle attacks a snake, it swoops down, and grabs the snake with its talons. The eagle immediately flies upward, while the snake is writhing and trying to strike but the snake cannot get its bearings. As the eagle takes flight, the danger is minimized, and it's able to fight the snake in the air. The eagle's sharp talons crush or tear off the snake's head. The eagle can decapitate and swallow its prey whole—all on the wing.[10] Instead of lowering ourselves into the enemy's trap, we can depend on our position in Christ. Since we are "raised up," we can take our spiritual battles to the heavenly places and let God fight our battles for us there. God's greatest joy is to lift us out of enemy territory and seat us in the heavenly places with Him.

Submission to what God wants may not be our natural response to His invitation. Thankfully, He is able to handle it. He knows the condition of our hearts, yet has not rescinded His request. "The foolishness of a man twists his way and his heart frets against the Lord" (Proverbs 19:3). We've all experienced the tension of wondering what to do, our own will or God's? What does God want? I remember praying through a major decision, and I chose to wait until I was sure God was leading me and I was doing His will, and not mine. If we chose to stay still until we feel peace, we can be assured God will show us the right path. "Be still and know that I am God" (Psalm 46:10).

Saying "no" to the flesh and "yes" to the Spirit is an hour-by-hour and often minute-by-minute decision. If we make it a priority to keep the truth in the forefront of our minds, sin will have no power over us anymore.

We behave according to what we believe. A description of our current spiritual position is found in Ephesians 2:6-7, "And God raised us up with Christ and seated us with him in the heavenly realms in Christ Jesus, in order that in the coming ages he might show the incomparable riches of his grace, expressed in his kindness to us in Christ Jesus." We are seated with Jesus far above Satan and all demonic powers. Not just slightly above, but far above. Dr. Anderson reminds us, "Your identity as a child of God and your authority over spiritual powers are not things you are receiving or will receive at some time in the future; you have them right now. You are seated in the heavenlies with Christ right now. You have power and authority over the kingdom of darkness and are able to do His will right now."[11] And that, dear one, is the abundant life Jesus died to give you.

Twisted Torment

The abundant life is what is promised to believers, however many find that it eludes them. Why? Often there is a "lie-knot" or mis-truth they have believed about a past event, trauma, or tragedy. There has been no resolution. They feel helpless while struggling with submission, and buried under confusion and damaged emotions. In Dr. Anderson's book, *Discipleship Counseling,* two separate women who were struggling with how to relinquish control came to his office. Here are their testimonies:

> Jane came to her appointment thinking her greatest need was to resolve a relational issue in her family, but what surfaced during the Steps was a extremely abusive marriage that had ended in divorce and a second marriage, which found Jane in the same cycle of abuse. Her past training and the pressure of family and friends had taught and reinforced the belief that submission is being passive to physical and emotional abuse. Her strategy for survival was crumbling and so was her ability to cope. (Jane found resolution and peace when she confessed her sin of control, renounced her fear of being controlled, and submitted to God's love and strength.)

> Beth was raised in a legalistic, churchgoing family. When she met and married Todd, who was a Christian, she fully expected that her life would be satisfying and that he would be able to meet all of her needs. Her fantasy faded as the marriage failed. Disillusioned and angry with her parents and husband, Beth developed a deep distrust in God. This led to open rebellion and despair. She dabbled in false religions and adopted a worldly lifestyle.

She was given some of my (Neil T. Anderson's) books and audiocassettes, but for months she was afraid to read them and listen to them. Through loving persuasion, she eventually called one of our staff couples, who befriended her and encouraged her. Later, she was taken through the Steps to Freedom.

The changes in her life are beautiful to see. The rebellion is gone, and she says, "I feel like I'm in love." And she is in love—with the lover of her soul, Jesus. Before, she used to "make things happen" by trying to control people or situations in the hope that her needs would be met. But she gave up her struggle for self-fulfillment, and now the Lord is filling her with a growing sense of peace and security. She says, "I no longer want the things I craved before; I just want to know Jesus better."[12]

Jane and Beth wanted "something more." They felt like they were lacking something spiritually, but like many of us, they weren't exactly sure what to do. There is an abundant life in Christ that scores of us have but are barely aware of, much less have experienced for ourselves. God has already given us everything we need in Christ. In Christ, we have His life abiding inside of us. We have become a new creation.

The Latin term, *Capax Dei,* means "an increased capacity for God." Theologians believed that we are all born with a capacity for God (*Capax Dei*). St. Augustine believed that this capacity makes it possible for the human person to be re-formed through God's gracious gift.[13] God cannot give us more of Himself than He has already given, but we can give Him more of ourselves. This action ushers us into a new level of commitment to sanctification, that is, giving God permission to do His work in us. If we are not remembering the truth, it's likely we are not resting in the condition that we are "complete in Him" (Colossians 2:10).

It's liberating to invite Christ to control us by submitting to His will. We don't have to stay helplessly ensnared any longer with our wrists and ankles bound up with lies, and on the back of the runaway bucking bronco of rebellion. When God reveals the "lie-knot" He wants to unravel, it's freeing to invite Him to cut away attitudes of mutiny or revolt. As we are relieved of these burdens, we free up emotional space in ourselves, and we make room for more of God. We can enjoy the abundant life we've been given, as we are reminded in John 10:10, "The thief comes only to steal and kill and destroy; I have come that they may have life and have it to the full." And we can revel in the fullness of God we have received.

Out of his fullness we have all received grace in place of grace already given (John 1:16).

And this, dear one, is the only way to live.

Chapter 7: Warped – I Don't Want Anyone to Tell Me What To Do!

Loosening the Lies

Individual or Group Study Questions and Guided Journal Opportunity

You have realized by now, there is a lot to "unraveling the lie-knot." It is a process. Aren't you glad our heavenly Father is not only part of the process, but He is involved in it, as an active part of it? Me too. Submission to God is not a sign of weakness, but a sign of willingness to agree with Him and commit to His will. Won't you take just a moment to pray a prayer of commitment to continue the development of your character?

Dear Heavenly Father,

Thank You for showing me, through Your Son's example, what submission to Your will looks like. I confess my sin of rebellion. I choose to submit to You. I choose obedience to Your Word. In Jesus' name. Amen.

T - Take time to pray through the acrostic using the truth statement.

Whether you turn to the right or to the left, your ears will hear a voice behind you, saying, 'This is the way; walk in it' (Isaiah 30:21).

Dear Heavenly Father,

Thank You for Your patience. Please reveal to me ways that I have been rebellious.

R - Remember the facts – Determine to get to the root of what or who caused the first snag.

Therefore, let us move beyond the elementary teachings about Christ and be taken forward to maturity, not laying again the foundation of repentance from acts that lead to death, and of faith in God (Hebrews 6:1)

Dear Heavenly Father,

Thank You for Your plans for my abundant life. Thank You that finding freedom in Christ through submission is part of the process. Show me any way I am being deceived.

U - Uncover your fear, unravel the lie-knot — Behind every fear is a lie that is believed.

He will not shout or cry out or raise his voice in the streets. A bruised reed he will not break, and a smoldering wick he will not snuff out. In faithfulness he will bring forth justice; (Isaiah 42: 2, 3)

Dear Heavenly Father,

Help to face my fear of submitting to those I don't agree with or don't trust. Father give me discernment and grace as I stand on Your promise. "In faithfulness You will bring forth justice."

T - Tell yourself the truth. Scripture spoken aloud ushers in healing and brings wholeness.

He has shown you, O mortal, what is good. And what does the LORD require of you? To act justly and to love mercy and to walk humbly with your God (Micah 6:8).

Dear Heavenly Father,

Thank You for Your plans. Help me to behave honestly and honorably. Help me to love mercy. Help me to give mercy. I choose to walk humbly with You. In Jesus' name. Amen.

H - Help is available by agreeing with God. Confess your sin, submit to God, declare the truth aloud over yourself.

On the last and greatest day of the festival, Jesus stood and said in a loud voice, 'Let anyone who is thirsty come to me and drink. Whoever believes in me, as Scripture has said, rivers of living water will flow from within them' (John 7:37-38).

Dear Heavenly Father,

Thank You for enabling me to understand and apply the principles of Biblical submission to new areas of my life. Help me to be open to allowing You to reveal more so I can walk even closer to You. You are so good. In Jesus' name. Amen.

Loosening the Lies

Individual or Group Study Questions and Guided Journal Opportunity

1. Do you agree with this statement from Nancy DeMoss Wohlgemuth, "The real war is a battle for control?" Why or Why Not?

2. Explain the concept of rebellion versus submission.

3. Share any new insight you have received from this chapter.

4. State the character qualities Daniel exhibited while serving an evil master.

5. The abundant life is what is promised to believers, why do you think so many find that this freedom in Christ eludes them?

6. Describe what it means to you to be "far above" and "battle in the heavenly places.

7. Has it helped to remind yourself that the battle takes place in the heavenly realms?

8. Explain the Latin term "*Capax Dei.*"

9. Would the concept of "making room for more of God" be something you may implement? Why or Why Not? Please share your next steps.

10. After learning God's truth, do you feel more threatened or more encouraged by the Biblical concept of submission?

Truth Tools

For rebellion is like the sin of divination, and arrogance like the evil of idolatry (I Samuel 15:23).

But Samuel replied: 'Does the LORD delight in burnt offerings and sacrifices as much as in obeying the LORD? To obey is better than sacrifice, and to heed is better than the fat of rams' (I Samuel 15:22).

Let everyone be subject to the governing authorities, for there is no authority except that which God has established. The authorities that exist have been established by God. Consequently, whoever rebels against the authority is rebelling against what God has instituted, and those who do so will bring judgment on themselves. For rulers hold no terror for those who do right, but for those who do wrong. Do you want to be free from fear of the one in authority? Then do what is right and you will be commended. For the one in authority is God's servant for your good. But if you do wrong, be afraid, for rulers do not bear the sword for no reason. They are God's servants, agents of wrath to bring punishment on the wrongdoer (Romans 13:1-4).

Freed by Faith

A prayer of adoration and devotion.

Dear Heavenly Father,

Thank You for Your kindness and goodness to show me the ways I have been rebellious toward You. Thank You for the healing and hope You have brought me through my decision to submit to Your will. I am grateful and thankful for this opportunity to trust You by submission. I am hopelessly devoted to You. In Jesus' name. Amen.

As long as you are proud, you cannot know God. A proud man is always looking down on things and people, and, of course, as long as you are looking down, you cannot see something that is above you.[1]

C.S. Lewis

Chapter 8:
Twirled - I Don't Need Anyone's Help!

Remote villagers in the African forest use snares to trap wild animals for their fresh meat. Snares are used by poachers to capture prey to harvest their hides. Snares are also used by farmers and homeowners to trap intrusive and irritating animals. The annoying intruders cause economic loss such as coyotes that kill livestock or beavers that damage trees or plug irrigation ditches. A snare is a confinement device that uses a loop of hemp, wire, or rope designed to capture furbearers around the neck, torso, foot or leg.[2] Using a snare is a simple, but effective capture device.

Snares are designed to capture an animal by their leg or neck, and when the snare's loop is purposefully set in the center of their movement path, the creature is trapped by surprise.[3] Unfortunately, innocent, non-target animals are snagged by these simple traps, too. One study found that snares captured four out of five animals that were non-target species.

A serious concern and problem with snares is that they're non-selective: they catch anything that strays into them. The unfortunate victims of snares include domesticated animals, threatened and endangered wildlife. Each year thousands of endangered lions, elephants, and wild dogs are captured, maimed, and killed by illegal traps. A disturbing fact is that snares often don't kill their prey, but leave it to suffer—dying slowly or hanging by a bloodied limb until the hunter arrives days later. Some animals manage to escape snares but four out of five are maimed in the process—losing a paw, or bearing deep scars around their necks, legs, or trunks.[4] The injured or maimed animal most likely bleeds to death or its life will end when it becomes prey to other animals. The unfortunate victims trapped by snares are either permanently injured or die as a result. According to LionAid, a UK-based conservation non-profit organization, an estimated 90% of wildlife caught in snares are killed and left to rot, while the few that are rescued or escape often sustain injuries that make it impossible to hunt or survive in the wild.[5]

There are numerous spiritual parallels to a non-target animal's unsuspecting capture by a snare and for believers, when we are innocently tempted, trapped, and enmeshed by pride. Daily we struggle with the choice to serve ourselves or God. Self-importance lurks to ambush us, ensnare us, and bring us down. Pride is non-selective. The enemy uses it to snag any saint not looking out for the deadly trap that the enemy has laid. Pride is a killer. A synonym for pride is arrogance, a heart condition that says, "I want my will. I can do it myself. It was my idea. I don't need anyone's help."

We've each experienced situations when our will is blocked. We feel out of control, realize we are, and we limp away. Our ego is damaged, we want to look good, and we hope to save face. In this chapter we will discuss the "lie-knot" of "I don't need anyone's help." We will look at a Biblical definition of pride - what pride is and what it is not. We will define humility - what it is and what it is not. We will discover practical steps to learn to humble ourselves and allow God's Word to lance the "lie-knot" of pride. Indeed, we can learn from the foibles of our past and the failures of others in history. Let's get started.

Evil Ensnarement

Pride first appeared in the Bible in Genesis 3. As we discussed in previous chapters, the devil used pride to seduce Adam and Eve to rely on their resources instead of depending on God. Through deceit and arrogance, the enemy snagged Eve by contradicting what God had told both of them not to do. God's original commandment to Adam is found in Genesis 2:16, 17, "And the Lord God commanded the man, "You are free to eat from any tree in the garden; but you must not eat from the tree of the knowledge of good and evil, for when you eat of it you will surely die." You can't get any clearer than that. God specifically told them what not to do, "I don't want you to eat of the tree of the knowledge of good and evil." But Adam and Eve disobeyed God and ate from the tree of the knowledge of good and evil.

Earlier in *Unraveling the Lie-Knot*, I wrote of Eve's twisted thinking. Her FOMO (fear of missing out) made her believe that God was withholding the opportunity from them to be godlike. Rejection of God's Word introduced Eve to unbelief and doubt. She questioned if God was reliable or if He could be trusted. The devil successfully drew Eve into the trap by suggesting God was lying to her. We continue to reap the consequences of the first couples' choices today. This concept is thoroughly explained by Thomas A. Tarrants III, Vice President of Ministry for the C.S. Lewis Institute, "Finally weakened by unbelief, enticed by pride, and ensnared by self-deception, she (Eve) opted for autonomy and disobeyed God's command. In just a few deft moves, the devil was able to use pride to bring about Eve's downfall and plunge the human race into spiritual ruin. This ancient but all-too-familiar process confronts each of us daily. "Each person is tempted when they are dragged away by their own desire and enticed. Then, after desire has conceived, it gives birth to sin, and sin when it is full-grown, gives birth to death" (James 1:14-15).[6] Tarrants reminds us of how the pride process brought about Eve's downfall and plunged the human race into spiritual ruin. James describes how each of us is tempted, lured, and enticed by our own desires. So how do we learn to turn away from our desires? I am glad you asked.

It's helpful to understand that the "lie-knot" attitude of "I don't need anyone else's help" is a subtle way we can be ensnared by the enemy's temptation, enticement, and trickery. If we are aware of this concept, we can become skilled at discerning his tactics through studying God's Word, what pride means, and how to respond with an attitude of humility. It helps to identify the sin of pride for what it is, a fatal snare. We can recognize the bait for its intended purpose, a deadly ambush. Author, speaker and radio host, Peggy Joyce Ruth, in her book, *Psalm 91: Real Life Stories of God's Shield of Protection* describes this condition,

> Have you ever seen a movie where a fur trapper travels deep into the mountains in the cold climate? He baits big, steel traps, covers them with branches, and then waits for some unsuspecting animal to step

into the trap. Those traps were not there by chance. The trapper has taken great care in placing them in very strategic locations. In times of a war, a minefield is set up the same way. Those land mines are methodically placed in well-calculated locations. These are pictures of what the enemy does to us. That is why he is called the trapper! The traps that are set for us are not there by accident. It is as if the trap has your name on it. They are custom made, placed, and baited specifically for each one of us. But like an animal caught in a trap, when ensnared, we suffer through a slow, painful process. We don't die instantly. We are ensnared until the trapper comes to destroy us.[7]

When King David was on the run from his enemies, he prayed, "Keep me safe from the traps set by evildoers, from the snares they have laid for me" (Psalm 141:9). We can pray like King David, using his words. In doing so, humble ourselves before God, the only One who can help us. Instead of taking the bait, and putting our toe into the snare, wondering if it will close on us, we can intentionally tip toe around or step over the temptation.

God's Word is our weapon, and through its power, we can win the fierce spiritual battle with pride. King David showed us how it works in a tangible way, and how to keep our focal point on the Lord. He talked truth by reminding himself to keep his eyes on the only One who could help him. And then King David spoke out the result of his humility - God would free him. "My eyes are ever on the Lord, for only he will release my feet from the snare" (Psalm 25:15).

I wonder what would have happened if Eve would have done this? We know what happened next. Satan successfully tricked Eve to shift her focus from the benefits of living in a perfect paradise to the one thing she didn't have - godlikeness. Eve took her eyes off of God's plan, looked at temptation, and listened to the enemy's voice. She could have asked God for help and prayed a prayer like this: ""When my spirit grows faint within me, it is you who watch over my way. In the path where I walk people have hidden a snare for me" (Psalm 142:3). If she would have been aware of the snare, she could have asked God for His help. But like a non-target animal, Eve unassumingly took the bait and, was caught in the noose, ushering separation from God into humankind. Sound familiar?

How often our attention is drawn away from being grateful for the blessings we have been given. We want what someone else has. We have an "I've got to have it" feeling and our desires, like Eve's, can be easily manipulated. When we obsess over the one thing we don't have, we fall into trouble and temptation and we are trapped by sin. Psalm 18:27 reminds us that "You (God) save, "the humble but bring low those whose eyes are haughty."'" When we are consumed with what we want, it's no surprise our desire increases. When our desire increases, we rationalize, thinking we can turn away from our sin at any time. When we are deceived, we rationalize, our will is eroded, and we are unable to resist. We no longer have the will-power to say no. And so we give in to sin. We get our way. God gives us our way, and later on we find out that His way would have been much better for us. If only we would have waited for His provision and been patient with His timing. There are many Biblical examples of pride which offer helpful lessons for our lives. Let's lean in for an Old Testament lesson on humility from the life of King Uzziah.

Conceited Captivity

At the age of 16, Uzziah became king of Judah, and reigned in Jerusalem fifty-two years. Early in his rule, he set his heart to seek God's will and did not desert the worship of the true God. His successful reign began by choosing accountability and committing to a mentoring relationship with the prophet Zechariah. The prophet instructed Uzziah in the fear of God. "As long as he sought the Lord, God gave him success" (2 Chronicles 26:5). God blessed the king with great wealth, political power, and military might. King Uzziah's management skills restored the bounty and prosperity of the southern kingdom of Israel that had diminished since the death of Solomon. "His fame spread far and wide, for he was greatly helped until he became powerful" (2 Chronicles 26:15).

King Uzziah was extraordinarily gifted, remarkably successful in war and peace, planning and execution, in building and planting.[8] Somewhere along King Uzziah's successful climb to the top, he became ensnared in the enemy's trap of pride. In the beginning, he lived with a fear of God and worshipped Him, but as he gained more fame, he did not continue to ask God for insight or direction. Instead of God-reliance, he became ensnared in self-dependence. In self-sufficiency, he broke away from the mentoring relationship with Zechariah. He failed to recognize God's part in his achievements and instead overestimated his own importance.

King Uzziah neglected to humble himself by giving gratitude to God. Instead of returning thanks to God for the gifts and abilities he received, he began to think more highly of himself. He developed an exaggerated sense of his own importance and ability. Pride of the heart is presumption. Proverbs 11:2 warns us "When pride comes then comes disgrace" and "Pride goes before destruction" (Proverbs 16:18). King Uzziah's self-importance was tangled up in his lack of thankfulness. The Smith's Bible Dictionary says that, "The end of Uzziah was less prosperous than his beginning. Elated with his splendid career, he determined to burn incense on the altar of God, but was opposed by the high priest Azariah and eighty others. The king was enraged at their resistance, and as he pressed forward with his censer, was suddenly smitten with leprosy."[9]

King Uzziah did not thank God for the leadership or administrative gifts God had given him. His great accomplishments, abundant success, and overflowing wealth went to his head. He thought he was above God's law and tried to perform the duties of the priests. Azariah and the other priests intervened, which gave King Uzziah yet another opportunity to repent from his disobedience to God. But King Uzziah refused. King Uzziah turned away from God, was struck with leprosy, and remained leprous until his death. Sadly, he is remembered for this arrogant act and punishment more than his great reforms.[10]

Each of us is susceptible to pride. The trap is subtly laid, and the enemy knows our weakness to forget God's part in our successes and victories. The remedy for pride? Thank God. Be grateful. Develop an attitude of gratitude for His blessings. As we return thanks and, express gratitude to God for His gifts, we remind ourselves that everything we have been given comes from Him. Our gifts all belong to Him. We can heed the insight of 1 Corinthians 10:12, "So if you think you are standing firm, be careful that you don't fall." We can prevent pride from becoming a sinful snare by choosing an attitude of gratitude and thanksgiving, and make praising God a habit. If we don't intentionally turn away from pride, our selfishness maims us. Or can entrap us to a standstill causing us to feel as if we are dead spiritually.

Snared by Self

"Have it Your Way" or "Be Your Own Boss" are cultural marketing sound bites thrown onto our path to ensnare us to put ourselves first. Billboards, commercials, and internet advertisements bombard us with the benefits of "looking out for number one." We are told self-sufficiency and independence is what's best for us, as these verbs are used as synonyms for happiness. These self-ruling bits of advice encourage us to "put ourselves in charge of our lives" and if we do, we are assured, "we will be content." This is deception.

We are not created for self-government and autonomy. We are created to depend on God. Isaiah 66:2 says, ""Has not my hand made all these things, and so they came into being?" declares the Lord. "These are the ones I look on with favor: those who are humble and contrite in spirit, and who tremble at my Word."" Dependence on God is not a sign of weakness. The way to maximize our potential and enjoy our lives to their fullest extent is to live in harmony with our Creator. Humbly submitting to God means we humbly submit to Him as our supreme Master. Recognizing His love, grace, and goodness, we can trust His kind direction, find peace in His lordship, and walk freely with joy as He guides our steps.

Years ago, I overheard my preschool son inform his elementary-aged sister, "You are not the boss of me." We may not want to admit it, but each of us has someone or something that is "the boss of us." The wise person allows God to be their boss. The question is who are we choosing to submit to? Proverbs 11:2 offers sound insight, "When pride comes then comes disgrace but with humility comes wisdom." For years, I allowed nicotine, alcohol and other addictive substances to be my boss. I thought I was in control, but I was led by my selfish desires, I told myself "I've got this," "I can quit anytime," "I am not an addict," "I don't need help from anyone." Others might allow food, spending, exercise, video games or any number of other things to trap them. God wants us to humbly come before Him and let Him lead.[11]

Why is pride such a temptation for us? And why is humility so elusive? It helps to have a thorough definition of pride. *Vine's Expository Dictionary of New Testament Words* defines pride as, "haughty, boastful, high-minded."[12] I like this additional description from *Seek and Find,* "Pride is a failure to accept and perceive the reality of our utter dependence on God. If we think we can save ourselves, that is taking the place of God and it is the result of a lack of humility. Only humility can accept and perceive the reality of our utter dependence on God. If we desire to run our own lives, that is taking the place of God and it is the result of a lack of humility."[13] Satan's chief aim is for mankind to accept selfishness and egotism as what we were created for and put on earth to do. Pride is the prominent feature of this world. "For everything in the world - the lust of the flesh, the lust of the eyes and the pride of life comes not from the Father but from the world" (I John 2:16).

As we saw in earlier chapters, God has designed us to submit to His will, and commit to His purpose, instead of our own. Pride is evidenced in self-centeredness but the root of pride is self-exaltation. In his book *Discipleship Counseling* Dr. Anderson describes pride and its consequences.

> Pride says, "It was my idea, and I can do it by my strength and resources." Pride is the origin of evil. Scripture says of Satan, "You said in your heart, 'I will ascend to the heavens; I will raise my throne above the stars of God, and I will sit enthroned on the mount of assembly on the utmost heights of Mount Zaphon. I will ascend above the tops of the clouds; I will make myself like the Most High.' But you are brought down to the realm of the dead, to the depths of the pit (Isaiah 14:13-15). Hell is where people say, "My will be done." Heaven is where we say, "Your will be done."[14]

Satan is called the prince of this world, and we see how self-interest is ruling and destroying this world. If only we could remember this verse, "The arrogant have hidden a snare for me; they have spread out the cords of their net and have set traps for me along my path," (Psalm 140:5). Every temptation we face is a snare meant to trap us to live our lives without depending on God. If we respond in pride, we are deceived. We think we are doing ourselves a favor, but the satisfaction quickly wears off. Like an innocent domestic or non-target animal, we naively step into pride's snare, the noose tightens. Refusing to ask God for help, or depending on Him, we struggle. The snare constricts and we become more intertwined. The trap has caught us and holds us fast.

Determined not to need anyone or ask for help, we become more tied up, and entangled, causing further spiritual and emotional injury. Kicking and thrashing about, we may be maimed by the trap of arrogance. We want to save face. If and when we are released, undoubtedly we'll be permanently marked by the scars. In the end, we may finally break loose, but we are spiritually wounded or begin a slow spiritual demise. C.S. Lewis observed, "Pride is a spiritual cancer. It eats up the very possibility of love, or contentment, or even common sense."[15]

We've described the effects of pride in the fall of humankind, it is also an attitude of contempt and indifference. Pride can be our undoing, and we must take time to search ourselves to determine if we are allowing it in our lives. We must refuse to tolerate pride. Pride caused the grandstander, Satan, to be cast out of heaven. Pride caused the self-aggrandizing Adam and Eve to be cast out of Eden. When we exalt ourselves, we are painting a target on our back. This target is an invitation for God to open fire. Pride is our greatest enemy. God is committed to opposing pride. The solution? God's grace. This is described Romans 5:1-2 (MSG) "By entering through faith into what God has always wanted to do for us - set us right with him, make us fit for him - we have it all together with God because of our Master Jesus. And that's not all: We throw open our doors to God and discover at the same moment that he has already thrown open his door to us. We find ourselves standing where we always hoped we might stand - out in the wide open spaces of God's grace and glory, standing tall and shouting our praise."

God gives us what we don't deserve. Accepting God's marvelous grace for ourselves and extending it to others is the best way to fight pride. James 4:3-6 reminds us, "When you ask, you do not receive, because you ask with wrong motives, that you may spend what you get on your pleasures. You adulterous people, don't you know that friendship with the world means enmity against God? Therefore, anyone who chooses to be a friend of the world becomes an enemy of God. Or do you think Scripture says without reason that he jealously longs for the spirit he has caused to dwell in us? But he gives us more grace. That is why Scripture says: "God opposes the proud but shows favor to the humble."" Humility begins with accepting the gift of a personal relationship with God, as He has freely given it to us. This gift of salvation was purchased through the sacrificial act of the death of Jesus Christ, and confirmed by our Lord's miraculous resurrection from the dead.

God does not force us to obey Him. We have a choice. When we ask God for help, it shows we trust Him. When we pray a prayer and invite God to assist us, we humble ourselves. God does the rest; He severs our self-life. Does it seem God's will is inconvenient? This thought is a "lie-knot," a snare set by the enemy. Don't believe it. "The teaching of the wise is a fountain of life, turning a person from the snares of death" (Proverbs 13:14). Dr. Anderson said, "Jesus counters by sharing the way of the Cross, the foundational principles for our lives in Christ, which is the repudiation of the old natural life and embracing the new joyful union with the resurrected life of Christ."[16] As we choose to allow Jesus to cut away the snare of the trappings of our old natural life, we are freed to embrace the joy of living the resurrected life in Christ. It's through our humble act of dependence on Jesus Christ that we can experience the fullness of joy God has promised us.

There will always be an easier way which involves less risk, but God's desire is for us to be strengthened in our faith. Galatians 2:20 reminds us, "I have been crucified with Christ and I no longer live, but Christ lives in me. The life I now live in the body, I live by faith in the Son of God, who loved me and gave himself for me." God does not hold us back or prevent our freedom, but wants to lead us into an abundant life. God is waiting for us to invite Him to cut us free from pride. He wants to crucify our fleshly desires. A humbly prayed prayer asking God for help, gives Him permission to do so. He liberates our spirit. God's power cannot operate in us until our self-will is cut off. Pride is a snare which traps us into moving away from God. Let's shift now to the opposite of pride -- a discussion on humility.

Liberated by Humility

Humility is confidence properly placed. It is our individual choice to declare our dependence on God's power and trust what He can do in us and through us. God wants us to reach our highest potential in Christ. Humility is not weakness. Humility is the Spirit-led position of a saint who says, "by God's grace, I allowed God to accomplish His will in me and through me." We might also want to define humility as "a decision to commit to spiritual cooperation with God's will and purpose for our lives." We are to "put no confidence in the flesh" (Philippians 3:3). The apostle Paul said of himself, "By the grace of God, I am what I am, and his grace to me was not without effect. No, I worked harder than all of them, yet not I but the grace of God that was with me" (1 Corinthians 15:10). In Christ, humility sees spiritual things through the truth of God's Word. As we believe and embrace the Biblical fact that we are loved and valued by our heavenly Father, we can fully appreciate and implement the truth of what God has done for us through the finished work of Jesus Christ.

We can place our trust in God's strength, and give Him permission to do what only He can do, by the power of His spirit. *Vine's Expository Dictionary of New Testament Words* gives a distinct definition of humility as "lowliness of mind, humility of mind."[17] The definition in *Seek and Find* reads, "Humility means that we are absolutely dependent on Christ the Head and Christ the Body. Humility shows you that God is working all things to bring about His good purpose, which is your conformity to the image of Jesus. Humility removes the human desire to go where God has not sent you. Pride is the lack of ability to see this."[18] As we are dependent on God, we can invite God into every area of our life and ministry and give Him the glory for the results. "This is to my Father's glory, that you bear much fruit, and showing yourselves to be my disciples" (John 15:8).

In the previous chapter, we discussed rebellion and how it pertains to control (or lack of control) of ourselves, circumstances, and other people. It's important to note that a position of rebellion interconnects with an attitude of pride. Often the root of an attitude of rebellion is enmeshed with the sin of pride. As noted earlier in this chapter, James 4:6 says, "God is opposes the proud but shows favor to the humble." By coming humbly to Christ, we choose to set aside our pride, and invite God to help us. This attitude is essential to enter into a faith relationship with Jesus Christ as Savior.

In doing so, we surrender ourselves to His control and we are restored to God's original plan and purpose for us. In Christ, we are accepted. In Christ, we are secure. In Christ, we are significant. We are no longer hopeless, worthless, or unworthy. I am excited to share the testimony of Cara Henderson whose parents were divorced when she was an adolescent, resulting in her struggle with fear of the future and control of her younger sister's life and future. Here's Cara's story:

> So my parents got divorced when I was 11 years old and at the time that happened. I am a very extroverted person and I have a younger sister who is a very introverted person. We experienced that life event of parental divorce really very differently. I felt like, as the older sister and as the more people person, that I had this responsibility to care for her. And so I took that on, and to an unhealthy level, although I didn't realize it for years. So I struggled a lot, when she moved across

the country and went to college somewhere where I couldn't watch her every day and be with her. And I worried about her a lot. Years later, she got married, and I experienced those same feelings of "Oh I don't know if I can let him take care of her. I really feel like she is my responsibility and I really need to be with her and make sure she's okay." Years after that, I was going through the Freedom In Christ material and really was praying through some stuff and reflecting on, and I felt like I heard God say, "You can let this go, I am in charge of her, I am taking care of her. You don't need to feel this pressure and you don't need to try to control this relationship that another person has with anyone." So that's really what I got out of it, is just that feeling of relief and of freedom to just let that go and let her be. You know, almost daily, there are opportunities for me to see something and to see that tendency in myself, to want to make things okay, which is not possible, and it's sort of a crazy thought. But just to allow myself to say, "Oh yeah, God is in control of this and I don't have to do this myself![19]

Cara's story is a confession of her pride. She wanted to control who took care of her little sister. Ultimately Cara realized she had to confess her sin of pride. She didn't trust God to love, provide, watch over her sister, even though Cara knew God loved her sister more than she ever could. Cara asked God for help. She willingly accepted the invitation by humbling herself and submitting to God.

As we choose to humble ourselves and submit to God's authority, we can do the same thing. We can rest in the authority given to us by God. To begin, we state our dependence on God (by humbling ourselves). In so doing, we acknowledge and declare what Satan refused to declare. In speaking out our intent to depend solely on God, we confess truth, and we expose pride. Romans 6:1-12, explains how life in Jesus Christ has overcome the law of sin and death. Paul explains how we are identified with Christ in His death, burial, resurrection, and life. Our responsibility is highlighted in Romans 6:11-12, "In the same way, count yourselves dead to sin but alive to God in Christ Jesus. Therefore do not let sin reign in your mortal body so that you obey its evil desires." By asserting the truth of God's Word, we affirm our intent to humble ourselves. Instead of living a self-sufficient and self-focused existence, we exchange it for a God-dependent and God-honoring life of abundant blessings with eternal benefits. And that, dear one, is the life we are created to live.

Aware of the Snare

Do these words sound familiar? Unworthy. Helpless. Defenseless. Hopeless. Unable. Powerless. Are these thoughts you currently have about yourself? Do these words describe how you've felt in the past? If you, like Cara, me, and countless others, have been victimized, wounded or abused, you've experienced how condemning these emotions can be. I've got good news. You don't have to suffer any longer. Turning to God and asking for His help is an act of humility, especially when we don't feel good about ourselves or others. One of the greatest marks of maturity in Christ is choosing to believe Him in spite of how we feel. God has provided a way to escape the temptation to stay ensnared in the "lie-knot" of "I don't need anyone's help." In Christ, we can claim in Psalm 91:3, "Surely he will save you from the fowler's snare and from the deadly pestilence."

You don't have to remain entrapped in the snare of feeling unworthy, helpless, defenseless, hopeless, unable, or powerless. In Christ, you are accepted, you are secure, you are significant, you are defended by God, you are righteous and holy, you are able, you are an enemy of the devil, and much more. Remember, "No temptation has overtaken you except what is common to mankind. And God is faithful; he will not let you be tempted beyond what you can bear. But when you are tempted, he will also provide a way out so that you can endure it" (1 Corinthians 10:13).

We have a choice, either to give in to the temptation, choose our own self-edifying and self-centered way, and choose not to ask God to help us. Or we can decide to humbly submit to God, ask for His help, and give the Holy Spirit's presence complete access. Great theologian, and well-loved author, C.S. Lewis stated in Mere Christianity that "even if we don't feel affection for another person, (including ourselves or God) we should act as if we did love him or her, for the emotions will follow the behavior."[20] As we yield ourselves and wield the sword of the Word of God, in one stroke we are cut free from the snare of pride.

In Christ, God has made us worthy. A proper sense of our worth to God comes from accepting the fact that we are loved and valued by Him. It can be explained by saying we set aside our pride, and with humility say "no" to the flesh and "yes" to the Spirit. We can respectfully accept the fullness of the promise found in Ephesians 4:13, "until we all reach unity in the faith and in the knowledge of the Son of God and become mature, attaining to the whole measure of the fullness of Christ." His purpose is not to merely bring us into the family of God and keep us as babies or children, but God is concerned with our maturity. He wants us to grow in wisdom.

As we permit this process, we will notice the fruit of the Spirit growing naturally. "But the fruit of the Spirit is love, joy, peace, forbearance, kindness, goodness, faithfulness, gentleness, and self-control. Against such things there is no law" (Galatians 5:22, 23). He wants our knowledge of the things of the Spirit to increase. He wants our ministry to be perfected and His Word to produce the fruit of the Spirit in us. Giving God permission to cut through our pride is essentially relinquishing our control and surrendering our self-life for His purposes. We may be surprised when we see Him produce a healthy crop to build His Kingdom.

Inviting God to help us is not a sign of weakness. It is an act of obedience to God by humbling ourselves through submission. Psalm 147:6 says, "The Lord sustains the humble but casts the wicked to the ground." Not only does God take pleasure in the act of humility, He loves to bless us. He delights by raising up the humble. Proverbs 3:34 says, "He mocks proud mockers but shows favor to the humble and oppressed." Robert J. Morgan, author and pastor of The Donelson Fellowship in Nashville, TN, said, "Emotions come and go, but attitudes come and grow, and our attitudes when based on scriptural realities, become the seedbed for ever-healthier emotions as we go through the day and throughout the years. The "as if" principle frees us from being enslaved to our emotions or to our circumstances. We can choose to act other than we feel, and over prolonged periods, we can work our way up from depression, discouragement, from loneliness, from lethargy and boredom. We can live enthusiastically."[21]

Now, we can anticipate the enemy will lay down the snare of pride, but we know what to do to avoid getting caught. By humbly asking God for help, we can "out-truth" him and steer clear of the trap. In Psalm 124:6-8, King David was on the run from His enemies and asked God to deliver him from destruction. He also thanked God for his rescue. "Praise be to the Lord, who has not let us be torn by their teeth. We have escaped like a bird from the fowler's snare, the snare has been broken and we have escaped. Our help is in the name of the Lord, the Maker of heaven and earth."

Like King David, myself, Cara, and you, if we humble ourselves before God and ask for His intervention, He welcomes the invitation, and can't wait to exalt us. "For the Lord takes delight in his people; He crowns the humble with victory" (Psalm 149:4).

Don't wait any longer to ask God to assist you. God gladly anticipates the opportunity to send His help. He can't wait to deliver you, heal your damaged emotions, and give you the finishing touch of victorious, enthusiastic living. And that, dear one, is the life you are created for. What are you waiting for?

Chapter 8: Twirled – I Don't Need Anyone's Help!

Loosening the Lies

Individual or Group Study Questions and Guided Journal Opportunity

Cast all your anxiety upon him, because he cares for you (1 Peter 5:7).

God is looking for women who repent and humble themselves before Him. He wants us to be responsive and receptive to His help. The process begins when we invite Him to care for us.

Why don't you pray this prayer of commitment?

Dear Heavenly Father,

Thank You for Your care for me. I confess, I have often thought my ways were better than Your ways. Forgive me. Help me to discern the areas I've not allowed You to access because of my pride. I didn't think I needed anyone's help. But now I see Your ways are better than any plans I might ever dream up for myself. Thank You for Your forgiveness. In Jesus' name. Amen.

T - Take time to pray through the acrostic using the truth statement.

Pride brings a person low, but the lowly in spirit gain honor (Proverbs 29:23).

Dear Heavenly Father,

I humble myself before You. Reveal to me areas I have been deceived because of pride. Thank You.

R - Remember the facts – Determine to get to the root of what or who caused the first snag.

If I had cherished sin in my heart, the Lord would not have listened; but God has surely listened and has heard my prayer (Psalm 66:18-19).

Dear Heavenly Father,

I confess my sin of pride. I receive Your forgiveness. Thank You for listening to my prayer. In Jesus' name. Amen.

U - Uncover your fear, unravel the lie-knot – Behind every fear is a lie that is believed.

Lord, do not your eyes look for truth? You struck them, but they felt no pain; you crushed them, but they refused correction. They made their faces harder than stone and refused to repent (Jeremiah 5:3).

Dear Heavenly Father,

Thank You for revealing what Your Word says about pride. I continue to seek You and yearn for Your truth. In Jesus' name. Amen.

T - Tell yourself the truth. Scripture spoken aloud ushers in healing and brings wholeness.

Therefore, if anyone is in Christ, the new creation has come: The old has gone, the new is here! (2 Corinthians 5:17)

Dear Heavenly Father,

If I could, I would shout this verse from the rooftops. I am grateful I don't have to struggle any longer to put myself first or compare myself to others' looks, accomplishments, or paychecks. I choose to put You first in everything. Thank You for the new me. In Jesus' name. Amen.

H - Help is available by agreeing with God. Confess your sin, submit to God, declare the truth aloud over yourself.

"Come near to God and he will come near to you. Wash your hands, you sinners, and purify your hearts, you double-minded" (James 4:8).

Dear Heavenly Father,

I have been proud by lifting my needs above others' needs. I have been proud by thinking if I looked better than others, I would exalt myself. There are other areas in which I have been proud. Reveal these areas to me. I desire for You to take away all areas in which I have been proud. Thank You, In Christ I am forgiven. In Jesus' name. Amen.

Loosening the Lies

Individual or Group Study Questions and Guided Journal Opportunity

1. Share ways you may have become ensnared, either knowingly or unknowingly, in the enemy's trap.

2. Explain a new concept you discovered in observing Eve's choice not to ask God for help.

3. Do you think things could have changed for King Uzziah if he would have been grateful to God?

4. Share what ways you imagine there may have been different outcomes.

5. Describe what pride means to you.

6. Give details about how we can express Godlike humility.

7. C.S. Lewis stated in Mere Christianity that "even if we don't feel affection for another person, (including ourselves or God) we should act as if we did love him or her, for the emotions will follow the behavior." Do you Agree or Disagree?

8. Explain the principle of "feelings follow actions."

9. Have you struggled to be cut free of the "lie-knot" of "I don't need anyone's help?"

10. After learning God's truth about submission, do you feel more threatened or encouraged about this concept?

Truth Tools

What causes fights and quarrels among you? Don't they come from your desires that battle within you? You desire but do not have, so you kill.

You covet but you cannot get what you want, so you quarrel and fight. You do not have because you do not ask God.

When you ask, you do not receive, because you ask with wrong motives, that you may spend what you get on your pleasures.

You adulterous people, don't you know that friendship with the world means enmity against God? Therefore, anyone who chooses to be a friend of the world becomes an enemy of God.

Or do you think Scripture says without reason that he jealously longs for the spirit he has caused to dwell in us?

But he gives us more grace. That is why Scripture says: "God opposes the proud but shows favor to the humble."

Submit yourselves, then, to God. Resist the devil, and he will flee from you (James 4:1-7).

Freed by Faith

A prayer of adoration and devotion.

Dear Heavenly Father,

I adore You for giving me the desire for a heart of repentance, a humble heart toward You. Thank You for Your support, as You teach me Your ways. Thank You for a renewed passion for Your presence. I praise You for the opportunity to abide in Your Word. In Jesus' name. Amen.

If you are paralyzed by your past, if Satan is destroying your gifts and your calling by his incessant replaying of old tapes, you're actually being hit by a double whammy. The original damage in the past is one thing—but now you're letting yourself be hurt and sidetracked again by the memory of what happened...we should not be ignorant of Satan's devices, and these ugly memories are one of the main weapons in his arsenal.[1]

Jim Cymbala

Chapter 9: Loosed - I Can Do This!

The extreme sport of skydiving is not for the faint of heart. Have you ever wondered why do people jump out of a moving aircraft at 10,000 feet above the ground? I know, me too. Here's what I've learned about people who skydive. In this select group of daredevils, many of them jump out of airplanes to face their fears. Some of these thrill-seekers say they "take the leap" to get rid of their worries or stress. Frequent jumpers talk about skydiving as their "therapy." Hmm...skydiving for therapy or curing my anxiety? Personally, I prefer something less edgy. For "therapy," I choose to confide in a close friend, take a run, indulge in an ice cream sundae, or visit with a trusted Biblical counselor. A staff member from the Long Island Skydiving Center said, "In free-fall, there are no worries or stress, everything else going on in your life just melts away and you feel there is nothing you can't do. We don't jump for a thrill, we jump for freedom."[2] Obviously, this type of extreme sport, whether as a hobby, to escape reality, or use as thrill therapy, is certainly not for everyone.

In January 2014, high above a small town southwest of Sydney, Australia, a 27-year-old Canadian skydiving instructor was jumping from an elevation of 14,000 feet. After over 2,000 successful dives, the parachutist was ecstatic for one more opportunity to experience the elation of the leap, not to mention the supercharged adrenaline rush.[3] But the unimaginable happened. After deploying the parachute at 3,000 feet, the lines of the main chute began twisting, sending him into an uncontrollable spin. Parachutes feature a three-ring release system allowing quick, emergency expulsion in case of a malfunction. But this time the system was jammed. As the parachute cords became frighteningly intertwined, the situation escalated, but the skydiver did some quick thinking.

A headline from *dailymail.co.uk* read, "Seconds from death: terrifying moment experienced skydiver's chute tangles sending him violently spinning toward the ground as he desperately tries to cut himself free."[4] The Canadian (who, for obvious reasons, did not wish to be named) said, "Under normal circumstances it's not very difficult to cut away your main parachute. However, this was far from a normal situation. Someone else had hooked half my gear up incorrectly and I missed it." Even under this deathly intense stress, the skydiver patiently attempted to untangle the ropes of the parachute, he gently and quickly worked at untwisting the matted cords. But his efforts were futile. They couldn't be unsnarled. As mentioned in the above quote, the skydiver was only a few seconds from hitting the ground without a parachute and he ran out of time. He knew his only option was to "cut away" and deploy his reserve chute a few seconds before the crash landing. "Cut away" is a skydiving term referring to disconnecting the main parachute from the harness-container in case of a malfunction to prepare for opening the reserve parachute.[5]

The backup parachute was deployed instantly. And as it was released, the canopy ejected out of the pack and spread out immediately. The skydiver was relieved when his feet firmly touched the ground. Apparently, the man was aware of other possible parachute malfunctions that could have happened. These often occur due to incorrect body position or faulty equipment, but even after over 2,000 jumps, the diver hadn't experienced such a severe interruption in a successful parachute drop such as this. The nearly fatal mistake was rare and could have been easily avoided. The parachute cord entanglement was caused by hasty and slipshod parachute packing. The skydiver's disaster had a scapegoat. It was caused by someone else's careless mistake.[6]

There are countless spiritual parallels to the conundrum of the parachute cord's entanglement that caused the skydiver's close call with death. We may find ourselves in a spiritual "free fall," as if our main parachute's cords become knotted up because of a hasty oversight, or someone else's blunder. We wonder if we can free ourselves before we hit the ground. The good news is that we can become skilled at untangling the "lie-knots," we've believed about God, ourselves, and others. Living in our freedom in Christ is a new way of life. As we mature, we can gain knowledge of practical strategies and use tools that will help us continually renew our minds.

In previous chapters, we discussed bitterness versus forgiveness, rebellion versus submission, and pride versus humility. In this chapter, we will discuss the "lie-knot" of "I can't control my emotions," "I am unable to overcome my addictions," or "I depend on using pornography to calm my stress, but I can quit at any time." The parachutist cut himself free from the tangled cords of the parachute so he could use the reserve parachute. In the same way, as we rely on God's Word, we can be cut free from the entanglement of any and every "lie-knot." We can cut through the lies with God's truth. Psalm 129:4 reminds us that "...the Lord is righteous; he has cut me free from the cords of the wicked." In Christ we can cancel the lie. This process only occurs as we declare the truth, "In Christ, I can do this!" God's Word renews our mind through its power. It replaces the lies with the truth. We don't have to worry about depending on our own reserves. With God's help we will be severed free from the cords of bondage into our new-found freedom. Let's get started.

Disentangling Deliverance

"I've asked God to deliver me from my obsession with marijuana. He hasn't done it for me. Why hasn't God come through?" Have you ever spoken these words? Okay, maybe not. You may not be fixated on marijuana. Maybe you're dependent on M & M's, movies, or men. Despite your addiction to the thing you are passionate about, you want deliverance. You want it now. I know. I get it. I've wondered the same thing for myself. I've struggled with each of the above addictions. I know the nagging, frustrating feeling of yearning to be fully delivered. I've experienced the vicious merry-go-round of shame and the anguish of sin-confess-sin-confess. I too, have asked God, "Why?" Let me explain.

Throughout my four decades of counseling hundreds of men and women, I have heard this very same question asked time and time again. "Why hasn't God delivered me?" And you may be thinking similar thoughts. I don't have all of the answers, but I can point you to God's Word and that's where we will find the tools to "cut away" the "lie-knot" of "Why hasn't God delivered me?"

First, let's look at what the word deliverance means. It's helpful to do Biblical word studies about spiritual concepts that confuse us. *The Vine's Expository Dictionary of New Testament Words*' definition of deliver, deliverance, deliverer is "to rescue from, to preserve from," and so "to deliver," the word by which it is regularly translated, is synonymous with "to save," though the idea is predominant in that of "preservation from."[7]

Who doesn't want to be preserved from, rescued now, or set free once and for all, from the thing or person that has ensnared us? Who wouldn't want to be liberated from the entanglement of habitual sin, past mistakes, snarled shame, blame, and unworthiness? We all want relief. Jesus showed us how to become "loosed," with Lazarus' resurrection. Spiritually, He has performed the same act of resurrection for each of us. In chapter three, you might recall, we discussed Jesus' visit to see his friends Mary and Martha. Jesus spoke to the lifeless corpse of Lazarus. Our Lord didn't just resuscitate the decaying body of His friend, He resurrected him. "When he heard this, Jesus called in a loud voice, "Lazarus, come out! The dead man came out, his hands and feet wrapped with strips of linen, and a cloth around his face. Jesus said to them, "Take off the grave clothes and let him go" (John 11:43, 44). Lazarus was unloosed, freed from death, and made alive again.

Through a restored relationship with God and because of the finished work of Jesus Christ, we've received rebirth and restoration. But wait, there's more. That's right. Jesus offers us our rescue. Most of us settle for just resuscitation. We don't see ourselves as completely resurrected into a new life. We still see ourselves as partly dead and partly alive. For a lot of us, our entire personality was formed around the wrong information. God's goal is for us to be free from the belief system that has held us hostage for too long. In Christ, we are a new creation and in Him we can learn how to be transformed by the renewing of our minds.

In 2 Corinthians 1:8-11, the apostle Paul wrote about his suffering and God's deliverance, "We do not want you to be uninformed, brothers and sisters, about the troubles we experienced in the province of Asia. We were under great pressure, far beyond our ability to endure, so that we despaired of life itself. Indeed, we felt we had received the sentence of death. But this happened that we might not rely on ourselves but on God, who raises the dead. He has delivered us from such a deadly peril, and he will deliver us again. On him we have set our hope that he will continue to deliver us, as you help us by your prayers. Then many will give thanks on our behalf for the gracious favor granted us in answer to the prayers of many." In this letter, Paul shared his love for the Corinthian church and expressed his absolute dependence on God.

Using himself as an example, Paul shared the revelation, and reality he had personally faced, for his total need for God's intervention. Paul's faith and choosing to believe God, in spite of his sufferings, feelings, or circumstances is an active example of the process of deliverance. As explained in the study notes of the Life Application Study Bible, "We often depend on our own skills and abilities when life seems easy, but we turn to God when we feel unable to help ourselves. Depending on God is a realization of our own powerlessness without Him and our need for His constant touch in our lives. God is our source of power and we receive His help by keeping in touch with Him. With this attitude of dependence, problems will drive us to God rather than away from Him."[8] Dependence on God is an obtainable way of life, not just a one-time activity. It's a choice, to continue to set aside our flesh by saying "no," and saying "yes" as we welcome the presence of the Holy Spirit.

Bondage Bargaining

To ask God for deliverance is a valid prayer we can pray. And we should pray for our personal deliverance from issues that entangle us. God wants to deliver us. If God reveals an area of concern to me, I must be honest. Not only do I want deliverance from the sin, I don't want to worry about the issue ever again. Furthermore, I do not want to even be tempted by the same sin at any time after I have been delivered. This is a "lie-knot" that states "If God really loved me, He would deliver me from this craving once and for all." Isn't that bargaining with God? Yes, it is. We don't need to bargain. Let me assure you, God has something much better in store. God has already made a deal with you and me. He is the one in control, not us.

When we negotiate with God, we are not in a place of humility. When Satan wanted to be equal with God, he tried to make a deal with God. He wanted control.

According to *Bible Sprout*, "Satan's fall was a direct result of his self-exaltation that was manifested in his pride, the first sin. The enemy's attitude is described in 1 Timothy 3:6 "He must not be a recent convert, or he may become conceited and fall under the same judgment as the devil." Motivated by pride, Satan set out on an irrational course to seize for himself God's authority over the universe. "How you have fallen from heaven, morning star, son of the dawn! You have been cast down to the earth, you who once laid low the nations! You said in your heart, "I will ascend to the heavens; I will raise my throne above the stars of God; I will sit enthroned on the mount of assembly, on the utmost heights of Mount Zaphon. I will ascend above the tops of the clouds; I will make myself like the Most High" (Isaiah 14:12-14).[9] This is a great explanation of Satan trying to make a deal with God as he exalted himself. The enemy wanted authority. He wanted to control the universe. God gave Satan the answer when he cast him out of heaven, and now Satan rules on the earth, as the prince of darkness. In the same way, we are given the choice, to give God control of our lives, or not.

Reality check: the process of being delivered may not be finished as soon as we would like. Unfortunately, we often want "fast-food freedom." I've learned deliverance is not like driving up to the takeout window at In-N-Out Burger™ and placing your order. You read the menu, figure out what you want, and speak your order into the intercom. At the next window you pay with your card, receive a receipt, and are then handed a bag of mouth-watering cheeseburgers, crunchy French fries, and a chocolate shake. There is no such thing as drive-thru deliverance. More often than not, God works in the process of deliverance by way of our moment-by-moment choices to choose truth. We can choose to say "No" to the flesh and "Yes" to the Holy Spirit. "Jesus said, "If you hold to my teaching, you are really my disciples. Then you shall know the truth and the truth shall make you free" (John 8:31, 32).

You and I can be cut free from "lie-knots" every time we read the Bible. In her book, *The Power of Praying for Your Adult Children*, Stormie Omartian said, "Deliverance means getting free of anything that holds us captive other than God. It means being rescued from someone or something that separates us from the Lord."[10] The process of deliverance is called sanctification, which we will discuss further in the next section.

Instead of demanding immediate deliverance, won't you rest in the assurance of the process of deliverance? Why not settle into your character development, as you allow God to fully transform you in the life-changing power of His grace? His specialty is working His will. When we "ask anything according to his will, he hears us. And if we know that he hears - whatever we ask - then we know that we have what we asked of him" (1 John 5:14,15). In His infinite wisdom, God waits, and all the while He is working His will. Instead of abdicating to our whim, or answering our why, God's intent is to usher us into wholeness. Why would we settle for anything less?

Scrambled Self-Control

Like it or not, we are in the midst of a spiritual battle. Sin no longer reigns over us, but it will try to tangle us up. We have been set free from the bondage of sin, and we are no longer entangled in the kingdom of unrighteousness. However, the struggle is real. We must be constantly on our guard, reminding ourselves we are dead to sin. We are no longer slaves. Before Christ Jesus released us from bondage, we didn't have a choice. Now we do. "For we know that our old self was crucified with him so that the body ruled by sin might be done away with, that we should no longer be slaves to sin" (Romans 6:6). Classic author W. Glyn Evans said, "There is no middle ground with the battle for my body. Either God or Satan is in control at any given moment. The control by one displaces the control by the other. The kingdom of one is enhanced or retarded by the relative degree of control he has over our bodies. I cannot excuse myself from the battle. I must enter it by an act of my will…"[11] The question is, will you submit your will to God's will?

Confession is the first step to repentance and will not be complete until we agree with God and face the truth. This is a key component to entering into the process of deliverance. In *Discipleship Counseling*, Dr. Anderson reminds us that, "Complete repentance means to submit to God, resist the devil and close the door. The door will be closed when all the bondages have been broken, all the mental strongholds have been torn down and the harmful relationship and sources that feed the problem have been cut off."[12]

As we discuss bondage versus freedom, let's consider possible areas we may be entangled by habitual sins of the flesh. Some examples are refusing to follow leaders we don't like or trust, anger because of an abrupt departure from a church staff or a family separation, or the tragedy of losing mobility because of an accident or illness. Because of these circumstances, do you have feelings of helplessness, or hopelessness? Or maybe you've had to face the loss of friends or church with a job change or move? Or have you had a recent loss of income with a demotion or layoff in your employment? Maybe you are now an empty-nester, or an adult child has recently married, and you are letting go of parenting him or her. Perhaps you've been incarcerated for several years, and a decade or two have slipped by as you have been behind bars.

Each of these situations may cause us to feel snagged or snarled by unhealthy attitudes, toxic habits, or infectious sins. We have the opportunity to resist sin, and we have the responsibility to do so. Our goal in this chapter is to reveal flesh patterns, that is, sins that tend to repeat themselves. For a list of sins of the flesh, we can look to Galatians 5:19-21 "The acts of the flesh are obvious: sexual immorality, impurity and debauchery; idolatry and witchcraft; hatred, discord, jealousy, fits of rage, selfish ambition, dissensions, factions and envy; drunkenness, orgies, and the like. I warn you, as I did before, that those who live like this will not inherit the kingdom of God." We can be transformed by the renewing of our mind, as we choose truth over the lies, we've believed. At the end of this chapter, you will have the opportunity to pray through sins of the flesh that may have become habitual sins. As you, like me, Cara, and others take personal responsibility for your part in the sin, God will help you, and you can learn to discern the truth. I am excited to share the testimony of an amazing woman named Rebecca Shirley, who overcame depression, discouragement, and despair.

> I was diagnosed with depression just after my grandson was born, so that was seven years ago. And I went out on the hills one day and I was really suicidal, really contemplating how I could end my life. I was just walking through the fields and I came across some fleece. When I picked it up, I just had this real sense for the first time in my life of God speaking aloud to me saying, "My sheep hear My voice." That was mind-blowing for me. So that was the start for the road to recovery.

I had my antidepressants and had some support from my friends, but Freedom In Christ was sort of the final breaking of that chain. When I realized who God said I was; that He loved me, that I was secure in Him, that I was accepted by Him, that He had a role for me to play, it meant that I could leave behind everything that was dragging me down. That was sort of the final test, it meant I could come off the anti-depressants and move on from there. Comfort eating – looking at me now, I am a fabulous size 12. Just under two years ago, I was a size 18, heading into size 20. When I got worried and upset, I would go to the biscuit tin, or the crisp packet, or the cakes, and I found food a real pleasure. I loved food, I loved good food. But it was also my real downfall and there were times when food held me a prisoner. So, when you are walking around a supermarket, and you see your favorite cakes, and your favorite sweets, and your favorite chocolate, you think to yourself, "I really want that." There were times when I was walking around the supermarket and I was crying. But because I'd done Freedom In Christ, and I knew God loved me, and I was secure in that, I could choose to make the right choices and I would say to myself, "You don't have to eat that, you're worth more than that." If I hadn't have done Freedom In Christ, I wouldn't feel secure, I wouldn't feel accepted, and therefore, I wouldn't have been able to make those difficult decisions when they were difficult. Because I knew that God loved me, and cared for me, and had a purpose for me, it meant that I realized I could take control of my eating – my eating didn't have to take control of me. If I hadn't done Freedom In Christ, I wouldn't be here today. I wouldn't be able to tell this story. Yeah, I am just such a different person than five years ago.[13]

Isn't Rebecca's story amazing? Did you notice the process of Rebecca's deliverance? She had not gotten into the intertwined mess overnight. She succumbed to temptation and became ensnared into sin. She became snagged in one of the cruelest harassments of the enemy. She was mercilessly condemned and felt helplessly enmeshed. Satan wears his "tempter" hat, as he deviously plans how to entangle us with his lies, enticing us to take the bait. He tells us we can't be happy, secure, or accepted without the things that we know will bring us bondage: over-indulgence in food, illegal drugs, or immoral sex. So, we give in. After we sin, he changes his hat to "accuser," and that's when we become enmeshed in the tangled cords of guilt and shame, stuck on the merry-go-round of sin-confess-sin-confess. Rebecca submitted to the material outlined in the *Steps to Freedom in Christ*.[14] She closed doors she had opened to the enemy, took personal responsibility for herself, and she learned to take every thought captive. In doing so, she was able to trade overeating, depression, and suicidal tendencies for the abundant life Christ died to give her.

Interwoven Dependence

As we move ahead in Christ, we face choices to confess our sin, submit to God and trust Him with the future. As long as we live, we can be sure we'll face obstacles and opportunities, trials and triumph, and decisions and determination. We can rely on the comfort of Proverbs 3:26, "for the Lord will be at your side and will keep your foot from being snared." We can ask God to reveal untruths and areas of bondage for what they are and choose to step over the trap laid for us. God will help us untangle the cords of deception. The process of sanctification is explained by Dr. Anderson in this paragraph:

> In the change of heart, a new root of life is created in the believer giving him a completely new orientation of life. The deepest core of the believer now seeks God whereas before it was in bondage to sin and sought only to preserve its own godhood. It is here in the knowledge of this new propensity of the heart, in the new deepest desires, that growth may begin and be nourished. Think about it for a moment...if all that has happened to us in salvation is forgiveness of sins and freedom from condemnation, but we are still fundamentally sinners at our core, oriented to sin in our deepest desires, how can we grow? The command of God for holiness comes to us from outside and we cannot respond to it. No amount of positive thinking can help this. But when the believer knows his full identity, that he himself is right now alive with the life of Christ, that his deepest being longs for God, God's Word, fellowship with God's people along with the other

means of growth, there is new hope of power for victory over sin in life, new hope for actual growth in obedience that positive thinking cannot provide.[15]

God wants us to take hold of our freedom and allow Him to change the default in our thinking. To do that, we have to replace the lie with the truth. To move forward from bondage to freedom, and to untangle the knots of bondage, we can renew our minds with the truth of God's Word. "Do not conform to the pattern of this world but be transformed by the renewing of your mind" (Romans 12:2).

A summary of this process is found in Steve Goss' *The Freedom In Christ Discipleship Course,* "All of us have mental strongholds, ways of thinking that are not in line with God's truth. Our success in continuing to walk in freedom and grow in maturity depends on the extent to which we continue to renew our minds and train ourselves to distinguish good and evil."[16] In the appendix of this book, you will find an additional section about *"Stronghold-Busting."* Once you have completed this book, and the *Loosening the Lies: Study Guide and Guided Journal Opportunity,* it helps to commit to truth through the accountability of developing a plan to persevere for forty days. It may seem overwhelming to attempt to work on many things at once. If we set out to allow God to help us work on one thing at a time. When we notice our thinking has been changed, we can move on to the next area. Believe me, it really works.

Loosed Liberation

I can't imagine the skydiver's terrified feelings during his helpless descent, as he unsuccessfully struggled to untangle the matted parachute cords. I wonder what his thoughts where when he realized the entanglement was caused by someone else's careless mistake.[17] He had to face the truth. His efforts were not working. The split-second he knew it was time to "cut away," is an example for us to ask God to deliver us. We've each faced our personal spiritual "free fall," and realized our hard work to untangle our "lie-knots" were futile. In choosing to take responsibility for ourselves and allowing God's Word to renew our minds, we can become skilled at untangling the "lie-knots" we've believed about God, ourselves, and others.

As we take on the task to say "No" to the flesh and "Yes" to the Spirit, we are giving Him permission to cut us free. This is inviting the Holy Spirit to continue to be at work in us, transforming us to be more like Christ.

Living in our freedom in Christ is a new way of life. As we mature, we can gain knowledge of practical strategies and apply tools that will help us continually renew our minds. Paul reminds us in Philippians 3:12-14, "Not that I have already obtained all this, or have already arrived at my goal, but I press on to take hold of that for which Christ Jesus took hold of me. Brothers and sisters, I do not consider myself yet to have taken hold of it. But one thing I do: Forgetting what is behind and straining toward what is ahead, I press on toward the goal to win the prize for which God has called me heavenward in Christ Jesus." We can commit for the long-term and cut away everything that holds us back or entangles us, from the abundant life and ministry God has planned. Let's "cut away," let God's Word free us, and soar into a life of abundance.

Chapter 9: Loosed – I Can Do This!

Loosening the Lies

Individual or Group Study Questions and Guided Journal Opportunity

Wouldn't it be great if you could break free of that irritating habit, distracting addiction, and annoying guilt? I hope you are beginning to realize - you can do this. And with God's help, by accessing His Word, you can "cut away," to be liberated and be the woman He created you to be. Exciting, huh? Let's continue.

T - Take time to pray through the acrostic using the truth statement.

Dear friends, I urge you, as foreigners and exiles, to abstain from sinful desires, which wage war against your soul (I Peter 2:11).

Dear Heavenly Father,

Show me the ways I am being deceived. Reveal to me how I'm being led to sin by following my sinful desires. Protect and prevent me from becoming entrapped by sin.

R - Remember the facts – Determine to get to the root of what or who caused the first snag.

"Be alert and of sober mind. Your enemy the devil prowls around like a roaring lion looking for someone to devour (I Peter 5:8).

Dear Heavenly Father,

Reveal the end of my "lie-knot" regarding bondage versus freedom.

U - Uncover your fear, unravel the lie-knot – Behind every fear is a lie that is believed.

No temptation has overtaken you except what is common to mankind. And God is faithful; he will not let you be tempted beyond what you can bear. But when you are tempted, he will also provide a way out so that you can endure it (I Corinthians 10:13).

Dear Heavenly Father,

Thank You for Your faithfulness. Show me the areas of temptation so I may avoid them. Thank You for giving me a way of escape.

T - Tell yourself the truth. Scripture spoken aloud ushers in healing and brings wholeness.

If we confess our sins, he is faithful and just and will forgive us our sins and purify us from all unrighteousness (I John 1:9).

Dear Heavenly Father,

I confess my sin of being drawn away into bingeing, by caving into my desires to eat unhealthy food. I submit my meal plans, taste buds, and desire for comfort from food to You.

H - Help is available by agreeing with God. Confess your sin, submit to God, declare the truth aloud over yourself.

Therefore, do not let sin reign in your mortal body so that you obey its evil desires. 13 Do not offer any part of yourself to sin as an instrument of wickedness, but rather offer yourselves to God as those who have been brought from death to life; and offer every part of yourself to him as an instrument of righteousness (Romans 6:12-13).

Dear Heavenly Father,

Thank You. In Christ, I have overcome the flesh. Jesus, You showed us how to live victoriously. Help me to depend on Your strength.

Loosening the Lies

Individual or Group Study Questions and Guided Journal Opportunity

1. What situation has made you feel helpless, plummeting through the atmosphere, struggling to untangle your parachute?

2. Explain (if any) your expectations of God regarding delivering you from habitual sin.

3. Express ways (if any) you have bargained with God to break you free from bondage.

4. Share a new concept you learned from the idea of expecting "drive-through deliverance."

5. Do you agree with Paul's perspective on deliverance from 2 Corinthians 1:9,10? "But this happened that we might not rely on ourselves but on God, who raises the dead. He has delivered us from such a deadly peril, and he will deliver us again."

6. Describe a "lie-knot" God may have brought to your mind.

7. What is your best advice to someone new at learning how to choose truth instead of lies?

8. After learning God's truth, do you feel more threatened or more encouraged by the Biblical concept of deliverance?

9. How can we become skilled at "unraveling lie-knots?"

10. How does it feel to ask God to reveal untruths and areas of bondage for what they are, and choose to step over the trap laid for us?

Truth Tools

Finally, be strong in the Lord and in his mighty power.

Put on the full armor of God, so that you can take your stand against the devil's schemes.

For our struggle is not against flesh and blood, but against the rulers, against the authorities, against the powers of this dark world and against the spiritual forces of evil in the heavenly realms.

Therefore, put on the full armor of God, so that when the day of evil comes, you may be able to stand your ground, and after you have done everything, to stand.

Stand firm then, with the belt of truth buckled around your waist, with the breastplate of righteousness in place, and with your feet fitted with the readiness that comes from the gospel of peace.

In addition to all this, take up the shield of faith, with which you can extinguish all the flaming arrows of the evil one.

Take the helmet of salvation and the sword of the Spirit, which is the word of God (Ephesians 6:10-17).

Freed by Faith

A prayer of adoration and devotion.

Warrior's Prayer

Heavenly Father,

Your warrior prepares for battle.

Today I claim victory over Satan by putting on the whole armor of God.

I put on the girdle of truth.

May I stand firm in the truth of Your Word so I will not be a victim of Satan's lies.

I put on the breastplate of righteousness.

May it guard my heart from evil so I will remain pure and holy, protected under the blood of Jesus Christ.

I put on the shoes of peace.

May I stand firm in the good news of the Gospel so Your peace will shine through me and be a light to all I encounter.

I take the shield of faith.

May I be ready for Satan's fiery darts of doubt, denial, and deceit so I will not be vulnerable to spiritual defeat.

I put on the helmet of salvation.

May I keep my mind focused on You so Satan will not have a stronghold on my thoughts.

I take the sword of the Spirit.

May the two-edged sword of Your Word be ready in my hands so I can expose the tempting words of Satan.

Enable me to cut through the every tangled "lie-knot" that has ensnared me.

Only You, Heavenly Father, can set me free from bondage.

By faith, Your warrior has put on the whole armor of God.

I am prepared to live this day in spiritual victory.

Amen[18]

Galvanize yourself against discouragement; treat it as any other sin. We're doing more than we know, and in His will, we're accomplishing more than we realize. His multiplication tables go further than our calculators. His Word doesn't return void, His promises don't fail, and our finest work is best pursued by faith. The true results are His alone, magnified by grace into glory.[1]

Robert J. Morgan

Chapter 10: Freed - Excited for God's Plan for Me!

An historical surgery took place on February 15, 1921. Dr. Kane applied local anesthesia to his patient and with his razor-edged scalpel, cut through infected skin and tangled tissues. He found and removed the toxic appendix. The patient assured the medical team he experienced minimal pain and discomfort. The patient's name? Dr. Evan Kane. The patient and the doctor were one in the same person.

In the 1920s, removing an appendix was considered a major surgery, requiring a large incision. The patient always needing general anesthetic. Dr. Kane had different views on this, and he believed the use of a local anesthetic would be more beneficial to the patient's speedy recovery. He had performed nearly four thousand appendectomies, so he knew the procedure well. The physician had observed patients after being "put under" general anesthetic. Their recovery and healing always took much longer than expected. Critics and skeptics mocked his opinions, so Dr. Kane set out to prove his point. To perform the surgery on himself, he propped his torso up on the operating table and used mirrors to see the infected section of his body. The brave and opinionated Dr. Kane removed his own appendix.[2] I recommend you don't try this at home.

Dr. Kane's example magnifies a valuable spiritual principle. Throughout the chapters of this book, we have discussed "lie-knots" of all sorts. These knots are like a noose around our neck or snare around our ankle, may cause us to feel snagged by unhealthy attitudes, toxic habits, irritating addictions, and infectious sins. As individuals, we are accountable to God, and by using His Word, we can be trained to cut through "lie-knots" and remove any spiritually lethal infection. We can be equipped to allow the truth of God's truth to sear the snarled and scrambled lies to heal our damaged emotions. With the Holy Spirit's help, we can open ourselves up to God's healing presence, and declare the truth of His Word.

In Christ, we have what it takes to strengthen ourselves and rely on His help to remove any toxic emotion, inflamed attitude, or infectious habit. As we choose to submit to God's plans for healing, hope, and restoration, our freedom can be maintained.

Before I send you off, there's one additional area of emotional and spiritual resolution to discuss. We will learn how to discern and cut through the "lie-knots" of the sins of our ancestors. Let's get started.

Family Ties

In earlier chapters, we discussed the concept of our historical or cultural quandary. The impact our home environment, educational circumstances, or even the names we were called can contribute to the entanglements of our "lie-knot." Through often-repeated phrases, quoted as if spoken by well-known authors or orators, we may have been given information contrary to the truth. Unknowingly, we have been given the wrong impression. To illustrate this circumstance with a common phrase, "Oh, what a tangled web we weave, when first we practice to deceive." This famous line was originally written by Sir Walter Scott in the late 1800s, in the poem *Marmion: A Tale of Flodden Field*.[3] Wait. You mean Shakespeare didn't write this? Nope. The catchphrase is regularly quoted as if the great Shakespeare spoke it into being. Although, he did use the expression often, Shakespeare did not write it.

This frequently quoted slogan is extensively used to describe life experiences and has become a common, household cliché for unfortunate circumstances. Thus, the definition of the axiom, "Oh what a tangled web we weave, when first we practice to deceive." It means that when you lie or act dishonestly you are initiating problems and a domino structure of complications which eventually run out of control.[4] Such is the case for ancestral sins that are passed down from one generation to another. For those from dysfunctional families or people whose families are involved with cults, the occult, or other areas of generational sin, there may be snares of bondage that have entrapped them to those past sins. They may not even realize it. Remember, when you are deceived, you don't know it.

We can't passively take our places in Christ.[5] By choosing to accept ourselves as new creations in Christ, we can actively take our places in the family of God.[6] Unbeknownst to us, we may have experienced the consequences of the sins of our fathers and mothers. These sins are called "generational curses" and can affect our future and the future of our family members. In this chapter, we are going to talk about curses versus blessings. We will discuss our personal role in actively and intentionally choosing to fully submit the area of generational sins to God. We have the choice. It's our option to permit Him to help us find the end of our "lie-knot" or try to break free on our own.

Interwoven Inheritance

As a result of generational sins, there are likely to be related spiritual attacks. Let me explain. We are not guilty because of our parent's sins, but because they sinned, we are vulnerable to what they have taught and modeled for us.[7] We have a responsibility to one another, but not for one another. We can rely on the comfort of Proverbs 29:25, "Fear of man will prove to be a snare, but whoever trusts in the Lord is kept safe." We can ask God to reveal to us untruths not yet previously resolved in the other steps. We may not be aware of the influence of ancestral sins from our family heritage and areas of deception that we may have encountered in our upbringing.

In her book, *The Beauty of the Broken,* Alisa Morgan, former president of Mom's In Prayer International said, "Families are broken in their expectations. Perhaps this is the largest fissure of all in the fallen family. Bottom line, we all expect families to produce the impossible. We've come to believe that our families can define, rate and actualize us as individuals."[8]

Family Matters

Indeed, family really does matter. The way our family functions or does not function influences our upbringing and our ability to manage ourselves and our lives. We may joke about dysfunctional families.

In an article in *All4Kids*, on the role of families in a child's development, experts state that "children who grow up in healthy, stable, and loving families will have a greater chance at future success. A child's behavior and development are directly influenced by how well his or her family functions. Children depend on adults to meet their needs and develop concepts of healthy human relationships."[9] The focus of this area of spiritual and emotional resolution is about how to overcome ancestral sins that are passed on from one generation to the next.

Sin cannot be inherited, but it's effects can be passed down from generation to generation. The concept of family curses is discussed in detail in the Old Testament. Specifically, under the Old Covenant, all of God's chosen people were to repent of their sins. It didn't matter whether the offense was personal or national, the bottom line was that the sins of a nation cannot be repented of without an individual's confession of their personal sin. In Jeremiah 32:17-18, we read of the tremendous power and love of God, as well as the profound effects of generational sin. "Ah, Sovereign LORD, you have made the heavens and the earth by your great power and outstretched arm. Nothing is too hard for you. You show love to thousands but bring the punishment for the parents' sins into the laps of their children after them. Great and mighty God, whose name is the LORD Almighty."

The punishment discussed here is because we all have sinned. It's not due to the environment, but because we, as humans have sinned. "Therefore, just as sin entered the world through one man, and death through sin, and in this way death came to all people, because all sinned—" (Romans 5:12) In his book, *Discipleship Counseling,* Dr. Anderson illustrates the concept of this condition,

> According to the dictionary, the word, "acquiesce" means to agree or consent quietly without protest." In our Christian life, acquiescence means spiritual passivity, and to live passively is to accept defeat by default. Spiritual freedom, however, can only be found when we

actively make a series of choices based on the truth of God's Word. For example, we were all born spiritually dead and separated from God because of Adam's sin (see Romans 5:12-15; Ephesians 2:1-3). When we were born again, we became new creations in Christ. But our minds were not instantly reprogrammed, and many of our old habits are still with us. Now that we are alive in Christ, you and I can be transformed by the renewing of our minds (see Romans 12:2). That renewal won't happen, however, unless you are "diligent to present yourself approved to God as a workman who does not need to be ashamed, handling accurately the word of truth" (2 Timothy 2:15). Spiritual victory is realized as we actively choose to place our faith or trust in Jesus Christ for justification and sanctification, rejecting dead works and other false means (see Romans 5:1; Ephesians 2:4-9).[10]

To actively take our place in Christ, we can ask God to help us become aware of ancestral sins. Some may have a difficult time bringing up the past, and yet others may be unaware of it. Here's when our reliance on the power of God's Word and the presence of the Holy Spirit makes all the difference. Without our knowledge, we may have had a curse put on us, had an oath made against us, or when someone swore against us, we were intentionally condemned. The moment these things occurred, the enemy's plan to harm us was put into motion. The Lord can help us specifically recall something that happened, even things we were not aware of.

Unless there is a truthful awareness and a resulting acceptance of the reality of the occurrence of the curse, (that it did happen and it was not a dream), the specific curse, hex or pronouncement cannot be dealt with. As believers, we can take our place in Christ, put on the armor of God, and stand against all assignments. Christ is our defense, and we can cut off any "lie-knots" that have us bound to the bondage of generational sins and curses. We don't have to be victims of our past any longer.

Eliminating Entanglement

In Sir Walter Scott's day, "a tangled web" meant a piece of badly woven cloth with many mistakes in it. This visual illustration tells us about the anatomy of a lie, doesn't it? If we define the meaning of the phrase metaphorically, once you start lying, it's hard to remember which lie you told to whom. And then you get caught in the lies and begin telling more lies to hide the lies you've already told. When someone tries to deceive another person, using lies and fabricating stories, there is usually an increasingly entangled deception. You know what happens. You tell one lie, and then you must make up more lies to support the first one. And then more lies are needed to support the others, and so the result is a matted, mangled mess.[11]

In the same way, generational curses require adding falsehood upon falsehood. The enemy would like us to become entangled to the point where we think it is no use to even try to break free. Our personal struggles or cultural challenges may not be as explicit as widespread observances in Third World countries such as the practice spiritism, voodoo, magic, and pagan rituals. Curses are present when people summon and send demons as part of a satanic ritual and are very common in North America.[12] Generational sins can be passed on by negative experiences we have mentally processed. At the time they happened, these upsetting incidences may have caused us to believe something about ourselves, our family, or God that is not true. We remain in bondage to our past not because of the traumatic experience itself, but because of the lies the experience caused us to believe.

I am excited to share an amazing testimony of someone who overcame generational curses. Once you see the way Tyrell James accepted personal responsibility for his freedom, you will understand why I share his story. I hope you will appreciate the reality check he received as he cut off the "lie-knot" caused by the failings of his biological father. As he did, he received a refreshing revelation and renewed hope through the unconditional love and commitment of his heavenly Father.

My dad, he was on crack cocaine for 30 years, so I saw him on a Saturday. He would come. He would literally have this urge to just be around for ten minutes, and we would talk and hang out. Then he would leave. It started to get worse, as I got from four-years-old to six-years-old. That's when he really left my life when I was six-years-old. It really had me feeling unimportant, not appreciated. I felt that I had no one I could talk to when it comes to having some advice from a man's perspective. I felt lonely. To live in a house with people who never took the time out to ask, "How are you doing?" I had an experience like that with my own father who told me I wasn't going to be anything in my life. So that fed into the lies that the environment was getting me to believe all my life. That the loneliness was going to be there, and I need to just deal with it. But Freedom In Christ really helped me to find out who I was and counteract the lies I was told. And finally, I was understanding the truth behind the situations or the emotions I had been fighting with all my life. Freedom In Christ, gave me that peace and the words to say, "this is just spiritual warfare and it's normal." I used to believe that I had no father that really loved me. Now I believe that Christ loves me more than life itself. I used to believe that poverty was the only thing that I was going to see for the rest of my life, now I believe that God will support all my needs and give me what I need abundantly. I used to believe that pain was all that I would ever experience, now I believe love is the greatest asset to ever have in life – through Christ.[13]

Tyrell's testimony underscores the impact generational curses can have on us as we walk with the Lord. Tyrell believed the truth about himself. He believed that every curse placed on him was broken when Christ became a curse for him by dying on the cross. "Christ redeemed us from the curse of the law by becoming a curse for us," (Galatians 3:13) As Tyrell mentioned, he made the choice, to understand and believe the truth about God's view of him.

For Tyrell, knowing, understanding, and believing God's truth made all the difference in his ability to cut himself free from the curses of the past. He didn't have to stay bound up in the lies he had been told by his father. The lies that had most likely been passed down through many generations in his family. Lies that said he wouldn't amount to anything, he would remain fatherless, or he, like his father, would be a cocaine addict or drug dealer. Tyrell actively took his place as a saint. He submitted to God and resisted the devil. The devil had no choice but to flee. You and I can do the same thing. We can ask God to show us any place in our lives where we are paying the consequences of anything that needs to be broken.

Uninhibited Unraveling

"Oh, what a tangled web we weave, when first we practice to deceive." Do you see how this phrase, is much like any lie we've believed about ourselves, our upbringing, or the past mistakes of our ancestors? Because of what we have been told, the lie was repeated over and over, and we've believed it to be true. Like a tangled web, woven by us or not, we've each had traumatic experiences that have trapped us and caused us to suffer. At the time we encountered the negative experience, we may not have had the understanding or the tools to break loose from the tangles that ensnared us or the deception that trapped us into believing the lies. Some of us may believe we will never be free from the past mistakes of our ancestors. We mistakenly think that because of their deeds, we have no choice but to continue in their ways. I beg to differ.

I've done the research and now, so have you. Because of the finished work of Christ on the cross, our past can be completely renewed. Pastor Rick Warren, best-selling author of *The Purpose Driven Life* said, "We are all products of our past, but we don't have to be prisoners of it."[14] We can break free from our past not only to free ourselves, but also to reverse the painful legacy we experienced. If we have been under a heritage of fear, divorce, anger, anxiety, or depression, through Christ, we can be liberated. Whatever we free ourselves of effects our children and grandchildren and will bless future generations. We can know the truth, and the truth of God's Word, as we understand and believe it, is what sets us free. "If the Son sets you free, you shall be free indeed" (John 8:36). Jesus didn't just come to help you cope with your past. Jesus came to help you resolve the effects of the past, completely. You can be entirely set free from the entanglement of your past mistakes and the sins of your ancestors. You can have complete, uninhibited, and total freedom -- once and for all. What are you waiting for?

Soul Surgery

You may recall that at the beginning of the book, I didn't know how to deal with my past trauma and shameful mistakes because I didn't understand what was going on with my soul. The enemy had me securely tied up in "lie-knots" that began with ownership of the labels I'd been given when I was bullied as a child. Later, as a teenager, I became more enmeshed as I abused street drugs, illegal alcohol, and acted out by having premarital sex. You guessed right; the matted mess of entrapment only increased in size. Decades later, I unknowingly added more cord to the humongous "lie-knot" of toxic feelings of rejection, unworthiness, and self-loathing. I deceived myself into thinking I could perform my way into feeling better about myself. The inner part of my personality and the way I presented myself, my mind, will, emotions were wounded and hurting. I didn't realize how much I had become ensnared and trapped by deception and how I'd permitted the "lie-knot" to keep me trapped in its snare. I allowed untruths to direct my thoughts, feelings, desires, decisions, and attitudes. Thankfully, God loves you and I too much to leave us trapped in the devil's snare of destruction.

Proverbs 22:5 reminds us that, "In the paths of the wicked are snares and pitfalls, but those who would preserve their life stay far from them." As human beings, we are comprised of our body, our soul, and our spirit. Regarding our physical being, we take care of our bodies with healthy eating and proper exercise habits. We choose good mental health as we keep our minds alertly focused on God's truth. It's essential to pay attention to the areas where our souls may have been wounded. We engage in proper "soul care" as we refuse toxic emotions of bitterness, hate, and anger. We're showing ourselves kindness, as we give ourselves permission to pay attention to our emotions. We can refer to the practice as proper "soul care," as we invite God to assist us with "soul surgery."

We can be set free from our past. The growth process may be immediate or step-by-step, depending on what God is teaching us. God's timing is perfect. It's affirming to find strength from His Word, as in Psalm 32:8, "I will instruct you and teach you in the way which you should go, I will counsel you with my loving eye on you." In partnership with God's Word and the Holy Spirit, we've learned it is our choice to ask God to help us unravel our "lie-knots." We can invite God to untangle any areas that have kept us ensnared. When we welcome Him to do so, He graciously responds, but it may be a lengthy or complex process.

As God reveals additional areas that haven't been uncovered, I am reminded of a quote from author and pastor John Eldredge, "A wound that goes unacknowledged and unwept is a wound that cannot heal."[15] Whether or not you agree with this quote, it is a fact. Sometimes it's hard to know what needs to be acknowledged and what needs to be wept over. God waits to be asked to help us know what to acknowledge.

King David understood the importance of the practice. Especially in his later years, he experienced a preciousness of pardon, and a keener sense of sin than in his younger days. In this understanding and his clear sense of the frailty of life, he wrote Psalm 103:1, 2, "Praise the Lord, my soul; all my inmost being, praise his holy name. Praise the Lord, my soul, and forget not all his benefits."[16] It's up to us to seek out ways to encourage ourselves in the Lord. Let's look to an example in I Samuel 30, from the earlier years in the life of David the conqueror.

Returning from Aphek, David and his mighty men were appalled to find their hometown, Ziklag, had been plundered and destroyed by fire. In addition, the battle-weary ensemble was horrified to discover their families, including David's wives and children had been kidnapped. "So, David and his men wept aloud until they had no strength left to weep" (I Samuel 30:4), David's soldiers turned against him. Instead of planning a rescue, the soldiers blamed David, and planned to kill him. We can learn a valuable lesson from what David chose to do next. "David was greatly distressed because the men were talking of stoning him; each one was bitter in spirit because of his sons and daughters. But David found strength in the Lord his God" (I Samuel 30:6).

I love this example of how David went to God. He made the hard choice to trust God. Each of us have the same alternative. It's an act of faith for us to turn to God or try to figure things out on our own. David found emotional, physical, and spiritual strength in God. We, too, can become skilled at leaning on the Lord our God. It takes practice, we don't have to be perfect. We can prefer to find our strength in the only One who can provide what we need.

It helps to rehearse your past victories. Take time to review the seasons of your life when God proved Himself to you and when He answered your prayers. Make a list of praise reports and things you are thankful for. Has God provided for your finances, protected your job, or showed you the way when you thought there was no way? Remind yourself of God's faithfulness in your past. Tell yourself over and over about the countless ways He has provided for you.

In addition, it helps to remind ourselves that we are under divine protection. What has God protected you from? Think of the things that should have happened, or could have occurred, but God and His angels protected you. As a teenage drug abuser, I attempted to escape life's challenges as

I misused prescription and street drugs. I experienced God's provision, as He protected me from ending my life with accidental drug overdoses and numerous intentional attempts at suicide. I praise God for being my deliverer.

In 2004, I faced a dark season of disease when diagnosed with stage four cancer – in my bone marrow in five places in my body. I depended on God as my Jehovah Rapha – my healer. I praise God for being my Jehovah Rapha – my healer. Over a decade ago, my first husband, Pastor Paul Giesbrecht was tragically killed in a motorcycle accident. As a new widow, I was facing supporting myself financially, encouraging my children and family members, and basically figuring out life as a middle-aged single woman, I learned to trust God as my El Roi – the God Who Sees Me.

The last thing that helps as we choose to depend on God to strengthen us, is to remind ourselves of who God is—God is God, God is in control. He is our protector, Way maker, miracle worker, shield and defender, Jehovah Jireh - provider, Jehovah Nissi - victory, Jehovah Shalom - peace, Jehovah-Rapha - healer. How has God been real to you lately?

Turn only to God's living Word for the truth of what He wants you to do next. Let His Word direct your life in everything, in every way. Protect your times alone with God so you know the sound of His voice. Listen for the whisper. As a shepherd boy, David trained himself to listen and to obey God's voice. He relied on this practice as he asked the Lord what to do next. "David inquired of the Lord, "Shall I pursue this raiding party? Will I overtake them?" (1 Samuel 30:8)

God's answers may not come to you in the ways you expect. David received help from a slave of one of the murdering enemies. In a field, they found and rescued an abandoned Egyptian slave "He said, "I am an Egyptian, the slave of an Amalekite. My master abandoned me when I became ill three days ago. We raided the Negev of the Kerethites and the territory belonging to Judah and the Negev of Caleb. And we burned Ziklag"" (1 Samuel 30:13, 14). Can you imagine? God sent His help through the hands of a slave of the enemy, who kidnapped David's family, robbed him of his livestock, and burned down everything David owned. In the same way, it helps to remember, God's ways are not our ways. He is the God of the unexpected. Be determined to seek God and follow His ways.

We abide in the natural world. Most of us are used to relying on resources from what we know. In an adventurous life in the Spirit, we can expect the unexpected, receive from God in the supernatural ways He provides. Be assured God will restore everything you have lost and bless you with a double portion. "David recovered everything the Amalekites had taken, including his two wives. Nothing was missing: young or old, boy or girl, plunder, or anything else they had taken. David brought everything back. He took all the flocks and herds, and his men drove them ahead of the other livestock, saying 'This is David's plunder'" (I Samuel 30:18-20).

Be determined to trust God. God will restore, rebuild, and renew. Even more than you ever thought He could or would. As you choose to continue to submit yourself to God's gentle hand of guidance, you can, like King David, encourage yourself in the Lord. In doing so, you are inviting God to help you. You are choosing to do proper soul care and inviting God's help with your "soul surgery" as He cuts you free from the "lie-knot."

Disentangled Truth

Dr. Kane's brave self-surgery was a heroic effort. In many ways, the choice you have made and the process you are undertaking, by allowing God to unravel the "lie-knot" is worthy of an award. In chapter one, we looked at a foundational Scripture about breaking free. "Therefore, since we are surrounded by such a great cloud of witnesses, let us throw off everything that hinders and the sin that so easily entangles. And let us run with perseverance the race marked out for us" (Hebrews 12:1). We discussed how the imagery suggests the event to be an athletic contest taking place in an amphitheater. The cloud of witnesses are the Bible heroes mentioned in the beginning of the verse: Abel, Enoch, Noah, and Abraham, each an example of persistence. Although these saints can't see or cheer on our progress from heaven, we can learn from them. David Guzik's commentary says, "...these witnesses are not witnessing us as we conduct our lives. Instead they are witnesses to us of faith and endurance."[17] The cloud of witnesses are our examples of how to move ahead despite something that may have kept us in knots. I wonder if you would feel comfortable adding your name to the list. I envision your name there.

The point of this book has been to help you embrace and implement a plan. Remember the warning found in the second half of the verse— "and the sin which so easily ensnares us." As we move ahead in deepening our faith in Christ, we face choices to trust Him more. We do this when we submit, confess our sin, declare the truth, and have hope for the future. As we live out our lives, we can be sure we'll face obstacles and opportunities, trials and triumph, and decisions and determination. We can rely on the truth of Proverbs 3:26, "for the Lord will be at your side and will keep your foot from being snared." We can ask God to reveal to us untruths and areas of deception for what they are and choose to step over the trap laid for us.

Freedom In Christ

The tangles of our "lie-knot" are unraveled as we become aware and truly own our identity in Christ. Each of us is a complete, clean, and holy child of God. When we are emotionally honest with God about how we feel, we can be right with Him. Our freedom comes from knowing the truth and a steadfast commitment to believing the truth. Children of God are not products of their past. They are products of Christ's work on the cross and His resurrection. No one can change our past, but we can choose to walk free of it.[18]

My prayer for you is that you maintain your freedom in Christ. This is possible by processing God's truths and choosing to do regular surgery on yourself. You can maintain your freedom by consistently inviting God to show you areas where you have been deceived. Refuse to be deceived and choose to search out God's truth. We cannot successfully run our own lives, and we don't have to. God is waiting for you to invite and allow Him permission to do what can only happen through His power. You can be free from all entanglements that are holding you back. You can be cut free from every trap, snare, or "lie-knot" that has been laid to keep you from experiencing the abundant life Jesus died to give you. What are you waiting for? "Free yourself, like a gazelle from the hand of the hunter, like a bird from the snare of the fowler" (Proverbs 6:5).

Chapter 10: Freed - Excited for God's Plan for Me!

Loosening the Lies

Individual or Group Study Questions and Guided Journal Opportunity

Thank you for finishing well. You have stayed with me through to the completion of this book. Well done! I am so glad you did. You and I have learned that the past does not have to be a place where we are held ensnared by "lie-knots." We can be cut free and untangled, to be launched into freedom. We can learn to "forget those things which are behind," and reach "forward to those things which are ahead," and we are to:

> Press on toward the goal to win the prize for which God has called me heavenward in Christ Jesus (Philippians 3:13-14).

Let's pray,

Dear Heavenly Father,

Thank You for showing me Your truth. I choose to completely let go of my past. I pray for Your truth to replace the "lie-knots" that have entangled me, so I may be freed from deception. I pray for Your peace to replace my anxiety and fear. I pray for renewal in my mind as You give me Your way of relating to my past mistakes and trauma. Thank You for hope. Thank You for Your supernatural power and unexpected touches of grace as together, You and I embrace the future. In Jesus' name. Amen.

Let's look to the acrostic using the word TRUTH.

T - Take time to pray through the acrostic using the T.R.U.T.H. statement.

> You were taught, with regard to your former way of life, to put off your old self, which is being corrupted by its deceitful desires; to be made new in the attitude of your minds; (Ephesians 4:22, 23).

Dear Heavenly Father,

Show me how to continue to renew my mind and maintain my freedom in Christ.

R - Remember the facts – Determine to get to the root of what or who caused the first snag.

Therefore, we do not lose heart. Though outwardly we are wasting away, yet inwardly we are being renewed day by day (2 Corinthians 4:16).

Dear Heavenly Father,

Thank You for renewing my mind daily.

U - Uncover your fear, unravel the "lie-knot" – Behind every fear is a lie that is believed.

Therefore, if anyone is in Christ, the new creation has come: The old has gone, the new is here (2 Corinthians 5:17)!

Dear Heavenly Father,

Thank You for the encouragement that You see me as new. Help me to see myself the way You do.

T - Tell yourself the truth. Scripture spoken aloud ushers in healing and brings wholeness.

Then you will know the truth, and the truth will set you free (John 8:32).

Dear Heavenly Father,

Thank You for the opportunity to speak the truth, Your truth over myself in love. I praise You for the grace and encouragement You give as You cut me free from the "lie-knot," and free me for abundant living.

H - Help is available by agreeing with God. Confess your sin, submit to God, declare the truth aloud over yourself.

Forget the former things; do not dwell on the past. See, I am doing a new thing! Now it springs up; do you not perceive it? I am making a way in the wilderness and streams in the wasteland (Isaiah 43:18, 19).

Dear Heavenly Father,

I have confessed my sin of bringing up my past mistakes. Thank You for forgiving me of every sin. Thank You for forgetting them and not using my past against me. Thank You for doing a new thing in me. In Jesus' name.
Amen.

Loosening the Lies

Individual or Group Study Questions and Guided Journal Opportunity

1. Express your opinion about the concept of resolving the past sins of your ancestors.

2. Explain how the "O what a tangled web we weave" model assisted your understanding.

3. Share a new concept you learned about "acquiescence."

4. Describe a "lie-knot" God may have brought to your attention that you were not aware of prior to learning about ancestral sin.

5. After learning God's truth, do you feel more threatened or more encouraged by the Biblical concept of generational sin?

6. Have you been made aware of your option for "soul care?"

7. Does Dr. Kane's act of performing an appendectomy on himself encourage you to allow time for the practice of "soul surgery?"

8. Describe a way David chose to "strengthen himself in the Lord" (I Samuel 30:6).

9. Express any new concepts you have learned about unraveling your "lie-knot" and maintaining your freedom in Christ.

10. Share your own personal testimony of how God has used "*Unraveling the Lie-Knot*" and Loosening the Lies: Study Guide and Guided Journal Opportunity to free you from the enemy's trap.

Truth Tools

I well remember them, and my soul is downcast within me. Yet this I call to mind and therefore I have hope: Because of the LORD's great love we are not consumed, for his compassions never fail. They are new every morning; great is your faithfulness. I say to myself, 'The LORD is my portion; therefore, I will wait for him' (Lamentations 3:20-24).

As the rain and the snow come down from heaven, and do not return to it without watering the earth and making it bud and flourish, so that it yields seed for the sower and bread for the eater, so is my word that goes out from my mouth: It will not return to me empty, but will accomplish what I desire and achieve the purpose for which I sent it (Isaiah 55:10-11).

Then they cried to the LORD in their trouble, and he saved them from their distress. He sent out his word and healed them; he rescued them from the grave (Psalm 107:19-20).

This has been my practice: I obey your precepts. You are my portion, LORD; I have promised to obey your words. I have sought your face with all my heart; be gracious to me according to your promise. I have considered my ways and have turned my steps to your statutes. I will hasten and not delay to obey your commands (Psalm 119:56-60).

Praise the LORD, my soul; all my inmost being, praise his holy name. Praise the LORD, my soul, and forget not all his benefits - who forgives all your sins and heals all your diseases, who redeems your life from the pit and crowns you with love and compassion, who satisfies your desires with good things so that your youth is renewed like the eagle's (Psalm 103:1-5).

Freed By Faith

A prayer of adoration and devotion

Dear Heavenly Father,

I praise You. I worship You. Lord, thank You for bringing me to this point of understanding. Thank You for showing me areas where I've been deceived. Thank You for mercy, grace, kindness, and love. Thank You for the strength You have given me to submit, confess, renounce, and declare the truth of Your Word. Thank You for the power of praying Your Word.

I am laid low in the dust; preserve my life according to your word. I gave an account of my ways and you answered me; teach me your decrees. Cause me to understand the way of your precepts, that I may meditate on your wonderful deeds. My soul is weary with sorrow; strengthen me according to your word. Keep me from deceitful ways; be gracious to me and teach me your law. I have chosen the way of faithfulness; I have set my heart on your laws. I hold fast to your statutes, LORD; do not let me be put to shame. I run in the path of your commands, for you have broadened my understanding (Psalm 119:25-32).

May your unfailing love come to me, LORD, your salvation, according to your promise; then I can answer anyone who taunts me, for I trust in your word. Never take your word of truth from my mouth, for I have put my hope in your laws. I will always obey your law, for ever and ever. I will walk about in freedom for I have sought out your precepts"(Psalm 119:41-45).

Thank you for your guidance, as You have brought me to this place. I accept my past and commit it to Your purpose and plans. I worship and praise You. I commit myself to You and offer You all I have, as we look forward to the future You have planned. In Jesus' name. Amen.

"For I know the plans I have for you," declares the LORD, "plans to prosper you and not to harm you, plans to give you hope and a future. Then you will call on me and come and pray to me, and I will listen to you. You will seek me and find me when you seek me with all your heart. I will be found by you," declares the LORD, "and will bring you back from captivity. I will gather you from all the nations and places where I have banished you," declares the LORD, "and will bring you back to the place from which I carried you into exile"

(Jeremiah 29:11-14).

Love Letter to My Readers

I can't wait to share with you something that can change your life. God sent His only son, Jesus Christ, to die in our place. He would have done this if you, or I, were the only person on earth. That's how much God loves us. God's love is unconditional; God's love is perfect. How do we know God loves us? His Word tells us.

"But God demonstrates his own love for us in this: While we were still sinners, Christ died for us" (Romans 5:8). God created us in His image—for a relationship with Him—but He gave us freedom of choice. We could choose to partake in a love relationship with Him or not. Because of our sin, we are separated from a Holy God. Romans 3:23 tells us, "For all have sinned and fall short of the glory of God." In Romans 6:23 we learn, "For the wages [payment] of sin is death, but the gift of God is eternal life in Christ Jesus our Lord." There is only one solution for the problem of separation from God—death. Some try to earn their way to heaven by working hard or being religious, but Hebrews 9:22 says, "Without the shedding of blood, there is no forgiveness of sins." Jesus Christ is the only answer to the problem. He died on the cross and rose from the grave, paying the "death penalty" for our sin. He provided a way for us to have a relationship with God.

As you read through John 3:16, aloud, fill in your name at the blanks. "For God so loved _____ that he gave his one and only Son, that if _____ believes in him, _____ shall not perish but have eternal life" What an amazing love. God sent His Son, His only Son, Jesus, to die for us. Which one of us would give our children—our only child— for the lives of someone else? God did, for you. Imagine God making way for a relationship with Him by giving His only Son as a sacrifice. You, however, must make a choice. You must choose to accept and believe.

Are you separated from God? I want you to be totally honest with God. Is there any reason why you cannot receive Jesus right now? God has loved you since before the beginning of time. He gave you a gift. His Son Jesus Christ died for you on the Cross and rose from the grave. Jesus cares for you, and He calls you, to decide for Him, today. He has a plan for your life. Don't miss out on the life God has for you. We can't clean up our act ourselves. I know. I've tried. We can't work our way to a relationship with God, and we can't get there by being religious. God has allowed Jesus' blood to cover our sins so that we can have fellowship with Him. In 1 John 1:9 we read, "If we confess our sins, he is faithful and just and will forgive us our sins and purify us from all unrighteousness." God is asking you to give yourself totally and completely to Him. Jesus had victory over death when He rose from the dead. Literally, Jesus Christ took on our sin; He was our substitute so that we might become the righteousness of God. When God sees us, He doesn't see our sin He sees us through Jesus Christ. Because of Jesus Christ's finished work on the cross, we have access to live life through His power. In Christ, we are new creatures. 2 Corinthians 5:17 says, "If anyone is in Christ, he is a new creation, the old has gone, the new has come!"

Pray this prayer to invite Jesus Christ to come in and control your life through the Holy Spirit. If you have already received Christ at one time in your life but feel you would like to recommit your life and your family to Christ, you can pray this prayer, too.

> *Dear Lord Jesus, I know that I am a sinner and need Your forgiveness. I believe that You died for my sins. I want to turn from my sins. I now invite You to come into my heart and life. I want to trust and follow You as Lord and Savior. In Jesus name, amen.*

God loves you, and so do I.

Sheryl [1]

What is a Stronghold?

A stronghold is "a belief or habitual pattern of thinking that is not consistent with what God tells us is true." It is something that has a *strong hold* on you. It usually results in behaviors that are out of character for a child of God. A *Stronghold-Buster* is a daily prayer practice that creates

1. An intentional rejection or renunciation of lies that you have believed and

2. An intentional choosing and declaration of what God says is true.

When we're adopted into the family of God, no one erases the "hard drive" of our emotions, memories, or mistakes. We have relied on the flesh for so long. Now we must reverse these flesh patterns and be taught how to depend on the Holy Spirit's guidance. Unfortunately, we come into a sweet relationship with our heavenly Father with false beliefs and dysfunctional coping mechanisms. In difficult times, we may be accustomed to relying on ourselves and develop coping skills that have become flesh patterns. The good news is that it is possible to unlearn negative ways of thinking and tell ourselves the truth.

Dr. Neil T. Anderson says that, "Strongholds are mental habit patterns of thought that are not consistent with God's Word." These strongholds can be dealt with and we can live free from bondage to them. The step towards finding the solution to freedom takes trust and transparency. As we immerse ourselves in and apply God's Word to our lives and believe it to be the truth, how we view God and ourselves changes. It begins in our hearts. Our lives often present a harsh reality, and yet God has declared greater and more permanent truths no matter what the circumstance. It is God's truths we are to choose to believe and set our minds upon in order to be set free from strongholds.

Anxious thoughts are to be expected as we've navigated through the past COVID-19 crisis and the uncertainty associated with the future. We are encouraged in scripture to take our thoughts captive and break down the mental habits that contribute to or perpetuate anxiety. 2 Corinthians 10:3-5 (ESV) we read that, "for though we walk in the flesh, we are not waging war according to the flesh. For the weapons of our warfare are not of the flesh but have divine power to destroy *strongholds*. We destroy arguments and every lofty opinion raised against the knowledge of God and take every thought captive to obey Christ." We capture thoughts and renew our minds by asking ourselves "does this thought belong in the mind of a follower of Jesus?" If so, embrace it and act on it. If not, reject and renounce it. We have a responsibility to take our thoughts captive and to "not be conformed to this world, but be transformed by the renewing of your mind" (Romans 12:2).

In 2 Corinthians 10:3-5, God presents us with a tool — a specific way to intentionally renew our minds according to the truth of God's Word. When we choose to take our thoughts captive and line them up with what God says is true, this scripture promises that we will have God's divine power to destroy strongholds. Pastor John Eldredge in his bestselling book, *Wild At Heart* said, "I will be honest, if you've given your heart over to something many times over, you've given it a good stronghold, and it's also tangled up in issues of wounds and sin, it's going to take some time to untangle and heal this, but it is worth the work. Don't just bury it."[1]

A *Stronghold-Buster* is not a magic incantation, or simply positive thinking. If we choose to renew our minds, we express our faith in Christ. This practice can help rewrite our default thinking from anxious and fearful, to confidence in the peace and security of a relationship with God through faith in Jesus Christ. In Christ, we are accepted. In Christ, we are secure. In Christ, we are significant. We are no longer hopeless, worthless, or unworthy.

Breaking down a stronghold often doesn't happen overnight, so we encourage you to read the following scriptures, pray the renunciation (verbal rejection), and pray the annunciations (verbal acceptance and agreement) out loud for 40 days. You may feel a bit hypocritical for the first 37 to 39 days because you don't 'feel like' what you are saying is true. But keep at it and trust God to renew your thinking by His truth.

I am excited to share the testimony of Virginia Higgenbotham, who at five-years-old, was tormented by nagging thoughts of unworthiness, unneeded, and shame for most of her life. Here's her story:

> I had a stronghold (a "lie-knot") to do with my views of other people and what they thought of me. I guess I grew up, being a fairly kind of science, nerdy type. Although I had friends, I wasn't popular. So that's the background, and then when I was older, I had a boyfriend who broke up with me by telling me I was boring. That single sentence had a massive impact on what I thought of myself. And I just realized I was assuming nobody was interested in anything I had to say, people thought I was boring and didn't want to be my friend. And that carried on for years, it wasn't until a few years ago I realized that's what I thought of myself. It actually wasn't right. And so it was figuring out that actually that was a stronghold (a "lie-knot") and I needed to do something about it, and I used a Stronghold-Buster for that. So the problem was figuring out what the lie was behind that particular stronghold. The lie wasn't that I was boring, because maybe I am, but I don't think I am. But that's not the issue. The issue was that I really cared about what other people thought about me and I needed to get really grounded in what God thought of me. I knew, I know God doesn't think I am. So I did a stronghold-buster that dealt with that. It dealt with the fact that God thought I was pretty amazing. He made me and all those sorts of things. I remember when I first started reading it out, I could hardly read it without crying. The bits about "it only matters what God thinks about me." It just didn't seem true at all. I just felt like this is a waste of time, it makes me feel sad, because I feel so rubbish inside. But actually, by the time I got probably three weeks into it, I could read it out and think, "Yes, that's true, that's amazing." I couldn't believe it. I was not expecting it to work, but it did, and it really changed the way I felt and thought about myself. Now I am just like everyone else, I guess, in a normal way. And God has really, really changed me through that.[2]

You can observe the process Virginia shared. Her choice to constantly renew her mind by reading aloud what God thought of her replaced the lies she believed about herself. Virginia, myself, and hundreds of others have experienced the same relief. Our minds have been renewed, we have replaced the flesh-patterns with a Spirit-filled peace and abundant life in Christ. Deception is overshadowed by truth. This is not positive thinking but choosing to think the truth because God has said it is true. And faith is believing that what God has said is truer than the circumstances in which we find ourselves in these days, and truer than whatever we have grown to believe because of the circumstances of our lives.

Pastor John Eldredge in his bestselling book, *Wild At Heart: Discovering the Secret of a Man's Soul* said, "I will be honest, if you've given your heart over to something many times over, you've given it a good stronghold, and it's also tangled up in issues of wounds and sin, it's going to take some time to untangle and heal this, but it is worth the work. Don't just bury it."[3] I have found it helpful to ask for God's help to focus on one stronghold at a time. As God shows me the lie I have believed, it's like finding the "end of the lie-knot." That's when the unraveling process begins, where God and I face the truth, and together, we write up a Stronghold-Buster for one area.

True belief is not indicated by your words only, but by whether you put these things into practice. (See James 2:22). If you have trouble implementing these truths, don't despair because there is no condemnation for those who are in Christ (see Romans 8:1). Keep choosing the truth, like the man who said to Jesus, "I do believe, help me overcome my unbelief" (Mark 9:24) We allow the limits of our faith to show us where we need God to help us grow in faith.

You can set up your phone or tablet to remind you daily to pray specifically about stronghold-busting and speak the truth over yourself. You may want to consider downloading the Freedom In Christ app called "The Freedom in Christ Course." Any Stronghold-Buster includes the following: identifying the lie, choosing scriptures to counteract the lie, and creating a prayer or declaration of truth based upon those scriptures.

Stronghold-Buster:

The lie: I cannot stand the stress and anxiety associated with the pandemic and all the changes it has brought about. OR, I'll only be secure if I know everything will return to normal as I desire.

Romans 6:23—For the wages of sin is death, but the gift of God is eternal life in Christ Jesus our Lord.

I John 5:12—Whoever has the Son has life; whoever does not have the Son of God does not have life.

Galatians 2:20—I have been crucified with Christ and I no longer live, but Christ lives in me. The life I now live in the body, I live by faith in the Son of God, who loved me and gave himself for me.

James 1:5—If any of you lacks wisdom, you should ask God, who gives generously to all without finding fault, and it will be given to you.

Colossians 3:1-3—Since, then, you have been raised with Christ, set your hearts on things above, where Christ is, seated at the right hand of God. Set your minds on things above, not on earthly things. For you died, and your life is now hidden with Christ in God.

Philippians 4:6-9—Do not be anxious about anything, but in every situation, by prayer and petition, with thanksgiving, present your requests to God. And the peace of God, which transcends all understanding, will guard your hearts and your minds in Christ Jesus. Finally, brothers and sisters, whatever is true, whatever is noble, whatever is right, whatever is pure, whatever is lovely, whatever is admirable - if anything is excellent or praiseworthy - think about such things. Whatever you have learned or received or heard from me, or seen in me - put it into practice. And the God of peace will be with you.

Isaiah 26:3—You (God) will keep in perfect peace (shalom) those whose minds are steadfast, because they trust in you.

John 14:27—Jesus said, 'Peace I leave with you; my peace I give you. I do not give to you as the world gives. Do not let your hearts be troubled and do not be afraid.'

John 16:33—I (Jesus) have told you these things, so that in me you may have peace. In this world you will have trouble. But take heart! I have overcome the world.

I renounce the lie that I cannot stand the stress and anxiety associated with the pandemic and the changes it has brought about. OR, I'll only be secure if I know everything will return to normal as I desire.

I announce the truth that, through faith in the saving work of Jesus Christ, I am forgiven and have passed from death to life (see also Ephesians 2:1-10 and Romans 3:21-26). I announce the truth that, as one who trusts in Jesus for life, I am not called to live on my own strength or wisdom. Rather, it is the life of Christ Himself, as I rely on Him by faith, that enables me to live with strength and wisdom. I announce the truth that as I set my heart and mind on the things of God and put these things into practice, I can trust He will give me peace. I announce the truth that I was not promised a comfortable life, because this world is broken as a result of the Fall. (See also Genesis 3, Romans 8:18-25) I announce the truth that Jesus has overcome the world and has given me His peace, therefore, I can have courage and not be afraid because the God of peace Himself is with me.[4]

If this has been helpful to you, consider other material produced by Freedom in Christ by visiting www.ficm.org.

May the God of hope fill you with all joy and peace as you trust in him, so that you may overflow with hope by the power of the Holy Spirit. (Romans 15:13)

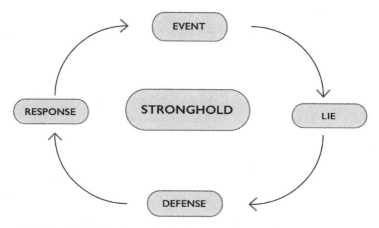

THE ANATOMY OF A STRONGHOLD
JESUS SAID, "YOU SHALL KNOW THE TRUTH AND
AND THE TRUTH SHALL MAKE YOU FREE"

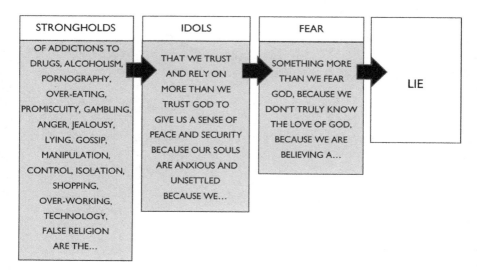

STRONGHOLDS	IDOLS	FEAR	
OF ADDICTIONS TO DRUGS, ALCOHOLISM, PORNOGRAPHY, OVER-EATING, PROMISCUITY, GAMBLING, ANGER, JEALOUSY, LYING, GOSSIP, MANIPULATION, CONTROL, ISOLATION, SHOPPING, OVER-WORKING, TECHNOLOGY, FALSE RELIGION ARE THE...	THAT WE TRUST AND RELY ON MORE THAN WE TRUST GOD TO GIVE US A SENSE OF PEACE AND SECURITY BECAUSE OUR SOULS ARE ANXIOUS AND UNSETTLED BECAUSE WE...	SOMETHING MORE THAN WE FEAR GOD, BECAUSE WE DON'T TRULY KNOW THE LOVE OF GOD, BECAUSE WE ARE BELIEVING A...	LIE

BODY

Tension or migraine headaches, nervous stomach, hives, skin rashes, allergies, asthma, some arthritis, spastic colon, heart palpitations, respiratory ailments, etc.

FLESH

(ROMANS 8:8)

The ingrained habit patterns still appeal to the mind to live independent of God.

A human mind and the mind of the spirit

MIND

Double-Minded

SPIRIT

(ROMANS 8:9)

Alive but quenched
(1 Thessalonians 5:19)

The born-again person has a spirit born of the Holy Spirit

FLESH · BODY · EMOTIONS · MIND · WILL

SPIRIT

EMOTIONS

Unstable

Driven by the natural man – the old unregenerated man

But the sons of God are led by the Holy Spirit.

Walk after the flesh   *Walk after the Spirit (seldom)*

FRUITS OF THE FLESH		FRUITS OF THE SPIRIT	
FLESH AND BLOOD CANNOT ENTER THE KINGDOM OF GOD		*FLESH AND BLOOD CANNOT ENTER THE KINGDOM OF GOD*	
IMMORALITY	OUTBURST OF	LOVE	GOODNESS
IMPURITY	ANGER	JOY	FAITHFULNESS
SENSUALITY	DISPUTES	PEACE	GENTLENESS
IDOLATRY	DISSENSIONS	PATIENCE	SELF-CONTROL
SORCERY	FACTIONS	KINDNESS	
ENMITIES	ENVYING		
STRIFE	DRUNKENNESS		
JEALOUSY	CAROUSING		

Stronghold-Busting

Work out the Lie you have been believing.

This is any way you have to think that is not in line with what God says in the Bible. Ignore what you feel because, by definition, the lie will feel true.

Speak out the effect that believing the Lie has had on your life.

Imagine how different your life would be if you did not believe this lie. What would you be able to do that you currently can't do?

Find as many Bible verses as you can that say what is actually true and write them down.

If there are a lot of verses, pick the top seven or eight.

Write a Declaration.

Base it on this formula: "I renounce the lie that.... I announce the truth that..."

If you prefer, you could use alternative language such as: "I reject the lie that... I embrace the truth that..." or "I say no to the lie that... I say yes to the lie that..."

Read the Bible verses and say the Declaration out loud every day for 40 days.

Remember that for a long time the verses and declaration will not feel true. Remind yourself that God is the Truth and that if He said it, it really is true. And it's not just true for other people, it's true for you! You can use the Freedom in Christ app to remind you to make your declaration.

STRONGHOLD-BUSTER EXAMPLE

Feeling irresistibly drawn to porn

THE LIE: that I cannot resist the temptation to look at porn.

EFFECTS IN MY LIFE: deep sense of shame, warped sexual feelings, unable to relate to other people as God intended; harmful to my marriage.

Romans 6:11-14

In the same way, count yourselves dead to sin but alive to God in Christ Jesus. Therefore, do not let sin reign in your mortal body so that you obey its evil desires. Do not offer any part of yourself to sin as an instrument of wickedness, but rather offer yourselves to God as those who have been brought from death to life; and offer every part of yourself to him as an instrument of righteousness. For sin shall no longer be your master, because you are not under the law, but under grace.

1 Corinthians 6:19

Do you not know that your body is a temple of the Holy Spirit?

1 Corinthians 10:13

No temptation has overtaken you except what is common to mankind. And God is faithful; he will not let you be tempted beyond what you can bear. But when you are tempted, he will also provide a way out so that you can endure it.

Galatians 5:16

So, I say, live by the Spirit, and you will not gratify the desires of the flesh.

Galatians 5:22-23

But the fruit of the Spirit is love, joy, peace, patience, kindness, goodness, faithfulness, gentleness and self-control.

I REJECT THE LIE - that I cannot resist the temptation to look at porn. I embrace the truth that God will always provide a way out when I am tempted, and I will choose to take it. I announce the truth - that if I live by the Spirit — and I choose to do that — I will not gratify the desires of the flesh and the fruit of the Spirit, including self-control, will grow in me. I count myself dead to sin and refuse to let sin reign in my body or be my master. Today and every day I give my body to God as a temple of the Holy Spirit to be used only for what honors Him. I declare that the power of sin is broken in me. I choose to submit completely to God and resist the devil who must flee from me now.

TICK OFF THE DAYS:

1	2	3	4	5	6	7	8	9
10	11	12	13	14	15	16	17	18
19	20	21	22	23	24	25	26	27
28	29	30	31	32	33	34	35	36
37	38	39	40					

STRONGHOLD-BUSTING

VERSE _____ DAY _____
SCRIPTURE # _____ DATE _____

1. WRITE SCRIPTURE HERE

2. TOOLS

- Read surrounding verses
- Read another version
- Used a concordance
- Spoke Scripture out loud

3. CONCORDANCE NOTES

4. SUMMARIZE THE MESSAGE IN YOUR OWN WORDS

5. THE LIE: HOW IS THE TRUTH DIFFERENT FROM HOW I THINK, FEEL AND ACT?

6. LORD, WHAT DO YOU WANT ME TO KNOW CONCERNING THIS SCRIPTURE?

7. WRITE A PERSONAL PRAYER OF DECLARATION AND READ OUT LOUD (USE I, YOU AND ME)

ADDITIONAL NOTES/THOUGHTS

STRONGHOLD-BUSTER

STEP 1 – INQUIRE

- Ask God to Reveal Strongholds
- Remember Satan Wants You to Stay in Bondage
- Desire to Be Changed!

STEP 2 – IDENTIFY

IDENTIFY THE LIE (i.e., Unloved, Abandoned, Rejected, Inadequate, Hopeless, Stupid, Ugly, etc.):

- The lie (the issue I'm struggling with) I have believed about myself is _____
  _____

IDENTIFY THE EFFECT THE LIE HAS ON MY LIFE:

- Believing this lie has caused me to _____
  _____

IDENTIFY GOD'S TRUTH (SCRIPTURE) TO REPLACE THE LIE

- Scripture Verse: _____
  _____

- Scripture Verse: _____
  _____

- Scripture Verse: _____
  _____

WRITE A DECLARATION OF TRUTH

- I renounce the LIE that _____
  _____

- Instead, I announce the TRUTH that _____
  _____

STEP 3 – IMPLEMENT

Persist! For 40 Days—Renew your mind with these Scriptures. Also use the Stronghold-Busting Pages as a great tool. Submit to His Transformation and ask for the Holy Spirit to help you in this process of renewing your mind!

1	2	3	4	5	6	7	8	9	10	11	12	13	14	15	16	17	18	19	20
21	22	23	24	25	26	27	28	29	30	31	32	33	34	35	36	37	38	39	40

End Notes

Chapter 1

1. Lysa TerKeurst, Uninvited: Living Loved When you Feel Less Than, Left Out, and Lonely (Nashville, TN: Thomas Nelson, 2016), pg. 258
2. http://blueletterbible.org/comm/guzik_david/studyguide2017-Hbr/Hbr-12 (7/15/2020)
3. www.pewresearch.org/fact-tank/2018/04/06/christian-women-in-the-u-s-are-more-religious-than-their-male-counterparts (3/15/2019)
4. Neil T. Anderson and Steve Goss, The Freedom In Christ Discipleship Course (Minneapolis, MN: Bethany House, 2017), pgs. 23-26
5. Ed Silvoso, That None Should Perish, Regal Books, 1994, p. 155.
6. Neil T. Anderson and Steve Goss, The Freedom In Christ Discipleship Course (Minneapolis, MN: Bethany House, 2017) DVD #1 Session 1

Chapter 2

1. Brennan Manning, https://goodreads.com/quotes/307891-weshould-be-astonished-at-the-goodness-of-god-stunned (3/10/2019)
2. Erin Smalley, https://www.focusonthefamily.com/marriage/lieswomen-believe/ (3/10/2019)
3. Neil T. Anderson, Victory Over The Darkness, (Minneapolis, MN: Bethany House , 2017), pg. 157
4. Neil T. Anderson and Steve Goss, The Freedom In Christ Discipleship Course (Minneapolis, MN: Bethany House , 2017) pg. 27
5. Life Application Study Bible, New International Version, (Wheaton, IL: Tyndale House Publishers, 1988), pg. 2568
6. Neil T. Anderson and Steve Goss, The Freedom In Christ Discipleship Course (Minneapolis, MN: Bethany House, 2017) pg. 29
7. Excerpt from Victory Over the Darkness by Neil T. Anderson, copyright © 2000, 2013, 2020, pgs. 36-37. Used by permission of Bethany House Publishers, a division of Baker Publishing Group.
8. Neil T. Anderson and Steve Goss, The Freedom In Christ Discipleship Course (Minneapolis, MN: Bethany House, 2017) Testimony of A Woman, DVD #6 Handling Emotions Well. 10:27-12:56
9. Sheryl Giesbrecht, Get Back Up: Trusting God When Life Knocks You Down, (Phoenix, AZ: Wheatmark, 2013), pg. 19

Chapter 3

1.   Ed Silvoso, Ekklesia, (Minneapolis, MN: Baker Publishing Group, 2019), pgs. 91-93
2.   Alexander the Great, The Gordian Knot, en.wikipedia.org/wiki/Gordian_knot (7/22/2020)
3.   https://psychology1.knoji.com/therapy-is-like-peeling-an-onion/ (11/15/2017)
4.   Dr. Michelle Bengston, Hope Prevails, (Minneapolis, MN: Baker Publishing Group, 2016), pg. 63
5.   https://www.everydayhealth.com/depression/facts-about-depression-whos-at-risk.aspx (9/8/2015)
6.   https://www.psychiatry.org/patients-families/depression/whatis-depression (11/15/2017)
7.   https://www.verywellmind.com/risk-factors-for-ptsd-followinga-traffic-accident-2797197 (5/8/2020)
8.   Webster's New World Dictionary, (New York, NY: Simon & Schuster, Inc ., 1988), pg. 373
9.   Sheryl Giesbrecht Turner: It'll Be Okay: Finding God When Doubt Hides the Truth, (Enumclaw, WA: Redemption Press, 2018), pages 42-43
10. John Stott, Romans: God's Good News for the World, (Downer's Grove, IL: Inter varsity Press, 1994), pg. 187
11. Neil T. Anderson, Victory Over the Darkness, (Bloomington, MN: Bethan y House Publishers, 2000, 2013), pgs. 65-66
12. https://www.markbatterson.com/blog/unlearning (3/27/2020)

Chapter 4

1.   https://www.thegospelcoalition.org/blogs/justin-taylor/what-isthe-most-important-thing-about-us/ (6/10/2020)
2.   www.https://kff.org/health-reform/issue-brief/the-implicationsof-covid-19-for-mental-health-and-substance-use (9/10/2020)
3.   Guy Winch, 12/8/2015, https://ideas.ted.com/why-rejectionhurts-so-much-and-what-to-do-about-it/ (10/15/2018)
4.   Henri Nouwen, Discernment: Reading the Signs of Daily Life, (New York, NY : Harper Collins, 2013) pg. 54
5.   https://themighty.com/2016/05/mental-health-conditions-arecosting-the-u-s-a-ton-of-money/ (12/10/2020)
6.   https://www.stlouisfed.org/open-vault/2018/october/fourways-spot-counterfeit-currency (1/12/2020)
7.   Neil T. Anderson and Steve Goss, The Freedom In Christ Discipleship Course (Minneapolis, MN: Bethany House, 2017) pgs. 36-39
8.   Stormie Omartian, The Power of Praying for Your Adult Children, (Eugene, OR: Harvest House Publishers), pg. 234
9.   https://www. telegraph.co.uk/news/2018/12/21/witchcraft-moves-mainstream-america-christianity-declines/ (3/10/2019)

10. http://www.charismanews.com/us/75184-tom-brady-s-wife-you-re-lucky-you-married-a-witch/ (3/19/2019)
11. https://en.wikipedia.org/wiki/Avengers:_Infinity_War#Plot
12. Neil T Anderson, The Bondage Breaker, (Eugene, OR: Harvest House, 2019), pg. 44
13. https://hellogiggles.com/lifestyle/modern-women-occult-empowering (3/10/2019)
14. https://www.merriam-webster.com/dictionary/occult (3/10/2019)
15. Neil T. Anderson and Steve Goss, The Freedom In Christ Discipleship Course (Minneapolis, MN: Bethany House, 2017) pgs. 45-58, 50-5
16. Martin Wells Knapp, Impressions, (Pantianos Classics, 1897), pgs. 43 & 14
17. Neil T. Anderson and Steve Goss, The Freedom In Christ Discipleship Course (Minneapolis, MN: Bethany House, 2017) DVD #2 Session #3 "World's View of Truth" Testimony of woman given away to Buddhist temple.
18. Neil T. Anderson, The Core of Christianity, (Portland, OR: Harvest House Publishers, 2003/2010), pgs. 76 - 77

Chapter 5

1. C.S. Lewis, A Grief Observed, https://www.bookroo.comquotes/c-s-lewis (10/20/2020)
2. https://Priceonomics.com/a-history-of-tug-of-war-fatalities (7/15/2020)
3. https://Merriam-webster.com/dictionary/tug-of-war (7/15/2020)
4. En.wikipedia.org/wiki/Tug_of_war
5. https://www.ctvnews.ca/nova-scotia-man-59-severs-fingers-during-tug-of-war-1.556764 (7/15/2020)
6. Neil T. Anderson and Steve Goss, The Freedom In Christ Discipleship Course (Minneapolis, MN: Bethany House, 2017) pgs. 28-31
7. Joyce Meyer, Healing the Soul of a Woman Devotional, (New York, NY : Hachette Book Group, Inc., 2019), pg. 147
8. https://www.goodreads.com/quotes/199214-take-the-first-step-in-faith-you-don-t-have-to#: (10/20/2020)
9. https://ficm.org/wp-content/uploads/2013/04/Standing-Free-ASteps-to-Freedom-Follow-up1.pdf 10/20/2020)
10. Neil T. Anderson and Steve Goss, The Freedom In Christ Discipleship Course (Minneapolis, MN: Bethany House, 2017) DVD #2 Session #2 "Choosing to Believe the Truth" Testimony of woman overcoming fear, anxiety, infidelity.
11. Neil T. Anderson, Victor y Over the Darkness, (Bloomington, MN: Bethany House Publishers, 2000, 2013), pgs. 35-37
12. Neil T. Anderson and Steve Goss, The Freedom In Christ Discipleship Course (Minneapolis, MN: Bethany House, 2017) pgs. 80-822
13. W. Glyn Evans, Daily With My Lord, (Chicago, IL: Moody Press), September 11
14. Francis Frangipane, The River of Life, (New Kensington, PA: Whitaker House), pg. 42

Chapter 6

1. Shelia Walsh, The Storm Inside: Trade the Chaos of How You Feel for the Truth of Who You Are, (Nashville, TN: Thomas Nelson, 2014), pg. 51
2. Skip Hipp, Henderson County, N.C. (WLOS) 2018 (7/25/2020)
3. Skip Hipp, http//www.frayedknotats.com/individual/hipp (7/25/2020)
4. Life Application Study Bible, New International Version, (Wheaton, IL: Tyndale House Publishers, 1988), pg. 94
5. Max Lucado, https://maxlucado.com/stronger-in-the-brokenplaces/ (10/25/2020)
6. Neil T. Anderson and Steve Goss, The Freedom In Christ Discipleship Course (Minneapolis, MN: Bethany House , 2017), pg. 96
7. https://joycemeyer.org/everydayanswers/ea-teachings/the-poison-of-unforgiveness (3/25/2019)
8. Sheryl Giesbrecht, Get Back Up: Trusting God When Life Knocks You Do wn, (Tucson, AZ: Wheatmark Publishers, 2013), pgs. 34-35
9. Neil T. Anderson and Steve Goss, The Freedom In Christ Discipleship Course (Minneapolis, MN: Bethany House, 2017) DVD #3 Session #7 "Forgiving From the Heart" Testimony of woman whose daughter was murdered.
10. https://www.azquotes.com/author/8044-Martin_Luther_King_Jr/tag/forgiveness (3/20/2019)
11. John Bevere, The Bait of Satan: Living Free from the Deadly Trap of Offense, (Lake Mar y, FL: Charisma House, 2014) Goodreads/quotes (10/25/2020)
12. Neil T. Anderson, The Steps to Freedom In Christ, (Bloomington, MN, Bethany House Publishers, 2017), pg. 12.

Chapter 7

1. A.W. Tozer, The Pursuit of God: The Human Thirst for the Divine, (Chicago, IL: Moody Publishers), pg. 35
2. Laurie Carlson, Harry Houdini for Kids: His Life and Adventures with 21 Magic Tricks and Illusions, (Chicago, IL: Chicago Review Press), pg. 37
3. Nancy Leigh DeMoss, Brokenness, Surrender, Holiness: A Revive Our Hearts Trilogy, (Chicago, IL: Moody Publishers, 2005), pg. 152
4. Life Application Study Bible, New International Version, (Wheaton, IL: Tyndale House Publishers, 1988), pg. 1751
5. Neil T. Anderson, Discipleship Counseling: The Complete Guide to Helping Others Walk in Freedom and Grow in Christ, (Ventura, CA: Regal Books, 1995), pgs. 283-4
6. http://En.wikipedia.org/wiki/Word_Association (9/20/2020)
7. http://blueletterbible.org/search/dictionary/viewtopic.cfm?topic=VT0002827 Vine's Expository Dictionary of New Testament Words 1 Strong's Number : G5226 (9/20/2020)
8. https://healingandrevival.com/BioAMurray.htm (9/20/2020)
9. Neil T. Anderson and Steve Goss, The Freedom In Christ Discipleship Course (Minneapolis, MN: Bethany House, 2017), pg. 86

10. http://audubon.org/news/snake-eagles-are-serpents-worst-nightmare (9/20/2020)
11. Neil T. Anderson, The Bondage Breaker, (Eugene, OR: Harvest House, 2019), pg.94
12. Neil T. Anderson, Discipleship Counseling: The Complete Guide to Helping Others Walk in Freedom and Grow in Christ, (Ventura, CA: Regal Books, 1995), pg.281
13. http://turveyabbey.org.uk/blog/?p=610 (10/20/2020)

Chapter 8

1. C.S Lewis, Mere Christianity. (New York, NY: Harper Collins, 1980), pg. 35
2. https://www.fishwildlife.org/application/files/5515/2002/6134/Modern_Snares_final.pd (9/20/2020)
3. https://nasdonline.org/332/d000129/proper-use-of-snares-forcapturing-furbearers.html (9/20/2020)l
4. http://alert-conservation.org/issues-research-highlights/2017/2/15/snares-legitimate-hunting-or-torturing-wildlife (9/20/2020)
5. https://www.earthtouchnews.com/environmental-crime/poaching/watch-young-lion-in-zimbabwe-rescued-from-illegal-snare/ (9/20/2020)
6. http://cslewisinstitute.org/Pride_and_Humility Single Page (9/20/2020)
7. Peggy Joyce Ruth, Angelia Ruth Schum, (Lake Mar y, FL: Charisma House, 2010), pgs. 17-18
8. Life Application Study Bible, New International Version, (Wheaton, IL: Tyndale House Publishers, 1988), pg. 907
9. William Smith, LL.D, Smith's Bible Dictionary, (Grand Rapids, MI: Zondervan Publishing House ,1979), entry 725
10. Life Application Study Bible, New International Version, (Wheaton, IL: Tyndale House Publishers, 1988), pg. 908
11. https://www.leadlikejesus.com/who-your-boss Sheryl Giesbrecht Turner (9/20/2020)
12. https://www.blueletterbible.org/search/dictionary/viewtopic.cfm?topic=VT0002208 (9/20/2020)
13. http://www.seekfind.net/Definition_of_pride___Define_Pride_from_Scripture.html#. XxIbmShKhEY (9/20/2020)
14. Neil T. Anderson, Discipleship Counseling: The Complete Guide to Helping Others Walk in Freedom and Grow in Christ, (Ventura, CA: Regal Books, 1995), pg.294-6
15. http://cslewisinstitute.org/Pride_and_Humility_SinglePage (9/20/2020)
16. Neil T. Anderson, Discipleship Counseling: The Complete Guide to Helping Others Walk in Freedom and Grow in Christ, (Ventura, CA: Regal Books, 1995), pg.298
17. https://www.blueletterbible.org/search/dictionary/viewtopic.cfm?topic=VT0001425 (9/20/2020)
18. http://www.seekfind.net/Humility_Seeing_Reality.html# XxIe9ChKhEY (9/20/2020)
19. Neil T. Anderson and Steve Goss, The Freedom In Christ Discipleship Course (Minneapolis, MN: Bethany House, 2017) DVD #4 Session #8 "Renewing the Mind" Testimony of woman with control issues over sister.

20. C.S. Lewis, Mere Christianity, (New York, NY: Harper Collins, 1980), pg. 101
21. Robert J. Morgan, Mastering Life Before It's Too Late: 10 Biblical Strategies for a Lifetime of Purpose, (New York, NY: Howard Books, 2015), pg. 182

Chapter 9

1. http://dailychristianquote.com/jim-cymbala-9/ (9/20/2020)
2. https://longislandskydiving.com/about-skydiving- long- island/articles/why-do-people-skydive (9/20/2020)
3. https://www.mensjournal.com/adventure/skydiver-survives-tangled-parachute-quick-thinking (9/20/2020)/
4. https://dailymail.co.uk/news/article-2661464/Skydiver-films-terrifying-moment-parachute-failed-sending-violent-spin (9/20/2020)
5. http://en.wikipedia.org/wiki/Cut-away (9/20/2020)
6. http://adventure.howstuffworks.com/10-things-go-wrong-airsports1.htm (9/20/2020)
7. https://www.blueletterbible.org/search/dictionary/viewtopic.cfm?topic=VT0000702 (9/20/2020)
8. Life Application Study Bible, New International Version, (Wheaton, IL: Tyndale House Publishers, 1988), pg. 2483
9. https://www.biblesprout.com/articles/hell/satan-cast-heaven/ (9/20/2020)
10. Stormie Omartian, The Power of Praying for Your Adult Children, (Eugene, OR: Harvest House Publishers, 2014), pgs. 80-81
11. W. Glyn Evans, Daily With My Lord, (Chicago, IL: Moody Press, 1989), July 26-Battle for the Body
12. Neil T. Anderson, Discipleship Counseling: The Complete Guide to Helping Others Walk in Freedom and Grow in Christ, (Ventura, CA: Regal Books, 1995), pgs.306-307
13. Neil T. Anderson and Steve Goss, The Freedom In Christ Discipleship Course (Minneapolis, MN: Bethany House, 2017) DVD #2 Session #4 "Our Daily Choice" Testimony of woman struggling with suicide, depression, overeating.
14. Neil T. Anderson, The Steps to Freedom In Christ, (Bloomington, MN: Bethany House Publishers, 2017)
15. https://ficm.org/ufaqs/the-importance-of-the-christians-identity-in-sanctification/ (9/20/2020)
16. Neil T. Anderson and Steve Goss, The Freedom In Christ Discipleship Course (Minneapolis, MN: Bethany House, 2017), pgs. 146-148
17. http://adventure .howstuffworks.com/10-things-go-wrong-airsports1.htm (9/20/2020)
18. https://davidjeremiah.blog/spiritual-warfare-prayer/ (9/20/2020)/

Chapter 10

1. Robert J. Morgan, Mastering Life Before It's Too Late: 10 Biblical Strategies for a Lifetime of Purpose, (New York, NY: Howard Books, 2015), pg. 252
2. Robert J. Morgan, Mastering Life Before It's Too Late: 10 Biblical Strategies for a Lifetime of Purpose, (New York, NY: Howard Books, 2015), pg. 161

3.   Sir Walter Scott, Marmion: A Tale of Flodden Field, https://www.gutenberg.org/files/4010/4010-h/4010-h.htm (9/22/2020),

4.   https://www.nosweatshakespeare.com/quotes/famous-shakespeare-quotes/oh-what-a-tangled-web-we-weave/ (9/22/2020)

5.   Neil T. Anderson, Discipleship Counseling: The Complete Guide to Helping Others Walk in Freedom and Grow in Christ, (Ventura, CA: Regal Books, 1995), pg.328

6.   https://ficm.org/faq/ What does acquiescence mean? (9/22/2020)

7.   Neil T. Anderson, Discipleship Counseling: The Complete Guide to Helping Others Walk in Freedom and Grow in Christ, (Ventura, CA: Regal Books, 1995), pg.332

8.   Elisa Morgan, The Beauty of Broken: My Story, and Likely Yours Too, (Nashville, TN: W Publishing Group, 2005), pg.23

9.   https://www.all4kids.org/news/blog/the-role-of-family-in-childdevelopment/ (9/22/2020)

10. https://ficm.org/faq/ What does acquiescence mean? (9/22/2020)

11. https://www.usingenglish.com/forum/threads/37081-Tangled-Web (9/22/2020)

12. Neil T. Anderson, Discipleship Counseling: The Complete Guide to Helping Others Walk in Freedom and Grow in Christ, (Ventura, CA: Regal Books,1995), pg.339

13. Neil T. Anderson and Steve Goss, The Freedom In Christ Discipleship Course (Minneapolis, MN: Bethany House, 2017) DVD #2 Session #6 "Handling Emotions Well" Testimony of man struggling with ancestral and generational identity.

14. Rick Warren, The Purpose Driven Life: What on Earth Am I Here For?, (Grand Rapids, MI: Zondervan, 2000), pg. 25

15. www.Biblestudytools.com/commentaries/treasury-of-david-psalms-103-1.html (9/22/2020)

16. http://blueletterbible.org/comm/guzik_david/studyguide2017-Hbr/Hbr-12 (9/22/2020)

17. Neil T. Anderson and Steve Goss, The Freedom In Christ Discipleship Course (Minneapolis, MN: Bethany House, 2017), pgs. 103-104

Love Letter to My Readers

1.   Sheryl Giesbrecht Turner: It'll Be Okay: Finding God When Doubt Hides the Truth, (Enumclaw, WA: Redemption Press, 2018), pages 147-149

Stronghold-Buster Appendix

1.   John Eldridge, Wild At Heart: Discovering the Secret of a Man's Soul, (Nashville, TN: Thomas Nelson, 2001), pg. 56.

2.   Neil T. Anderson and Steve Goss, The Freedom In Christ Discipleship Course (Minneapolis, MN: Bethany House, 2017) DVD #4 Session #9 "Relating to Others" Testimony of woman with self-image, acceptance issues, stronghold-buster.

3.   John Eldredge, Wild At Heart: Discovering the Secret of a Man's Soul, (Nashville, TN: Thomas Nelson, 2001), pg. 56

4.   Sheryl Giesbrecht Turner, CFMU Virtual Practicum Notebook, Knoxville, TN: FICM USA (9/1/2020)

Dedication

To Jesus – The Truth

Thank You, Lord Jesus Christ, You are the Truth. You don't just show us the way to the truth. You invite us to know You and to encounter You because You are truth. You are full of truth, overflowing with grace, You are the very essence of truth. May each one who reads, studies, and analyzes Your Word experience You as the ultimate Truth. Amen.

Jesus answered, 'I am the way and the truth and the life. No one comes to the Father except through me.' John 14:6

The Word became flesh and made his dwelling among us. We have seen his glory, the glory of the one and only Son, who came from the Father, full of grace and truth. John 1:14

Then you will know the truth, and the truth will set you free. John 8:32

The Lord is near to all who call on him, to all who call on him in truth. Psalm 145:8

Guide me in your truth and teach me, for you are God my Savior, and my hope is in you all day long. Psalm 25:5

Acknowledgments

With special thanks:

To my editor, LaRae Weikert, for your desire to help move our "unraveling the lie-knot" message forward, so it is available to women, men, friends, and families who love them. Your commitment and collaboration, attention to detail, Biblical accuracy, accessibility to the reader, and devoted prayers enabled this project to be finished.

To my husband, Jim Turner, for sharing me during these past two years of phone calls, zoom meetings, research, study, and editing through another book deadline. Your selfless love as my husband can only be equaled by your servanthood with our home and church commitments.

To my mother, Shirley Adkins, for praying me during the preparation, processing, and production of another book project. Your tireless prayers, daily encouragement, and words of wisdom are deeply cherished.

To my heart-sister prayer partners, Saundra Dalton-Smith, and Heidi McLaughlin. Your commitment to our monthly prayer times, sharing God's Word and accountability as fellow authors and speakers, keeps me encouraged and focused on the Kingdom work God has for us. It's a joy to be serving in the same vineyard.

To my From Ashes to Beauty, Inc. Board Members. Carol Wilcox, Merleen Johnson, Sue England, and Kaye Camp for your consistently positive input and your enthusiasm about the book. Your cheerleading, chocolate-feeding, accountability, and prayers have strengthened and emboldened me to keep me focused on my message.

To my Freedom In Christ Southwest Region Team family, Hank and Carol Wilcox, Cheryl Hestley, Heather Daniels, Myra Salgado, Shawna Effle, Frank Sung, Sharon Chapman, Ken, and Jan Hardison. Your prayers and encouragement have helped me navigate through to the finish line.

To my Freedom In Christ National Care and Training Team loved ones, Joe and Lory Matthews, Judy Ingvardsen, Mark and Frieda DePenning, and Terry Pausch. Your prayers of care and concern have carried me through to completion of this manuscript.

To my Freedom in Christ International Publishing Team group, Marianne Becker, Steve Goss, and Rob Reed for partnering with me to bring this book into print. I pray the message will be a blessing to all who encounter it as we offer tools of truth. Thank you for inviting me to join the team.

Author Information

Sheryl Giesbrecht Turner's focus is exchanging hurt for hope – a message she shares with audiences as a media personality, author, and speaker. A dynamic teacher and motivating leader, Giesbrecht Turner has endured many changes and challenges, moving her to a deep faith and reliance on God. Sheryl loves to share how God's Word can heal painful hurt and help believers move forward after past trauma with the help of the Holy Spirit. She offers personal examples of how to access abundant life in Christ, offering the hope she's been given as a delivered drug addict, stage four cancer survivor, and former widow. Her desire is for believers to understand God's truth, and they, too, can be set free from past offenses, be healed, and whole emotionally.

A pastor's wife for twenty-eight years, Sheryl served as Focus on the Family's columnist for pastors' wives for four years. Hundreds of her columns and magazine and devotional articles have appeared in *Focus on The Family Magazine, Just Between Us, Discipleship Journal, Contemporary Christian Music, Walk Thru the Bible's - InDeed* and *Tapestry, Charisma, Faith Filled Family, iBelieve, Live Living, Spirit-Led Woman.*

Sheryl is a monthly contributor to Lead Like Jesus BlogSpot. She is the author of five books, *The Kindred Moments Prayer Journal, Get Back Up:Trusting God When Life Knocks You Down, Experiencing God Through His Names,* and *It'll Be Okay: Finding God When Doubt Hides the Truth.*

Sheryl is passionate about reaching out to the poor and needy locally through The Mission at Kern County and worldwide through various international ministry partners. She is a Lead Like Jesus facilitator and part-time staff member with Freedom In Christ Ministries. She has been personally involved with equipping hundreds for ministry and facilitating the training of thousands internationally.

Giesbrecht Turner's television and radio show, *Transformed Through Truth*, is hosted by the Holy Spirit Broadcasting Network. Viewed and heard daily by internet, Roku, and YouTube audiences, the program's content is intended to encourage and strengthen the viewer's faith and offer God's hope to those in need.

The joys of Sheryl's life are her adult children, their spouses, and her fourteen grandchildren. She is excited about the current chapter in her life, her marriage to Dr. Jim Turner. Sheryl enjoys baking pumpkin bread, running in the foothills, walking the dog, and hiking in The Yosemite Valley with her husband. Sheryl holds a Bachelor of Arts from Biola University, a Master's in Ministry, and a Doctor of Theology.

Sign up to receive Sheryl's weekly blog on her website:

www.sherylgt.com or www.fromashestobeauty.com

Follow Sheryl on Social Media!

Facebook: Sheryl Giesbrecht Turner or @SherylGiesbrechtAuthor

Twitter: @SGiesbrecht

Parler: @Sherylgiesbrecht

Instagram: sherylgiesbrecht

LinkedIn: Sheryl Giesbrecht

Scribd: Sheryl Giesbrecht

Freedom in Christ Resources

Can We Help You Make Fruitful Disciples?

A church with growing, fruitful disciples of Jesus is a growing, fruitful church that is making a real difference in the community where God has placed it. A key question for church leaders is: "How can I help our people become mature, fruitful disciples as quickly as possible so that they go out and make a real impact?"

A fundamental part of the answer is to help them understand the principles that underlie all of Freedom In Christ's discipleship resources for churches:

* TRUTH - Know who you are in Christ.
* TURNING - Ruthlessly close any doors you've opened to the enemy through past sin and don't open any more.
* TRANSFORMATION - Renew your mind to the truth of God's Word (which is how you will be transformed).

Freedom In Christ has equipped hundreds of thousands of church leaders around the world to use this "identity-based discipleship" approach. As churches base their discipleship around these principles, they report not only changed individual lives but whole changed churches. When churches start to look less like hospitals, full of those who are constantly struggling with their own issues, and more like part of the Bride of Christ, they make an increasing impact on their community.

Our mission is to equip the Church to transform the nations by providing church leaders with transformational discipleship resources that can be used right across their church. Some are specially tailored to the communication styles of different groups such as young people and millennials. Others build on our main Freedom In Christ Course. You can see some of them on the following pages.

Our heart is to help church leaders develop a long-term, whole-church discipleship strategy. Our offices and Representatives around the world run training courses and have people on the ground who like nothing better than to discuss discipleship with church leaders. If you think we can help you in any way as you look to make fruitful disciples, please get in touch. Find your local office at: FreedomInChrist.org

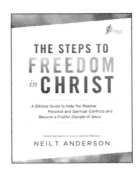

THE STEPS TO
FREEDOM
in CHRIST

A Biblical Guide to Help You Resolve
Personal and Spiritual Conflicts and
Become a Fruitful Disciple of Jesus

Bestselling Author of *Victory Over the Darkness*

NEIL T. ANDERSON

Take Hold Of The Freedom That Is Yours In Christ!

- Do you want to become an even more fruitful disciple of Jesus?
- Are you tired of not fulfilling your full potential as a Christian?

All Christians need to come to know and understand their identity, position and authority in Christ. Knowing those truths helps a believer in Jesus become a growing, fruitful disciple (follower) of Christ. Dr. Neil T. Anderson has been greatly gifted by God to present the biblical truths of our identity and freedom in Christ in a wonderful God-directed, liberating way. These truths are described in the books Victory Over the Darkness, and The Bondage Breaker which became the foundation of Freedom in Christ Ministries. But this teaching did not originate with Dr. Anderson, it is straight from the New Testament and is new covenant Christianity brought to us initially by the apostles Paul, Peter and John and further developed by the early Church fathers.

The Steps to Freedom in Christ is a biblically-based ministry tool which is derived from James 4:7—"Submit to God, resist the devil and he will flee from you." It is a gentle process of following the Holy Spirit's prompting to deal with the effects of any sin committed by you or against you.

Going through the Steps to Freedom in Christ is taking personal responsibility for your life and spiritual growth. It is a systematic approach of examining your heart and life before the Lord and asking Him to reveal areas of your life where there are unresolved sin issues in the light of Scripture. Accordingly, you choose to confess, repent and renounce whatever is standing between you and your spiritual freedom, identify lies believed, and replace them with God's truth.

The Freedom In Christ Course

Now in its third edition and translated into well over 30 languages, The Freedom In Christ Course can transform the way you help Christians become fruitful disciples. Focused on firstly establishing every Christian in the sure foundation of their identity in Jesus, it gives them the tools to break free and stay free from all that holds them back, and a strategy for ongoing transformation. It has ten teaching sessions presented by Steve Goss, Nancy Maldonado, and Daryl Fitzgerald plus The Steps To Freedom In Christ ministry component presented by Steve Goss and Neil Anderson.

With a specially designed app, extra teaching films, a worship album, Leader's Guide, Participant's Guide, and tons of extras, The Freedom In Christ Course offers you everything you need to make disciples who bear fruit that will last!

"Men, women, and middle and high school students have been radically transformed."

Bob Huisman, Pastor, Immanuel Christian Reformed Church, Hudsonville, MI, USA

"I recommend it highly to anyone serious about discipleship."

Chuah Seong Peng, Senior Pastor, Holy Light Presbyterian Church, Johor Baru, Malaysia

"The Freedom In Christ Course changed me and put me in a position to minister to people in a much more effective way."

Frikkie Elstadt, Every Nation Patria, Mossel Bay, South Africa

"Our church has changed as a result of this course. Those who come to Christ and who do the course end up with a rock-solid start to their faith."

Pastor Sam Scott, Eltham Baptist Church, Australia

disciple – FIC's Message For The Millennial Generation

Church leaders report that discipling those in their 20s and 30s is one of their biggest challenges. disciple is a powerful tool to help you. It speaks the language of 20s and 30s and invites them to dive into the greatest story ever told, God's story. They will learn how to take hold of their freedom and discover their mandate.

- 10 sessions designed to run for approximately 90 minutes each.
- Impactful Starter Films introduce the theme for each session.
- Extra films (via the app) on topics including sex, the occult, and fear.
- Chat and Reflect times allow teaching to take root.
- App with extra teaching films, daily devotional, daily nuggets of extra teaching, and Stronghold–Buster-Builder with reminders.

"Thank you so much for caring enough to do this. You have no idea how much it means to us that you have taken the time to understand and help us overcome all the stuff that comes at us."

"You really get us and understand us, you don't patronize us and talk down to us."

"God is doing incredible things in the young people at our church and I'm just grateful this course has been able to facilitate that."

"disciple is really user-friendly. The young adults really engaged and there were definite light bulb moments."

The Lightbringers For Children

The Lightbringers is a powerful resource for churches and parents to use with 5-to-11-year-olds. It is designed to equip them to become fruitful disciples who stay connected to Jesus into their adult lives. They will understand:

* Who they are in Jesus.
* What they have in Jesus.
* How to become fruitful disciples who follow Jesus closely.

It consists of ten action-packed sessions plus specially written versions of The Steps To Freedom In Christ ministry component and has versions for two age groups (5-8 and 9-11). It's great for churches, Bible clubs, and families.

The Church Edition includes a comprehensive 276-page Leader's Guide plus downloadable videos, songs, activity sheets, and PowerPoint presentations. The Family Edition is an online-only version designed to be delivered in the home.

"Parents, educators, children's leaders, and pastors rejoice! There is no longer a void in quality children's curriculum that instills the essentials of identity in Christ and freedom in Christ."

"The Lightbringers is a fantastic resource to help children know their identity in Christ and how to view the rest of the world through that lens."

"It has awesome content, is easy to follow, and will fill what has been a huge gap in kids' ministry up to this time."

The Grace Course

If you don't first know God's love for you in your heart – not just your head – it's impossible for your life to be motivated by love for Him. Instead, you are likely to end up motivated more by guilt or shame or fear or pride. You may be doing all the "right" things, believing all the right things and saying all the right things, but there will be precious little fruit.

* Six sessions plus The Steps to Experiencing God's Grace.
* Present it yourself or use the video presentations.
* Video testimonies illustrating the teaching points, practical exercises, times of listening to God, and Pause For Thought times.
* Works especially well as a course during Lent.

"For the first time in the decades that I've been a Christian, I'm suddenly 'getting' grace – it's amazing and it's shocking!"

"I realized that it's not about my performance – He just wants my heart."

"It was AMAZING! During the last session after we had finished nobody moved for what seemed like ages. When the silence eventually did break, people began to spontaneously share all that the course had meant to them. Testimonies to what the Lord had done just flowed out, some were life-changing."

"The Grace Course does a marvelous job in introducing the concept of grace in a simple, engaging and, at times, even humorous way. It is short and to the point, taking an incredibly deep theological issue and making it understandable and practical."

Freed To Lead

Freed To Lead is a 10-week discipleship course for Christians who are called to leadership – whether in the marketplace, public service, the Church or any other context. It will transform your leadership, free you from drivenness and burnout, enable you to survive personal attacks, use conflict positively, and overcome other barriers to effective leadership.

- Ten sessions plus Steps to Freedom for Leaders
- Video testimonies and Pause For Thought discussion times
- Ideal for church leadership teams before rolling out across the church

"The Freed To Lead course has been the most amazing leadership development experience of my career, having been called to both marketplace and church leadership for over 20 years. It dispels worldly leadership myths and practices and provides Biblical foundations for Godly leadership. I wholeheartedly recommend this course for anyone who aspires or is currently called to Godly servant-hearted leadership in any arena."

"An outstanding course – inspirational and motivational, affirming and encouraging."

"It has reinforced my conviction that my identity is first and foremost in Christ, whatever leadership role I may hold."

FREEDOM**STREAM**

On-Demand Videos For Our Courses

You can access all of our video material for small group studies online for one low monthly subscription. Try it for free!

Access to all the main Freedom In Christ small group courses so you can browse or use the entire range including:

- The Freedom In Christ Course
- The Lightbringers – Freedom In Christ For Children
- Freedom In Christ For Young People
- disciple (the Freedom In Christ message for 18s to 30s)
- The Grace Course
- Freed To Lead
- Keys To Health, Wholeness, & Fruitfulness.

Free video training courses for course leaders and their teams:

- Making Fruitful Disciples – the Biblical principles of discipleship
- Helping Others Find Freedom In Christ.

No need to buy several DVD sets if you have multiple groups running. Access is for all members of your church so participants can catch up if they miss a session.

For further information, pricing, and to start your free trial go to:

FreedomInChrist.org/FreedomStream

Get In Touch

Freedom In Christ exists to equip the Church to make fruitful disciples who make a real impact in their community. Our passion is to help church leaders develop a discipleship strategy right across their church that will be effective for years to come. How can we help your church?

We offer:

- A series of introductory and training events for church leaders.
- Advice on establishing a discipleship strategy for your church built around our discipleship resources.
- Training and equipping for those in your church who will be involved in implementing that strategy.

For contact details of Freedom In Christ in your country or to find out how to order our resources, go to:

FreedomInChrist.org

FREEDOM
IN CHRIST
Transforming Discipleship

Join Us!

If, like us, you are excited about seeing this message of "**Truth, Turning, and Transformation**" spread throughout the Church around the world, please join us.

Join our team of international supporters

Freedom In Christ exists to equip the Church worldwide to make fruitful disciples. We rely heavily for financial support from people who have understood how important it is to give leaders the tools that will enable them to help people become fruitful disciples, not just converts, especially when we are opening up an office in a new country. Typically, your support will be used to:

- Create new resources such as this one
- Help establish new Freedom In Christ offices around the world
- Translate our resources into other languages
- Partner with other organizations worldwide to equip leaders
- Equip church leaders around the world.

Join the team of supporters in your country

We are passionate about working with those who have themselves been touched by the Biblical message of freedom. Financial support enables us to develop new resources and get them into the hands of more church leaders. As a result, many people are connecting with this life-changing message. There are always new projects – small and large – that don't happen unless there's funding.

To find out more please go to: FreedomInChrist.org/friends